J. Thompson

The Complete Practical Pastry Cook

J. Thompson

The Complete Practical Pastry Cook

ISBN/EAN: 9783744792103

Printed in Europe, USA, Canada, Australia, Japan

Cover: Foto ©Andreas Hilbeck / pixelio.de

More available books at **www.hansebooks.com**

THE COMPLETE

Practical Pastry Cook,

— IN —

THREE PARTS.

PART I.—Pies, Tarts, Pastry Cakes, Etc.

PART II.—Sweet Sauces and Puddings.

PART III.—Savory Pies and Puddings—
Patties Vol-au-Vents, Etc.

CHICAGO:
J. THOMPSON GILL, Manager Confectioner and Baker Publishing Co.,
1889.

PREFACE.

We have aimed in the preparation of this book to make it the most complete work on pastry which it is practicable to compile. In doing so we have been forced to restrict the scope of the subject exclusively to those preparations in which puff and other crusts are used; namely pies, tarts, pastry-cakes, puffs, puddings, . Charlotte Russe, raised pies, patties, vol-au-vents, souffles timbales, Fondues, boudins, fritters (beignets) Rissoles, etc. To have extended the work beyond these limits would have encroached on other subjects. The work is particularly complete on the subject of puddings, raised pies, patties. With these few words of introduction we commend it to the attention of the trade, trusting it will give as much satisfaction as our other works on kindred subjects.

THE COMPLETE

Practical Pastry Cook.

—IN—

THREE PARTS.

• ————

PART I.

Pies, Tarts, Pastry, Cakes, Etc.

CONTAINING THOSE RECIPES OF MOST USE TO THE BAKER AND CON-
FECTIONER IN THIS SPECIAL BRANCH OF THE BUSINESS.

————

CHICAGO:

J. THOMPSON GILL, MANAGER BAKER AND CONFECTIONER PUBLISHING CO.

1884.

CONTENTS.

CHAPTER I.

PASTRY IN GENERAL.

Wherein the Art Consists—Materials Used—Flour—Butter—Lard—Suet—Clarified Beef Drippings—Cleanliness—The Mixing and Rolling—Puff Paste—Greasing of Tins and Moulds—How to Ascertain the Right Heat of the Oven—The Baking of Pastry—To Prevent Pastry Being Burnt—To Glaze Pastry—To Ice Pastry.

The art of making puff and other pastes used by the pastry cook requires much practice, dexterity and skill; it should be handled lightly, made with cool hands, and in as cold a place as possible, a marble slab and a glass rolling pin being much better for the purpose, than those made of wood. In warm weather especially select the coolest spot possible for the process. Furthermore, to ensure rich paste being light, great expedition must be used in the making and baking, for if it stand long before being put in the oven, it becomes flat and heavy. In making pastry, the following general directions should be carefully attended to:

Flour should be of the best quality, perfectly dry and well sifted before being used; if in the least damp, the paste made from it will certainly be heavy.

Butter, unless fresh is used, should be washed from the salt, and well squeezed and wrung in a cloth, to get out all the water and buttermilk, which, if left in, assist to make the paste heavy.

Lard should be perfectly sweet, which may generally be ascertained by its appearance and flavor.

Suet should be finely chopped, perfectly free from skin, and quite sweet; during the process of chopping, it should be lightly dredged with flour, which prevents the pieces from sticking together. Beef suet is considered the best; but veal suet, or the outside fat of a loin or neck mutton make good crusts; as also the skimmings in which a joint of mutton has been boiled, but *without* vegetables.

Clarified Beef Dipping answers very well for kitchen pies, puddings, cakes, or for family pies. A very good short crust may be made by mixing with it a small quantity of moist sugar; but care must be taken to use the dripping sparingly, or a very disagreeable flavor will be imparted to the paste.

Strict cleanliness must be observed in pastry making; all the utensils used should be perfectly free from dust and dirt, and every article required for pastry be kept entirely for that purpose.

In mixing paste, add the water very gradually; work the whole together with the knife blade, and knead it until perfectly smooth. Those who are inexperienced in pastry making should work the butter in by breaking it in small pieces, and covering the paste rolled out. It should then be dredged with flour, and the ends folded over and rolled out very thin again; this process must be repeated until all the butter is used.

BAKING OF PASTRY.

The heat of the oven should be regulated according to the article to be baked, or those things should be made first which will suit the heat of the oven.

Light paste requires a moderately quick oven, for if the oven is too hot, it will be colored before it is properly baked, and if it is taken out of the oven, it will fall and become flat; a cool oven will not cause it to rise suffi ciently, and puff paste baked in an oven with anything that causes much steam, will not be so light as otherwise.

Pastry, when baked sufficiently, may be easily slid about on the tin or pan while hot, and puffs or patties or small pies may be lifted from the tin without breaking, by putting the fingers round the edges and carefully lifting them, which cannot be done unless they are baked enough to be taken from the oven.

Puff Paste requires a brisk oven, but not too hot, or it would blacken the crust; on the other hand, if the oven be too slack, the paste will be soddened, and will not rise, nor will it have any color.

Tart tins, dishes for baked puddings, patty tins, etc., should all be buttered before the article intended to be baked is put in them.

Things to be baked on sheets should be placed on buttered paper.

Raised pie paste should have a soaking heat, and paste glazed must have rather a slack oven. It is better to ice tarts, etc., when they are three parts done.

To ascertain when the oven is heated to the proper degree for puff paste, put a small piece of the paste in, previous to baking the whole, and then the heat can be thus judged of.

When pastry is not done through, and yet the outside is sufficiently brown, cover it over with a piece of white paper until thoroughly cooked; this prevents it from getting burnt.

To *glaze* pastry, which is the usual method adopted for meat or raised pies, break an egg, separate the yolk from the white, and beat the former for a short time. Then, when the pastry is nearly baked, take it out of the oven, brush it over with this beaten yolk of egg, and put it back in the oven to set the glaze.

To *ice* pastry, which is the usual method adopted for fruit tarts and sweet dishes of pastry, put the white of an egg on a plate, and with the blade of a knife beat it to a stiff froth. When the pastry is nearly baked, brush it over with this, and sift over some powdered sugar; put it back in the oven to set the glaze, and in a few minutes it will be done.

Great care should be taken that the paste does not catch or burn in the oven which it is very liable to do after the icing is laid on.

CHAPTER II.

PUFF PASTE.

Its Simplicity—What It Is—Precautions Necessary—How to Make Puff Paste in Summer—In Cold Weather—How to Roll it Out—How to Proceed if the Butter Breaks Through—To Choose Butter for Puff Paste—To Prepare Butter for Puff Paste – How to Bake Puff Paste—How to Make it Rise in Leaves or Flakes – Feuilletage—Ude's Recipe for Puff Paste—Soyer's Recipe for Puff Paste—Puff Paste, American and French Methods — Rundell's Recipe for Puff Paste—Puff Paste, an Easy Method—Medium Puff Paste—Half Puff Paste.

The production of a first-class puff paste is commonly regarded as a matter of considerable difficulty, but by the exercise of proper precautions it is, on the contrary, an extremely simple affair. The paste, before being placed in the oven, consists of alternate laminæ of butter or fat, and ordinary flour dough, the latter being, of course, the thickness of the two. During the process of baking the elastic vapor disengaged, being in part restrained from flying off by the buttered surface of the dough, diffuses itself between these laminæ, causing the mass to swell up, and to form an assemblage of thin membranes or flakes, each of which is more or less separated from the other. Indeed, these flakes resemble those of an ordinary, rich, unleavened dough when baked; but collectively they form a very light crust, possessing an extremely inviting appearance and an agreeable flavor.

The precautions above referred to, are, (1) the use of perfectly dry flour, and its conversion into dough with a light hand, avoiding unnecessarily working it; (2) the use of butter freed from water or buttermilk, and which has

been reduced to precisely the same degree of plasticity
as the dough between which it is to be rolled; (3) con-
ducting the operation in a cool apartment, and after two
or three foldings of the dough, exposing it to a rather
low temperature before proceeding further with the pro-
csss; (4) and lastly, baking the paste in a moderately
smart but not too hot an oven. A piece of puff paste ¼
inch thick, when baked, will rise to the height of 2 inches,
thus increasing its volume eight times.

In summer it is impossible to ensure success in making
puff paste without the use of ice, it being matter of the
first necessity that it should be kept cool and firm, two
requisites that tend materially to facilitate the working
of the paste, and also contribute very considerably to
give it that very extraordinary degree of elasticity, when
exposed to the heat of an oven, so well known to expe-
rienced pastry cooks. To effect this properly a good
plan is to procure thin oblong tin pans, of the following
dimensions: The first 20x16 inches, and 3 inches deep;
the second 18x14, 2 inches deep; and the third 16x12
inches, 3 inches deep. Place pounded rough ice in the
largest; set the second-sized tin on this with the puff
paste in it; lastly, put the smallest pan, also filled with
ice on the top of the paste; by this method puff paste
may be easily made to perfection during the hottest days
of summer.

In extreme cold weather, when butter is very hard, it
will be necessary to press it in a cloth or on the slab, to
give it more expansion, and thus facilitate its incorpora-
tion with the paste. Care must be taken in mixing the
paste, not to make it too stiff, especially in summer, as
in that case, it becomes not only troublesome to work,
but it also effects its elasticity in baking.

In winter the precaution of letting the paste lay before rolling out a third or fourth time, may be dispensed with, if it is required in a hurry, as the butter being firm and the weather cold, it will admit of its being done so.

After giving the paste the second rolling, it is well to let it stand for half an hour, after which it will roll much easier and more evenly.

Roll as much as possible, and give as many folds as possible, without the butter breaking through the dough. Success in making good puff paste depends in a great measure upon the ability to use the rolling pin level and evenly, and in such a manner as to roll without breaking the dough and thus allowing the butter to come through.

If this accident should however happen, cover the paste with a piece of "plain dough," dust it well with flour and continue the rolling. It is a good plan to keep a piece of plain dough in reserve for this purpose.

If the dough is not kneaded firmly in making puff paste, the butter will run out in cooking.

TO CHOOSE BUTTER FOR PUFF PASTE.

Butter which is short and crumbly when broken, is seldom of any use for puff paste; it should be good, firm and solid. There are butters which have a soft and oily feel, without any degree of toughness when worked or moulded; these should not be used, as they are generally poor and weak. In summer, however, the softness of butter is no criterion, as the heat naturally renders it so.

TO PREPARE BUTTER FOR PUFF PASTE.

In summer get a pail of cold spring water, into which throw 3 or 4 pounds of pounded ice, previously washed and 1 oz powdered salt; break the butter into small pieces, put it into the pail and let it remain 20 minutes, until quite firm and hard; it should then be well moulded on a marble slab or paste board, and again immersed in ice water until wanted for use, when it should be pressed in a clean cloth or napkin.

If ice cannot be procured, the following mixture may be used: 1 oz crystalized muriate of ammonia, 1 oz nitrate potash, and 2 ozs sulphate of soda; powder each separately and put them into just sufficient water for the butter to float freely. When taking the butter out for use, wash it well in cold water.

If the butter is too soft, the dough clings to the slab and it will lose its smooth appearance; if the butter is too hard, the dough will not rise any better.

Do not put the paste into the oven until it is sufficiently hot to raise it; for the best prepared paste, if not perfectly baked, will be good for nothing. Brushing the paste as often as rolled out, and the pieces of butter placed thereon, with the white of an egg, assists it to rise in *leaves* or *flakes*. As this is the great beauty of puff paste, it is as well to try this method.

PUFF PASTE—FEUILLETAGE (UDE'S RECIPE.)

Equal quantities of flour and butter—say 1 ℔ of each; ½ saltspoon of salt; the yolks of 2 eggs; rather more than ¼ pt water. Ascertain that the flour is perfectly *dry*, and sift it; squeeze all the water from the butter, and wring it in a clean cloth till there is no moisture remaining. Put the flour on the marble slab; work lightly into it 2 ozs of the butter; then make a hole in the centre and put therein the yolks of 2 eggs, the salt, and about ¼ pt water (the quantity of this latter ingredient must be regulated by the cook, as it is impossible to give the exact proportion of it); knead up the paste quickly and lightly, and when quite smooth, roll it out square to the thickness of about ½ inch. Presuming that the butter is perfectly free from moisture, and as *cool* as possible, roll it into a ball, and place this ball of butter on the paste; fold the paste over the butter all around, and secure it by wrapping it well all over. Flatten the paste by rolling it lightly with the rolling pin until it is quite thin, but not thin enough to break through; keep the slab and paste dredged lightly with flour during the process of making it. This rolling gives it the *first* turn. Now fold the paste in three, and roll out again; and should the weather be warm place it on ice during the several turns, or the paste may be entirely spoiled. Roll out the paste again *twice*; put it by to cool; then roll it out *twice* more, mak- . ing six *turnings* in all. Lastly, fold the paste in two and it will be ready for use. If perfectly baked and well made, this crust will be delicious and should rise in the oven about 3 or 4 inches. The paste should be made rather firm in the first instance, as the ball of butter is liable to break through. Great attention must also be paid to keeping the butter very cool, as if it is in a liquid and soft state, the paste will not answer at all. Should the cook be dexterous enough to succeed in making this, the paste will have a much better appearance than that made by the process of dividing the butter into four parts, and placing it over the rolled out paste. The above paste is used for vol-au-vents, small articles of pastry, and in fact, everything that requires very light crust.

PUFF PASTE—SOYER'S RECIPE.

Put 1 ℔ flour upon the pastry slab; make a hole in the centre into which put a pinch of salt; mix with very *cold* or iced water into a soft, flexible paste with the right hand; dredge it off a little with flour until it is cleared from the slab, but do not work it any more than possible; let it remain 2 or 3 minutes on the slab; then take 1 ℔ fresh butter (from which the buttermilk has been squeezed in a cloth and brought to the same consistency as the paste); place it upon the paste, pressing it out flat with the hand; fold over the edge of the paste so as to hold the butter, and reduce it with the rolling pin to the thickness of about ½ inch, when it will be about 2 feet in length; fold over one-third, over which again pass the rolling pin; then fold over the other third, thus forming a square; place it with the ends, top and bottom towards you, shaking a little flour both under and over, and repeat the rolls and turns twice again, as before. Flour a baking sheet, put the paste on this, and let it remain on ice, or in some cool place for ½ hour; then roll it twice more, turning it as before; place it again upon ice for ¼ hour; give it two more rolls, making seven in all, when it is ready for use when required.

The yolk of an egg and the juice of a lemon are sometimes added with the salt.

PUFF PASTE—AMERICAN AND FRENCH METHODS.

4 ℔s flour (amber white). 4 ℔s butter.
1 qt cold ice water.

Wash the butter well, so as to extract all the salt out of it, and to give it a smooth texture; place it on the ice to harden; make the flour and water into a paste; roll out thin; place the butter in the centre, and gather the paste all around it; take the rolling pin and roll as thin as possible in the form of a square; double it up and roll it out again, if the butter does not get greasy and stick to the rolling pin; if so, put it into a cloth and place in the ice-box until the mass gets hard. It will take from one to three hours. Take it out and roll five or six times, until the dough is nice and clear, and has a fine grain. Place in the ice-box till ready for use; bake in a hot oven.

The French put in the above mixture $\frac{1}{2}$ doz eggs, and work them into the paste before putting in the butter. This does very well for patties, but is not required for pie dough.

PUFF PASTE—RUNDELL'S RECIPE.

Take $\frac{1}{4}$ peck of flour; rub into it 1 ℔ of butter, making a "light paste" with cold water, just stiff enough to work well; lay it out $\frac{1}{2}$ inch thick; put a layer of butter all over it; sprinkle on a little flour, double it up, and roll it out again; by repeating this with fresh layers of butter three or four times, or oftener, a very light paste will be formed. Bake in a moderately quick oven.

PUFF PASTE—AN EASY METHOD.

To every pound of flour allow 1 ℔ of butter, and not quite $\frac{1}{2}$ pt water. Work the flour into a smooth paste with the water, using a knife to mix it with; roll it out to an equal thickness of about an inch; break 4 ozs of the butter into small pieces; place it on the paste; sift on a little flour; fold, roll out again, and put on another 4 ozs of butter. Repeat the rolling and buttering until the paste has been rolled out four times, or equal quantities of flour and butter have been used, not omitting every time the paste is rolled out, to sprinkle a little flour over that and the rolling pin, to keep both from

2

sticking. Handle the paste as little as possible, and do not press heavily upon it or the rolling pin.

PUFF PASTE—MEDIUM.

To every pound of flour allow 8 ozs of butter, 4 ozs of lard, and not quite $\frac{1}{2}$ pt water. This paste may be made as ordinary puff-paste, only using less butter, and substituting lard for a portion of it. Mix the flour into a smooth paste with not quite $\frac{1}{2}$ pt water; roll it out three times, the first time covering the paste with butter. Keep the rolling pin and paste slightly dredged with flour to prevent them from sticking, and it will be ready for use.

HALF PUFF PASTE

Is puff paste made with half the quantity of butter, and giving the paste only 3 or 4 folds.

CHAPTER III.

PIE CRUSTS AND THE MANUFACTURE OF PIES.

Common Crust for Kitchen Pies and Puddings—Common Pie Crust (top)—Common Pie Crust (bottom)—Domestic Pie Paste (1)—Domestic Pie Paste (2)—Domestic Pie Paste, Without Butter or Lard—Lard or Flead Crust—Raised Pie Crust—Raised Pie Crust (French)—Short Crust (1)—Short Crust (2)—Short Crust (3)—Soyer's Method with Pies—How to Make Pies—General Directions—Use of the Jagger—Suiting the Crust to the Flavor of the Fruit Used—How to Make Deep Fruit Pies—Raised Pies.

COMMON CRUSTS FOR KITCHEN PIES AND PUDDINGS.

To every pound of flour allow 6 ozs clarified beef drippings, and ½ pt water. After having clarified the drippings, weigh it, and to every pound of flour allow the above proportion. With a knife work the flour into a smooth paste with the water, rolling it out three times, each time placing on the crust 2 ozs of the dripping broken into small pieces. If this paste is lightly made, if good dripping is used, and *not too much of it*, it will be found good; and by the addition of two tablespoonsful of fine moist sugar, it may be converted into a common short crust for fruit pies.

COMMON PIE CRUST—TOP.

16 lbs flour.　　　　　9 lbs hard, solid lard.
3 qts cold water.

Mix lard and flour lightly together; add water; mix lightly, or rather shake it up, as it were, so that the dough will sponge well.

COMMON PIE CRUST—BOTTOM.

16 lbs flour.   6 lbs hard, cold lard.
3 qts cold water.

The scraps left from making the tops of pies are used for the bottoms, as far as they will go.

DOMESTIC PIE PASTE (1).

2 lbs butter, washed in cool   3 lbs pastry flour (sifted).
  ice water, or
1½ lbs butter and ½ lb lard.

Mix the butter and flour together (not too fine), as it is better to have the butter in good sized lumps. Make a hollow in the centre and mix in enough ice water to make a stiff dough. If not used immediately place in a cool situation until wanted.

DOMESTIC PIE PASTE (2).

1 lb flour.   ½ lb hard lard.
Salt to taste.

Mix as for domestic pie paste (1). This makes a good and cheap pie crust, if eaten whilst it is fresh baked, but it lacks the flavor of that made with butter.

DOMESTIC PIE CRUST—WITHOUT BUTTER OR LARD.

Put into a good sized bowl, a cup of thick sweet cream; add sifted flour to it by degrees, not stirring it about, but chopping it in with the edge of a knife, until thick enough to roll without sticking. This paste scorches very easily, and must also be baked as soon as possible after it is made.

LARD OR FLEAD CRUST.

To every pound of flour, allow ½ lb lard or flead, ½ pt water, and pinch of salt. Clear the flead from skin, and slice it into thin flakes; rub it into the flour, add the salt, and work the whole into a smooth paste with the above proportion of water; fold the paste over two or three times; beat it well with the rolling pin; roll it out, and it will be ready for use. The crust made from this will be found to be extremely light, and may be made into cakes or tarts; it may also be very much enriched by adding more flead to the same proportion of flour.

RAISED PIE CRUST (1).

To every pound of flour allow $\frac{1}{2}$ pt water, $1\frac{1}{2}$ ozs butter, $1\frac{1}{2}$ ozs lard, and a pinch of salt. Put the water into a saucepan, and when it boils add the butter and lard; when these are melted, make a hole in the middle of the flour; pour in the water gradually, beat it well with a wooden spoon, and be particular in not making the paste too soft. When it is well mixed, knead it with the hands until quite stiff, dredging a little flour over the paste and slab to prevent them from sticking; when well kneaded, place before the fire, with a cloth covered over it, for a few minutes; it will then be more easily worked into shape. This paste does not taste so nicely as a richer one, but it is worked with greater facility, and answers just as well for raised pies, for the crust is seldom eaten.

RAISED PIE CRUST—FRENCH.

1 ℔ flour.	4 ozs butter.
1 teaspoon salt.	$1\frac{1}{2}$ gills cold water.

Make a well in the flour and add the other ingredients; work into a fine paste in the following manner: When the ingredients have been worked into a paste this must be brought to the edge of the slab; use the palms of both hands, applying them alternately with great force, to spread and divide the paste into small parts; sprinkle a few drops of water over the paste, and knead it together; this is called breaking and kneading and must be repeated 3 or 4 times. This paste must then be gathered up, placed in a clean rubber, and firmly kneaded by pressing upon it with the elbow. It will then be ready for use.

SHORT CRUST (1.)

To every pound of flour allow 8 ozs of butter, the yolks of 2 eggs, 2 ozs sifted sugar, and about $\frac{1}{4}$ pt milk. Rub the butter into the flour, add the sugar, and mix the whole as lightly as possible to a smooth paste; work the yolks of the eggs well beaten, and the milk. The proportion of the latter ingredient must be judged by the size of the eggs; if they are large, so much will not be required; and more, if the eggs are smaller.

SHORT CRUST (2.)

To every pound of flour allow 2 ozs of sifted sugar, 3 ozs of butter, and about $\frac{1}{2}$ pt boiling milk. Crumble the butter into the flour as finely as possible; add the sugar and work the whole up to a smooth paste with the boiling milk. Roll it out thin and bake in a moderate oven.

SHORT CRUST (3.)

To every pound of flour, allow $\frac{1}{2}$ or $\frac{3}{4}$ lb of butter, 1 tablespoon of sifted sugar, $\frac{1}{3}$ pt water. Rub the butter into the flour, after having ascertained that the latter is perfectly dry; add the sugar, and mix the whole into a stiff paste with about $\frac{1}{3}$ pt water. Roll it out two or three times, folding the paste over each time, and it will be ready for use.

This crust is used specially for fruit tarts.

PIES—SOYER'S METHOD.

To make a pie to perfection—when the paste (half puff or short) is carefully made, and the dish or form properly full, throw a little flour on the paste-board; take about ¼ ℔ of paste, which roll with the hand until (say) an inch in circumference; moisten the rim of the pie dish, and fix the paste equally on it with the thumb. When the paste for the cover or upper crust is rolled of an equal thickness throughout, and in proportion to the contents of the pie (½ inch is about the average), fold the cover in two, lay it over one-half of the pie, and turn the other half over the remaining part; press it slightly with the thumb round the rim; cut the rim of the paste neatly, form rather a thick edge, and mark this with a knife about every quarter of an inch apart; observe to hold the knife in a slanting direction, which gives it a neat appearance; lastly make two small holes in the top, and egg over the whole with a paste brush, or else with a little milk or water. Any small p rtion of paste remaining may be shaped to fanciful designs, and placed as ornaments on the top.

For meat pies, observe that if the paste is either too thick or too thin, the covering too narrow or too short, and requires pulling one way or the other, to make it fit, the pie is sure to be imperfect, the cover no longer protecting the contents. It is the same with fruit; and if the paste happens to be rather rich, it pulls the rim of the pie to the dish, soddens the paste, makes it heavy, and therefore indigestible as well as unpalatable.

HOW TO MAKE PIES.

The making of pies is so simple an operation that few words will suffice to give all needed instructions on the matter. The object is to get a good even bottom and a sightly, well-fitting top. The methods adopted for doing this are varied according to the conveniences at hand or the quantity of pies to be made. The general principle may be illustrated, by taking a piece of dough large enough for the bottoms of two pies; roll it very lightly into a long, round shape, and cut into four equal parts; roll the bottoms out; place them on the pie tin, pressing them smoothly to the form; fill the pies; roll out the covers and top the pies, not forgetting to use the jagger; mark on the top of the pie the first letter of fruit, etc., used in filling the pie with stamps made for this purpose; cut the scrap off with the hand if it is common dough, or if puff-paste cut with a very sharp knife; use the scrap for the bottom of the next pie, etc. Where, however, pies are made in quantities, the bottoms are placed on by one set of hands, the filling done by a second set, and again a third set put on the covers and finish the pies ready to be placed in the oven. The object of making holes in the top crust of the pie with the jigger or pie-mark, is to let the steam escape which is generated in baking, otherwise the crust would be apt to burst open on the side.

Most workmen trim the pie by using the palms of both hands to cut off the superfluous paste, as if they were clapping their hands together; this is said to raise the crust and give a larger appearance to the pie.

In conclusion we may add that pies may be made of almost any variety of fruit, either green or dried; but

very often the flavor is destroyed for want of a true
knowledge of making them. A great deal depends on the
manipulation of the pie dough, as well as on the regula-
tion of the oven in which it is baked. No matter what
kind of a covered pie is made, if the dough is not suitable, the flavor of the pie is destroyed. Take, for instance, a dough made of lard and baked in a slow oven;
all the fat goes into the fruit, and consequently spoils
the flavor of the pie. Lard makes a good crust if
properly handled, otherwise it will not; but butter is
always the best. Puff paste makes the finest cover for
pies of all kinds, especially for apple, peach, or mince
pies. What is commonly known as domestic pastry
answers the purpose very well where ice is not plentiful,
or if wanted for immediate use, and not requiring as
much butter as puff-paste, it comes cheaper.

DEEP FRUIT PIES.

Fruit pies in deep dishes, such as made by the English and French, are preferable to ordinary fruit pies, because more juice and fruit is obtained. The best
method of making these is as follows: Take a deep,
oval pie dish, china, not tin; line the edge with paste,
also about half its depth inside; place a small cup, an
egg cup is best, and one that will stand a little above
the edge of the dish; fill the dish with fruit, and add a
little water if the fruit has not too much juice. Some
fruits, such as currants and raspberries, have enough
juice. Also add sugar to taste; cover this with a crust
of short paste, wash it with water or white of an egg,
and dust with powdered sugar. Make a few fancy cuts
on it before baking, and after it is washed and sugared;
do not cut too deep. These cuts give it a rich looking

appearance. The cup in the center collects the juice, and if the whole of the pie is not eaten at one meal, what is left can be supplied with juice by simply lifting the cup and allowing the juice to escape. The edge of this pie, to be artistic, should be pinched up with the finger and thumb, then notched with a knife. If fruit is used which gives too much juice, it can be prevented from boiling over by mixing a little flour with the sugar, about one teaspoonful of flour to twelve of sugar.

RAISED PIES.

To form: Take as much pastry as it is intended to use for the pie; cut off as much as will be wanted for the cover, and form the remainder to the shape of a cone. Flatten the sides with the palms of the hands, and when they are quite smooth, squeeze the point down a little, and press the knuckles of the left hand into the middle of the pastry till the inside is hollow. Knead it well with the fingers, and be careful to have every part of an equal thickness. Fill the pie, roll out the remainder of the pastry to the size of the top of the pie, moisten the edges with a little egg, and lay on the cover. Press this down securely, and pinch it with pastry pinchers. Make a small hole in the centre of the pie, and ornament with pastry leaves, chains, or any fanciful designs. Brush all over with egg, and bake in a well-heated oven. When the pie is done enough, take it out, and pour in a little good gravy, which will jelly when cold. If a mould is used, butter it, and line it with good firm pastry. Fill the pie, roll out the cover, moisten the edges of the pastry, lay it on, and press it down securely, so that the edge of the pie may be raised slightly above the cover. Pinch the edges with the pastry nippers; make a small hole in the center, and lay upon the pie pastry ornaments of any description. Brush over with egg, bake in a well-heated oven. Take the pie out, draw out the pin which fastens the side of the mould, and take it out carefully. If it is not sufficiently browned, put it into the oven a quarter of an hour longer. · Raised pies should be served on a neatly-folded napkin, and garnished with parsley.

CHAPTER IV.

VARIOUS PASTES USED BY THE PASTRY COOK—PATTY CASES—VOL-AU-VENT.

Almond Paste—Confectioners' Paste - Croustade Cases - French or or Swiss Paste—Gum Paste—Nouilles Paste—Office Paste - Patty Cases (1) - Patty Cases (2) - Tart Paste—Timbale Paste Vol-Au-Vent (1)—Vol-Au-Vent (2).

ALMOND PASTE.

1 ℔ sweet almonds.	⅛ oz gum tragacanth,
1½ lbs fine white sugar.	soaked and squeezed through a napkin.

Blanch the almonds; pound quarter of them with a little rose water to prevent oiling; when pounded to a paste, pound another quarter, and so on until all are done; then put the paste through a hair sieve, and put it into a preserving kettle with the sugar; place over a slow fire; keep stirring about 25 minutes, clearing it from the sides of the pan; when it feels tough take it out and put into a mortar with the gum tragacanth; add the juice of a lemon and pound until quite cold, when it is ready for use.

If not used directly, roll up in a ball and place upon a plate under a basin to keep moist. Stands can be made of this paste, or it may be converted into any fancy ornament.

CONFECTIONERS' PASTE.

1¼ lbs flour.	2 yolks of eggs.
10 ozs sifted sugar.	1 gill hot water.

Spread out the flour with a hollow in the center on

the slab, placing the yolks and sugar therein; add half the water and work the ingredients together with the fingers; when well mixed add the remainder of the water, and vigorously work all together into a firm, smooth, compact paste; roll this up in a cloth till wanted for use.

CROUSTADE CASES.

Roll out $\frac{1}{2}$ ℔ Timbale Paste to the thickness of about $\frac{1}{8}$ inch; take a circular tin cutter about 4 inches in diameter, and stamp out a dozen flats; press one of them in the end of a circular piece of wood, about 6 inches long by $1\frac{1}{2}$ ins. diameter (or failing this, cut a carrot to that shape). Line a dariole mould, previously slightly spread with butter, with the paste so prepared; use the thumb to make the paste lie evenly in the mould; trim away the edges; raise the sides a little; then fill each croustade so finished with flour, mixed with $\frac{1}{4}$ part of chopped suet, and bake them of a light color; when done empty them and place them on a dish.

The tops must be stamped out with a small circular fluted cutter, from some puff paste, rolled seven times; put these on a baking sheet previously wetted to receive them; egg them over with a soft brush; place a much smaller circular piece of paste on the top of each; egg these over, and then bake them of a bright color; when done, trim them and place each on top of one of the croustades after they are garnished.

Croustades and patties are garnished with scollops or ragouts of chicken, game, all kinds of fillets of fish, the the tails of crayfish, prawns, and shrimps, with oysters in scollops, or small dice, and also lobsters cut up in small

dice. They may be sauced either with Supreme, Bechamel, or Allemande, lobster, oyster or crayfish sauces.

FRENCH OR SWISS PASTE.

This paste is made precisely the same as Puff Paste,
the difference is simply in the cutting and baking. Take
the paste and roll it out about ½ inch thick; cut it into
strips about 3 inches long and ½ inch wide; lay them on
the baking plate with the cut side uppermost, placing
them about 3 inches apart; bake in a moderately quick
oven. While they are baking, instead of rising, they
will spread out like a fan; take them out and dust over
them some fine powdered sugar; put them again into
the oven one minute to melt the sugar, and they will be
glazed.

GUM PASTE.

Dissolve a sufficient quantity of Gum Tragacanth in
rose water; make it into a paste with double refined
sugar, well beaten; color with vegetable colors different
portions of the paste, according to fancy. Keep moist
for use.

NOUILLES PASTE.

1 ℔ flour.	Water sufficient to melt
10 yolks of eggs.	the salt.
1 teaspoonful salt.	

Form a hollow in the centre of the flour; put in the
salt and water, and add the yolks of 8 eggs; work well
together, at first rubbing between the hands, and then if
necessary add two more yolks of eggs; finish working
the paste by pushing it from you with the palms of the
hands, using considerable pressure; sprinkle a few drops
of water over it; knead the paste into a ball and keep it

wrapped up in a cold cloth till wanted for use. This paste must be kept very stiff.

OFFICE PASTE.

1 ℔ flour.	2 whole eggs.
8 ozs powdered sugar.	2 yolks.

Make a well in the flour; add the sugar and eggs; work into a stiff compact body. If the paste should appear dry, and present any difficulty in kneading, another yolk or two may be added.

This paste is mostly used for making ornaments for the second course.

PATTY CASES (1.)

Make 1 ℔ Puff Paste, give it seven turns, wetting the last turn before folding it; roll the paste out so as to leave it scarcely $\frac{1}{4}$ inch thick; about 3 minutes afterwards take a fluted circular tin cutter about 2 inches in diameter, and use this to stamp out as many patties as may be required; previously to stamping out each patty the cutter should be first dipped in very hot water, as the heat thus imparted to the cutter causes it to slip easily through the paste, and produces the same effect as if it were cut with a sharp knife; in consequence of there being little or no pressure on the edges, the paste has thus a much better chance of rising while baking, especially in the summer season.

As soon as the patties are cut out they should be immediately placed in rows, on a baking sheet, previously wetted over, about 2 inches apart; then egg them over with a soft brush dipped in beaten egg, being careful not to smear the edges; stamp them in the centre, making a slight incision through the surface, with a plain circular tin cutter about 1½ inches in diameter (this cutter must also be dipped in hot water each time it is used.) The patties should then be quickly put in the oven and baked of a light color; when done, let the covers or top be removed; pick out the inner crust carefully with the point of a small knife, and then place the patties with their tops on a baking sheet lined with clean paper.

PATTY CASES (2).

These should be made from the best paste. Get three cutters of different sizes; roll out the paste about ¾ inch thick; cut out as many pieces as required with the large cutter; cut out the same quantity of pieces with the second sized cutter; and with the third size, cut out some small thin pieces to put on the top of these;—then with the second cutter, cut the paste partly through, what was had from the large cutter, leaving as near as possible, an equal edge round out; wash the top with egg, and bake them on an iron-plate;—dip each of the cutters into boiling water before using, which prevents the edge being drawn, and they rise more evenly.

When baked take out the centre of the large pieces with a knife, as far as the mark of the cutter and about three parts of the depth of the paste; fill these vacancies or holes with some prepared patty meat, put the other pieces on top, and send to the table quite hot.

TART PASTE.

1 lb flour.   8 ozs butter.

Rub the flour and butter together till the latter crumbles into pieces; mix into a moderately stiff paste with cold water; continue rubbing it with the hands on the board or slab until the paste becomes smooth and supple, having no degree of toughness, and shines on the surface. This paste will take considerably less water to mix it in summer than in winter.

This is used for making raspberry tarts, and all covered tarts, and occasionally for large fruit, and other pies.

TIMBALE PASTE.

1℔ flour.	½ ℔ butter.
1 teaspoon salt.	Yolks of 2 eggs.
Nearly ½ pt water.	

Make a well in the centre of the flour; place in this the yolks, salt, butter and ⅔ of the water; work together with the hands into a somewhat firm paste; dip the fingers into the flour to separate any of the paste that may adhere to them; sprinkle a little water over it, and then work the whole together into a ball, and keep it in a cloth till wanted for use.

VOL-AU-VENT (1).

A vol-au-vent presents one of the handsomest forms in which the remains of dishes can be served. It is generally filled with a mince, or ragout, or fricasse—or whatever other name may be chosen—of dressed meat; and after the vol-au-vent case is made, there is abundant opportunity for the cook to display his skill, either in the richness and delicacy, or in the savoury nature of its contents. A vol-au-vent can be made successfully only with the lighest puff paste. If the puff paste is not exceedingly light, the vol-au-vent will not rise properly, and so will have a very bad appearance. In rolling it. care must be taken to keep it perfectly square and even at the ends, as unless this is done the pastry cannot rise evenly. The pasty for a vol-au-vent ought to have

six turns, and five minutes should be allowed to elapse
between each turn.   After it has been turned five times,
brush the pastry over with lemon juice, and when it is
doubled for the last time, fold it in such a way that,
when finished, it will be the exact size of the inside of
the dish in which it is to be served, and a little more
than an inch thick.   Cut it evenly all around with a
knife that has been made hot in water, so as not to drag
the pastry.   Place a stew-pan lid, or any other shape of
a suitable size, within an inch and a half of the outer
edge of the pasty, and with a sharp knife make an incision a quarter of an inch deep all around the edge of the
lid.   Press the inner circle away from the outer one
with the point of the knife to prevent them closing
again; this inner cake, when baked, will form the cover
of the vol-au-vent.   Put the vol-au-vent in a well-heated
oven; in half an hour or three-quarters of an hour, if it
should appear baked through, take it out of the oven,
lift up the cover with the point of a knife where it has
been marked, and scoop out the soft, crummy centre
without at all injuring the walls of the case.

VOL-AU-VENT (2).

Take some paste as for Patty Cases, give it an extra
half turn; make it about $1\frac{1}{2}$ inches thick; cut it out with
a large oval or round cutter, or in any shape, with a
a knife, to suit the form and size of the dish; heat the
knife or cutter in hot water; mark it round about an inch
from the edge; ornament the centre part by cutting any
design with a knife; egg the top and bake it in a moderate heat;—when rather more than three parts done, take
it out and remove the centre piece, reserving it for a

cover;—scoop out the remaining part of the paste from the centre, leaving it ½ inch thick at the bottom; put in the oven again to dry or finish baking; it should be 4 or 5 inches high and quite straight; fill it with any sort of ragout or fricasse, as for patties.

These are occasionally filled with a compote, or a made dish of fish, or served as a sweet entree, filled with a cream or fruit.

CHAPTER V.

PIES AND TARTS.

Distinction of the Terms, Pies, Tarts and Tartlets—English Nomenclature—Stripping—Glazing, etc.,—Tarts and Tartlets, (1) —Tarts and Tartlets, (2)—Tarts of Puff Paste—Fruit Pies and Tarts—Berry Pies—Fruit Tarts, Soyer's Method—Ornamentation—Mosaic Boards—Patty Cases—Vol-au-Vents.

In England the term *pie* is applied almost exclusively to savory or meat pies, *tart* being the name for what the Americans designate promiscuously by the former word. Consequently *tartlet* corresponds with our term, tart. It is well to understand this distinction when referring to English works on pastry, in order to avoid mistakes. As the general directions for making pies have been given before, (Chapter III,) it will be only necessary here to note some special memoranda in regard to the manipulation of both pies and tarts or tartlets, before giving the formulæ for their fillings.

1. *Stripping.* Pies and tarts are sometimes covered with a net work of strips of pastry, in place of a full top cover, or no cover at all. To do this, after the dough covered pie plates have been filled, cut long strips from the dough, about the width of the finger; roll this out flat, about ⅛ inch thick; plait these strips over the filling, laying the first one across the centre, the second crossing the first, then two others from each side of the first, and lastly two from each side of the second, keeping them about ¼ inch apart, so that two strips alternately cross from side to side, until the whole filling is covered, as it were, with a net work. The ends must then be cut

off even at the edge, the ridge of the pie washed with
egg and then bordered with one of the before mentioned strips; wash the pie with egg, being careful that
none of it runs off on the sides.

For tarts, the strips must, of course, be made propor-
tionately narrower, in order to make a net work on so
small a surface.

2.   All pies of puff paste must be glazed well with
pulverized sugar while in the oven, or else covered with
snow of the white of eggs and sugar, sprinkled with water, and baked in a more than medium hot oven.

TARTS AND TARTLETS, (1.)

Tarts or tartlets are generally made in the following
manner: Have some puff paste rolled out thin; press
out the slices; put them into appropriate tin moulds,
and add the filling.   Or, after having rolled out the
dough about $\frac{1}{4}$ inch thick, press out the under crust
about 3 or 4 inches in diameter; put it on the baking
pans; wash it with eggs, and put on an edging of about
$\frac{1}{2}$ inch in height; put in the filling and bake as usual.

TARTS AND TARTLETS, (2.)

Place a layer of puff paste in the pans, about $\frac{1}{2}$ inch
thick; make it thinner in the centre than at the edges,
by pressing the thumb round the centre; trim it off
close to the pan with a knife; fill with any fruit or filling
desired; cover with a net-work of strips of paste, by
stringing them across the tart.

TARTS OF PUFF PASTE.

Roll out 1 ℔ puff paste to the thickness of 1-6 inch;
with a circular tin cutter about $1\frac{3}{4}$ inches in diameter,
stamp out forty flats; again, use a smaller cutter meas-

uring 1 inch in diameter, to stamp out the centre of
these; gather up the trimmings, knead them together,
and roll them out ⅛ inch thick, stamping out as many
flats as there are rings; place them on a wetted baking
sheet and moisten the edges with a soft brush dipped in
water; stick the rings of paste on these; shake some sugar over them, and bake of a very light color, (at a moderate heat.) When the tarts are done, mask the bands
or rings with a little meringue-paste; dip them either
in some chopped, or very finely shred pistachios or almonds, and place them in the screen to dry. Previously
to serving these tartlets, they may be filled either with
cherries, currants, plums, etc., or any kind of preserved
or prepared fruits.

FRUIT PIES AND TARTS.

When the larger kinds of stone fruits are used for making pies and tarts, such as peaches, apriots, etc , the stones
must be taken out and cracked, and the kernels placed
upon the top of the fruit in the dish. Add a spoonful of
water, and sugar enough to sweeten; cover with pie paste,
and finish as usual. For making cherry or damson pies
follow the same directions, except that the stones should
not be removed.

Gooseberries, currants, raspberries, strawberries, etc.,
may be treated in the same way. These fruits may also
be prepared for tartlets, as well as plums, etc., by boiling them gently for a few minutes in sufficient syrup;
the fruit should then be drained in a sieve, and the syrup
reduced to one third its original quantity, and kept with
the fruit in a small basin to fill the tartlets with.

Berry pies are generally so juicy that they do not cut
well; to obviate this difficulty, the beaten white of an

egg may be added to thicken the juice; but a better way is to add a small quantity of rolled crackers or cracker crumbs. A little flour is sometimes sprinkled over the berries after filling the pies.

FRUIT TARTS—SOYER'S METHOD

They may be made from the trimmings of any puff paste which remains, and should be enveloped in paper, and kept in a cold place, or in the flour tub. Make them as follows: Have ready twelve or more small tart pans, which butter; line each with a bit of puff paste cut with a small cutter; force up the edges with the thumb and finger; put a small ball (made of flour and water) in each, and bake them nicely in a very hot oven; when done, take out the ball, (which may be kept for other occasions,) from the tarts, and shake powdered sugar over the bottom of each; glaze with a salamander, turn them over, and shake sugar in the interior, which also salamander; fill with any kind of preserve, fruit or marmalade.

They may be made with cream as follows:—Make the tarts as before, placing cream instead of the ball of flour, made thus; put ½ pt. milk in a stewpan, when boiling, add half a stick of vanilla; reduce the milk to half ; in another stewpan have the yolks of 2 eggs, ¼ oz. powdered sugar and 1 oz. sifted flour, with a pinch of salt; pour in the milk, taking out the vanilla; place over a slow fire and keep stirring till it thickens; when cold, fill the tartlets; bake nicely in a slow oven; when cold, add a little jam; have ready a meringue of 4 eggs; lay a teaspoon of each upon them, spreading it quite flat with a knife; ornament the top with some of the mixture, put into a paper cornet; sift sugar over; place in a slow oven till a light brown color, and the meringue is quite crisp; if the oven is too hot, cover with a sheet of paper; dress and serve in a pyramid upon a dish. They ought to be of a light color.

ORNAMENTATION.

Pies, tarts, etc., may be ornamented by means of stars, roses, leaves and other fanciful designs, stamped out of the paste. Cutters for making a great many patterns can be procured from any dealer in bakers' supplies. Touch the tops of the designs with the white of egg; sift sugar over them, and sprinkle with a very little water; put them on a plate and bake them; or the ornaments may be baked with the pies.

MOSAIC BOARDS.

These boards may be procured of all sizes and patterns. To cut out impressions from them, it is necessary to use small circular flats of raised pie-paste, which must be placed on the board, and pressed into the design, by rolling it with a paste-pin; the superfluous paste must then be cut or shaved away, and the mosaic of paste that remains in the design shaken out of the board.

PATTY CASES AND VOL-AU-VENTS.

Both patty cases and vol-au-vents when filled with preserved fruits, etc., make a nice species of tart.

As a general rule the same fillings can be used for either pies, tarts or tartlets.

Directions for using the salamander will be found under Chapter I, Part II.

CHAPTER VI.

PIE AND TART FILLINGS.

Adelaide Pie—Apple Pie, Sliced—Apple Pie, Quarters, Eighths, etc.—Apple Pie, Stewed (1)—Apple Pie, Stewed (2)—Apple Pie, Custard—Apple and Rice Pie (Soyer's)—Apple Pie with Quince—Apple Pie, Creamed—Apple Pie, English—Apple Tarts (1)—Apple Tarts (2)—Banana Pie—Blackberry Pie—Cherry Pie (1)—Cherry Pie (2)—Cherry Pie, Seedless—Cherry Tarts—Chocolate Custard Pie—Chocolate Pie—Chocolate Tarts—Cocoanut Pie (1)—Cocoanut Pie (2)—Cocoanut Pie (3)—Cranberry Pie—Cracker Pie—Cream Pie—Cream Pie a la Meringue—Currant Pie (1)—Currant Pie (2)—Currant Tarts—Custard Pie (1)—Custard Pie (2)—Custard Pie (3)—Damson Pie—Dewberry Pie—Dried Fruit Pies—Farina Pie—French Plum Pie—Gooseberry Pie—Gooseberry Tarts—Grape Pie—Huckleberry Pie—Irish Potato Pie—Jelly Pie—Lemon Pie—Lemon Pie, Cheap—Lemon Cream Pie—Lemon Marang Pie—Marlborough Pie—Mince Pie (1)—Mince Pie (2)—Mince Pie (3)—Mince Pie, Common—Mock Apple Pie—Mosaic Tarts—Orange Pie—Peach Pie (1)—Peach Pie (2)—Peach Custard Pie—Pear Pie—Pine-apple Pie—Plum Pie—Prune Pie—Pumpkin Pie (1)—Pumpkin Pie (2)—Pumpkin Pie, Dried—Pumpkin Pie, Grated—Punch Pie—Quince Pie—Raisin Pie—Raspberry Pie—Rhubarb Pie (1)—Rhubarb or Pie-Plant Pie (2)—Rice Pie—Squash Pie—Strawberry Pie—Strawberry Meringue Pie—Sweet Potato Pie—Transparent Pie—Vanilla Cream Pie—Vanilla Tarts—Washington Cream Pie.

ADELAIDE PIE.

1 oz candied citron peel.	3 eggs.
1 oz " lemon peel.	3 yolks of eggs.
1 oz " orange peel.	2 ozs butter.
½ doz macaroons, beaten fine.	2 ozs sugar.
	1 tablespoon rice flour.
1 gill milk.	

Boil the rice flour with the milk until thick; add the butter; when cold, add it to the eggs, sugar, and macaroons, which have been beaten ten minutes together;

lastly add the citron, lemon and orange peels, chopped up finely; bake in a deep pie plate with top and bottom.

APPLE PIE—SLICED.

Pare and slice some sour apples; bottom the pans and put the apples therein, with sufficient sugar to sweeten them; sprinkle over a little salt and cinnamon; add 1 or 2 ozs of butter to each pie; add water until the plate is two-thirds full; cover with puff paste. Lemon zest may be used in place of the cinnamon to flavor.

Sour apples are the best for pie purposes, and they should be sweetened to taste.

APPLE PIE—QUARTERS, EIGHTHS, ETC.

Proceed as for sliced apple pie, quartering, etc., the apples in place of slicing them.

APPLE PIE—STEWED (1.)

Boil one peck of apples very soft in enough water to cover them; strain; sweeten with about 6 ℔s white sugar, and boil about 20 minutes longer, flavoring with nutmeg.

Apples stewed may be used as the basis of a great number of pies, and flavored with lemon, orange, etc., to taste.

APPLE PIE--STEWED (2.)

Peel, core, stew and strain the apples; add light brown sugar, and ground cinnamon or mace, until sweet enough and of the right flavor; stir them up well to get the different articles thoroughly mixed.

APPLE PIE—CUSTARD.

Proceed as for Peach Custard pie, substituting thick, stewed apples.

APPLE AND RICE PIE—SOYER'S.

Peel some apples, cutting them in rather thin slices; boil ¼ lb rice in water till tender, and put in a sieve; when dry put in a basin and add 2 ozs sugar, in which a little cinnamon has been mixed, with 2½ ozs butter; stir lightly; put a layer of rice and a layer of apple alternately till full; add a little more sugar on the apples; make the border of the dish damp, and put a thin rim of paste round it; moisten the rim of paste, place a plain pancake over it, fixing it by damping the rim of the cake; fix artistically another thin band of the same paste; trim neatly, egg over, sprinkle sugar, bake and serve hot. In omitting the rice, apple alone may be used, or any other fruit introduced.

APPLE PIE WITH QUINCE.

Peel the apples, remove the cores, cut them in slices, and arrange them neatly in a pie dish; add the quince, which must be sliced thin and stewed with a little water, sugar, and a bit of butter, in a small stew-pan over a slow fire; add sugar enough to sweeten the quantity of apples required, and some grated lemon peel; cover the pie with puff-paste, first placing a band of paste upon the wetted edge of the dish, and then, after wetting the band, place the cover upon its place, and having pressed it down all round, cut the edge evenly, and scollop it with the back of a knife; decorate the top with leaves of paste; egg it over and bake; when done, dredge it over with sugar, and salamander.

APPLE PIE—CREAMED.

Pare, cut in quarters and core a sufficient quantity of baking apples; sweeten to taste, adding some grated lemon peel, a few cloves, and a small quantity of water; put round the dish an edging of puff-paste, to keep the apples moist; put into the oven till the apples are baked. When the apples are cold, cover them well with a cold boiled custard; ornament the top with leaves and stars.

APPLE PIE—ENGLISH.

Lay some paste crust round the sides of a deep dish; quarter the apples and take out the cores; put in a thick layer of apples, cover with half the sugar intended for the pie, some lemon peel grated fine and a few cloves; put in the rest of the apples and sugar, and add a little lemon juice; boil the cores and peelings of the apples in water with a blade of mace until they are soft; press it through a colander; boil it with sugar, and pour it in the pie with a little quince or marmalade; put on the upper crust and bake.

APPLE TARTS (1.)

Roll out 1 ℔ tart paste rather thin; stamp out forty circular flats, with a fluted cutter suited to the size of the tartlets, and use them to line the moulds; fill each tartlet with a spoonful of apple marmalade; cover them with a mosaic of paste, egg them over, place them on a baking sheet, and bake them of a light color; when done, shake some fine sugar over them, and use the red-hot salamander to give them a glossy appearance.

APPLE TARTS (2.)

Line the tart pans, as for Apple Tarts (1); garnish them with halves of small apples, previously turned and divested of the cores, and afterwards parboiled in a little syrup in which a piece of a lemon has been squeezed. Bake the tarts, and when they are done dilute some apricot jam with a little of the syrup; use this to mask the apples in the tarts; place a preserved cherry on the centre of each.

BANANA PIE.

Slice raw bananas, add butter, sugar, allspice and vinegar, or boiled cider or diluted jelly; bake with two crusts. In the South they use cold boiled sweet potatoes in this way, and regard the pie as choice.

BLACKBERRY PIE.

Bottom the tins and fill with picked blackberries; sweeten to taste; cover and bake.

CHERRY PIE (1.)

Fill the pies with ripe cherries; sweeten to taste.

CHERRY PIE (2.)

Line a pie-tin with rich crust; nearly fill it with the carefully seeded fruit, sweeten to taste, and sprinkle evenly with a teaspoonful of corn starch or tablespoonful of flour; add a tablespoonful of butter cut into small bits and scattered over the top; wet the edge of the crust, put on upper crust, and press the edges closely together, taking care to provide holes in the centre for the escape of the air. Pies from blackberries, raspberries, etc., are all made in the same way, regulating the quantity of sugar by the tartness of the fruit.

CHERRY PIE—SEEDLESS.

Seed 1 peck cherries, adding $\frac{1}{2}$ ℔ sugar to every pound; bake with or without crust.

CHERRY TARTS.

Stone 2 ℔s cherries; put them into a small sugar-boiler with ¾ ℔ pounded sugar; toss them in this, then set them on the fire, and allow to boil for about five minutes; the cherries must be strained on a sieve, and the syrup reduced about one-third, and then added to the cherries, and kept in a small basin.

Line 2 doz small tart-pans with short paste, or tart paste (the flats being stamped out with a fluted cutter); knead as many small pieces of paste as there are tarts, and after dipping them in flour, press one of them into each of the tarts; place them on a baking sheet, and put them in the oven (moderately heated) to be baked of a light color. When they are nearly done, withdraw them, and take out the pieces of paste; shake some fine sugar over them, and glaze them with the red-hot salamander. Just before serving the tarts, fill them with the cherries.

CHOCOLATE CUSTARD PIE.

Simmer 1 quart of milk; add ¼ ℔ of chocolate, grated; sweeten to taste; incorporate 4 well-beaten eggs. Line deep pie-pans with rich paste; pour in the mixture; bake in moderately quick oven.

CHOCOLATE PIE.

To one pint of boiling milk add one tablespoonful of rice flour, the yolks of five eggs, well-beaten, a little salt, and one pint of cream; sugar to taste; ¼ ℔ of grated chocolate, well dried; let them boil, stirring; let it cool. Line deep buttered tins, pour in the mixture and bake.

CHOCOLATE TARTS.

Rub 4 fillets of chocolate smooth in milk; heat over the fire; add corn starch and milk, and stir until sufficiently thick. When cold, beat in the yolks of 1 or 2 doz eggs; sweeten to taste, and flavor with vanilla; bake in open shells lining patty pans. Cover with a meringue made of the whites of the eggs and powdered sugar, when they are nearly done, and let them color slightly; serve cold.

COCOANUT PIE (1.)

1 qt milk.　　　　　3 ozs flour.
½ ℔ sugar.　　　　½ ℔ grated cocoanut.
8 eggs.

Mix eggs, milk, sugar and flour; add ¼ ℔ cocoanut; fill and bake without top. After it has baked have 4 eggs well-beaten; add while beating 1 oz sugar; add ¼ ℔ more cocoanut to the whites with 4 ozs sugar; mix lightly and spread on the pies; set in the oven to brown.

COCOANUT PIE (2.)

Proceed as for Custard pie, adding ½ cupful of grated cocoanut, and leaving out ½ pt milk.

COCOANUT PIE (3.)

1 ℔ flour.　　　　8 eggs.
2 ℔s sugar.　　　½ pt milk.
½ ℔ butter.　　　Meat of 2 cocoanuts, grated

These pies should be made on very small plates or patty pans; bake with only a bottom crust.

CRANBERRY PIE.

Boil 1 ℔ cranberries in 1 pt water until soft; add 1 ℔ fine white sugar, and let simmer 15 or 20 minutes. Line a pie-plate; put in the cranberry jam; wash the edges, and lay three narrow bars across, fasten at the edges, then three more across, forming diamond shaped spaces; lay a rim of paste; wash with egg wash, and bake in a quick oven until the paste is cooked.

A little corn starch dissolved in cold water, is sometimes added with the sugar.

CRACKER PIE.

1 qt milk.	¼ ℔ sugar.
3 or 4 crackers.	Vanilla flavor.
½ doz eggs.	

Boil crackers and milk; when melted take off the fire and let cool; add the other ingredients; bake without crust, with frosting on top.

CREAM PIE.

1 qt. white wine.	1 oz corn starch dissolved
1 ℔ sugar.	in cold water.
8 yolks and 2 whites of eggs.	Zest of a lemon.

Boil sugar and wine; add yolks and whites well whipped, stirring till it boils again; add corn starch and lemon zest; when cool, fill into dishes and bake.

CREAM PIE À LA MERINGUE.

Boil 3 qts. milk; take 8 ozs. corn starch, 10 whole eggs or 20 yolks, and 1 ℔ sugar; beat the eggs, corn starch and sugar together, and pour into the boiling milk; stir briskly over a slow fire, until it thickens to the consistency of a stiff batter. This constitutes the cream, one pint of which will fill an ordinary pie; bake as custard pie; when baked, ornament with a meringue mixture; place back in the oven to color; when it is done, flavor with vanilla.

CURRANT PIE, (1.)

Leave no stems on the currants; fill the pie with ripe currants, adding 6 ozs. sugar to each pie.

CURRANT PIE, (2.)

Stew ripe currants in sufficient sugar; strain, and proceed as for cranberry pie.

CURRANT TARTS.

Carefully pick over a pint of green currants, put in a sauce pan, add a little water, and scald; pour off the water and mash them up with six ounces of white sugar, three ounces of fresh butter beaten to a cream, white of 2 eggs, one cup of red currant jelly; line the tart pans with paste, put in the mixture, and bake.

CUSTARD PIE, (1.)

Boil 1 qt. milk; stir in 1 tablespoon corn starch dissolved in cold water; sweeten and flavor to taste; stir in thoroughly 3 beaten eggs; bake with only a bottom crust.

CUSTARD PIE, (2.)

| 1½ pts. milk. | ¼ ℔ sugar. |
| 4 eggs. | Lemon zest to flavor. |

Beat well together and strain.

CUSTARD PIE, (3.)

| 15 eggs. | 2 ozs. flour. |
| 1 ℔ sugar. | ½ gal. milk. |

Mix eggs, flour and sugar together first; add milk.

DAMSON PIE.

Cover damsons with water and boil till very soft; rub through a sieve and add 1 ℔ sugar to every pound of fruit.

4

DEWBERRY PIE.

Proceed with dewberries as for raspberry pie.

DRIED FRUIT PIES.

Dried apples, peaches, prunes and plums, etc., may be used; cook in water and strain through a sieve; add $\frac{1}{2}$ to $\frac{3}{4}$ ℔ sugar to pound of fruit; flavor with lemon, etc., to suit taste.

FARINA PIE.

2 eggs, 1 pt. milk, 1 tablespoon corn starch, a pinch of salt, and sugar to taste. Set the milk over the fire; let it simmer, but not boil; soak the corn starch in a little cold milk, and when the other milk is hot, stir the starch in; add the beaten eggs, and sweeten to taste; let all boil a little till it thickens; take it off; add any flavoring desired, and pour it into the crust; bake half an hour. When baked, glaze the top with the beaten white of an egg and a little sugar; set back in the oven for a few minutes to brown it a little.

FRENCH PLUM PIE.

Steep the fruit over night in water; add sugar to taste; flavor with lemon.

GOOSEBERRY PIE.

Boil over a slow fire 1 gal. gooseberries in 1 pt. water; when soft, strain through a sieve; add 6 ℔s of sugar to the juice, if for immediate use, if not, add 8 ℔s sugar; in both cases boil $\frac{1}{2}$ hour.

GOOSEBERRY TARTS.

Top and tail the gooseberries. Put into a porcelain

kettle with enough water to prevent burning, and stew slowly until they break. Take them off, sweeten *well*, and set aside to cool. When cold pour into pastry shells, and bake with a top crust of puff paste. Brush all over with beaten egg while hot, set back in the oven to glaze for three minutes. Eat cold.

GRAPE PIE.

Boil grapes with as much water as will cover them; when boiled to a thick liquor, add ½ lb sugar to each pound grapes. Preserved grapes may be used if desired.

HUCKLEBERRY PIE.

Wash and pick the berries; sweeten to taste.

IRISH POTATO PIE.

One pound mashed potatoes rubbed through a cullender, one-half pound butter creamed with the sugar, six eggs, whites and yolks beaten separately, one lemon squeezed into the potato while hot, one teaspoonful nutmeg, one teaspoonful mace and ½ lb white sugar. Mix and bake same as sweet potato pie.

JELLY PIE.

Take 1 doz. soda crackers, rolled fine, with sufficient jelly; beat them well together, adding a little water.

LEMON PIE.

Yolks 1 doz eggs.	4 ozs pounded almonds.
1 oz corn starch.	3 ozs citron.
Juice and zest of 4 lemons.	½ pt wine.
½ lb sugar.	

Heat over a fire till it thickens; add the beaten whites of 6 eggs; fill the pies and bake.

LEMON PIE—CHEAP.

Boil 1 peck apples, mashing them through a strainer; add 8 or 10 grated or ground lemons; cut the lemons open; take out the seeds before grating; sweeten to taste.

LEMON CREAM PIE.

Proceed as for Cream Pie a la Meringue, by grating the rinds of 3 or 4 lemons according to the quantity required. Care must be taken not to let any of the juice get into the cream, as it would make the cream sour, and ruin the pie. Put the grated rind into the cream and stir; flavor with lemon extract and ornament the same as other pies.

The only way the whole of the lemon can be used is to substitute water for milk, using a little more egg. This makes a good, nice pie, and is equally as good as that made with cream.

LEMON MARANG PIE.

$\frac{3}{4}$ lb sugar.	2 grated lemons with
6 ozs butter.	juice.
$\frac{1}{2}$ doz eggs.	1 oz flour.

Beat butter and sugar, add eggs and lemon; make the bottom of puff paste dough; ornament with kiss batter and bake in a moderate heat.

MARLBOROUGH PIE.

$\frac{1}{2}$ pt stewed apples.	$\frac{1}{2}$ gill brandy.
3 eggs.	1 oz chopped citron.
1 oz butter.	8 macaroons.
1 gill cream.	

Beat the macaroons fine; add apples and eggs, beating

well; then the melted butter, cream, citron and brandy;
bake in deep pie-plate with thin rim of paste.

MINCE PIE (1.)

Mince very finely some beef suet, and of this take 1½
℔s; pick some currants, stone and chop finely some
Malaga raisins, and take 1½ ℔s of each. Peel and core
a quantity of apples, and weigh out 1½ ℔s of these,
mince them also finely, and mix these four ingredients
in a basin, adding to them 1 ℔ of moist sugar, ½ ℔ of
mixed orange, citron, and lemon, candied peel, also
finely minced. Squeeze the juice of a lemon in the
mixture, and, lastly, put in half the thin rind of it,
chopped as finely as possible. Work the mixture with a
spoon for a little time; put half a teaspoonful of salt
into half a tumblerful of brandy, with powdered mixed
spice and ginger, according to taste; add this to the
mince, work it a little more to get it well mixed, and put
it by in a covered jar. It should remain seven or eight
days before being used, and it will keep for several
weeks. Butter slightly a number of patty-pans, take a
piece of the paste, roll it out to the thickness of a
quarter of an inch, and line the pans with it. Put a
wineglassful of brandy into the mince, stir it well, and
put a small quantity of it into each pan; brush the
paste round with white of egg, and put on a cover of
paste rolled out to about one-third of an inch thick.
Press the edges well together, brush the top with cold
water, strew finely powdered sugar over, and bake about
half an hour.

Mince pies are frequently made about Christmas time
in the shape of mangers, to represent the cradle of
Bethlehem.

MINCE PIE (2.)

10 ℔s beef.
20 ℔s apples, chopped
    fine.
6 ℔s raisins.
6 ℔s currants.

1 ℔ citron.
10 ℔s sugar.
2 ozs ground cloves.
2 ozs ground cinnamon.
1 oz nutmegs.

Mix with 2 qts good brandy and the meat broth; press
the mass in a pot; when used, thin it with cider. The
above will keep 2 or 3 months in a cold but not damp
place. Some makers use part sugar and part molasses.

MINCE PIE (3.)

8 ℔s beef suet, chopped
    fine.
10 ℔s apples, chopped fine.
8 ℔s mixed lemon, orange
    and citron peels, chop-
    ped fine.

4 ℔s sugar.
Mixed spices to taste.
Add 1 pt brandy.

Mix the whole and keep in close jar for use.

MINCE PIE (3*.)

Prepare the spices in manner and proportion as follows: To 4 ozs cinnamon add 2 ozs nutmeg, 4 ozs
cloves, 2 ozs ground ginger, 1 oz coriander seed, the
zest of 1 doz each oranges and lemons; pound and sift
the spices, mixing with the orange and lemon zests; keep
well corked in dry bottles.

Procure 4 ℔s stoned raisins, 4 ℔s cleaned currants, 2
℔s Eleme figs, 2 ℔s preserved ginger, 4 ℔s mixed candied peel, 6 ℔s coarse chopped beef suet; 4 ℔s tripe,
and 4 ℔s boiled salt beef chopped fine together; 6 ℔s
peeled apples, to be chopped with the raisins and currants; the candied-peel is to be shred small; mix all together on a clean table, adding 6 ℔s moist sugar, and

the spices; when thoroughly mixed, put the mincemeat into stone jars, and two days after, pour into each its fair proportion of 2 bottles of brandy and two bottles of port wine. The addition of 4 ozs pounded bitter almonds would be an improvement.

MINCE PIE—COMMON.

This may be made with chopped apples, suet, molasses, ground cinnamon, raisins, etc., according to quality desired.

MOCK APPLE PIE.

Proceed as for Cracker pie, flavoring with lemon.

MOSAIC TARTS.

Prepare 2 doz puff paste tartlets (see chapter 5); fill each of them with a spoonful of apricot or greengage jam; wet round the edges and place a mosaic of paste on the top of each; egg them over slightly, and bake them of a light color; when they are done shake some fine sugar over them, and glaze with the red-hot salamander.

ORANGE PIE.

$\frac{1}{4}$ ℔ almonds, chopped fine.　5 ℔s apples, cut fine.
1 pt wine.　1 ℔ sugar.
　　Zest of $\frac{1}{2}$ doz oranges.

Mix well; slice the oranges and lay over the pies; bake with bottom crust and rim.

PEACH PIE (1.)

Stone the peaches, and either slice them thinly or cut them in quarters or eighths; fill the dishes and sweeten, adding a little water; or pounded almonds, grated lemon peel and wine may be added. If the fruit is not ripe, it is preferable to boil the peaches soft in only sufficient water to prevent burning; when cold enough, remove the stones and sweeten with sugar to taste.

PEACH PIE (2.)

Proceed with peaches as for stewed apple pie (1.)

PEACH CUSTARD PIE.

Proceed as for Custard pie, laying on the bottom some cooked fresh or canned peaches; add the custard.

PEAR PIE.

If mellow pears are used, proceed as for Apple pie; but if stewing pears are made used of, they must first be stewed with a little water, sugar, a few cloves and lemon peel. When the pears are cold, put them in the dish; cover with pie paste and half bake it; sprinkle it over with water and the white of an egg whisked together; shake sifted sugar over the surface, and put it back in the oven to finish baking of a light color.

PINE-APPLE PIE.

Remove the outer rind of a well ripened pine-apple; cut in thin slices; add ¾ ℔ sugar and cook over a slow fire, adding ½ pt red wine and ¼ oz cinnamon; let cool and fill the pies.

PLUM PIE.

Proceed with plums as for Damson pie.

PRUNE PIE.

Give the prunes a scald; take out the stones and break them; put the kernels into a little cranberry juice, with the prunes and sugar; when cold fill the pies.

PUMPKIN PIE (1.)

1 doz medium sized pump-	2 lbs butter.
kins.	4 lbs sugar.
2 gals scalded milk.	2 doz eggs.

Peel and boil the pumpkins, strain through a sieve and add milk, butter and sugar.

PUMPKIN PIE (2.)

Cut the pumpkins in halves, and remove all the seeds; cut them into small pieces, and put the whole onto boil with about 1 pt water poured over them; this moistens it sufficiently at first, and if the pumpkin is stirred frequently it will not burn,—as it softens by cooking, it has sufficient moisture of its own. Let it stew an hour or more after it becomes soft; strain it through a colander into a large pan; to each quart of pumpkin, add 1 qt milk and 4 eggs; sweeten to taste, and flavor with cinnamon and ginger. After all is prepared, set the pan containing the mixture upon a kettle of warm water, that the whole may become warm while preparing the crusts; bake the crusts a little before pouring the pumpkin in; fill, and bake immediately in a hot oven.

PUMPKIN PIE—DRIED.

Dry the pumpkin after the following manner: Boil it a good while: spread it upon plates, or drop a spoonful at a time upon buttered paper, which is laid on tins, forming cakes, as it were, and set the tins into a slow oven after the baking has been removed; it dries in this way without getting dusty.

In making the pies, take for each pie three cakes of pumpkin and 3 eggs; sugar to taste; soften the pump-

kin in warm milk; strain through a colander; spice
with cinnamon, and bake in a deep dish.

When well dried, the pumpkin will keep over a year.

PUMPKIN PIE—GRATED.

An excellent pie is made by grating the raw pumpkin,
adding one egg and a cup of cream for each pie; sugar
and spice to taste.   A little butter is an improvement.

PUNCH PIE.

1 qt white wine.   1½ ozs corn starch dis-
1 ℔ sugar.   solved in cold water.
Yolks of 8 eggs.   Lemon flavor.
2 whole eggs.

Boil wine and sugar; add the eggs and corn starch
beaten well together; let come to a boil; when cool fill
the pies.

QUINCE PIE.

6 ℔s quinces, sliced.   3½ ℔s sugar.
1 pt wine.   Zest of a lemon.
1 pt cider.   ⅛ oz cloves.

Boil and press through a sieve.

RAISIN PIE.

Take 1 ℔ raisins; turn over them 1 qt boiling water;
keep adding so that there will be 1 qt when done; grate
the rind of a lemon into ¼ ℔ sugar, adding three tablespoons of flour and 1 egg; mix well together and turn
the raisins over the mixture, stirring the while.

Prunes may be used instead of raisins.

RASPBERRY PIE.

After picking and cleaning the berries, add ½ ℔ sugar

to every pound. If desired to keep for 3 or 4 days boil for ½ hour with the sugar and a little water.

RHUBARB PIE.

8 ℔s rhubarb, cut and 1 qt water.
    peeled.   6-8 ℔s sugar.

Boil the rhubarb in the water until it gets thick; add sugar and some grated lemon peel; when boiling again add 1 oz corn starch dissolved in a little cold water; leave it on the fire a few minutes longer.   ·

RHUBARB OR PIE PLANT PIE.

Select the largest stalks; peel off the skin carefully; slice them fine, and when the undercrust is prepared upon a plate, spread them over as full as for apple pie; sprinkle over with sugar to taste, and a little water; dredge with flour, adding a few bits of butter; cover with crust and bake. While warm, grate white sugar over.

RICE PIE.

Boil 1 ℔ rice in about ½ gal milk until very soft; rub through a sieve and add 1 doz eggs well beaten, a little salt and 1 ℔ sugar; flavor as desired; bake as for Custard pie.

SQUASH PIE.

Boil winter squash soft, and strain it through a colander; for every pint of squash add 1 pt milk or cream; add 4 eggs well beat, and cinnamon and sugar to taste; strain and bake in a deep pie dish.

STRAWBERRY PIE.

Proceed with strawberries as for Raspberry pie.

STRAWBERRY MERINGUE PIE.

Procure some good strawberries that are clean and do not need washing, as it is well known that washing destroys the delicate flavor of the berries. Pick them clean, taking care not to multilate them in the least. Make a dough as follows: Take 2 ℔s of the best pastry flour; rub into it ¼ ℔ fresh butter, the same as for soda biscuit, adding 1 oz baking powder; make a hollow in the middle, put in 2 eggs, ½ ℔ sugar, a little salt, and enough milk to make a nice dough. Roll the dough as an ordinary pie crust, and line the pie plates; dock the crust with a fork so that it will not get displaced from the bottom of the tin; bake in a moderate oven with great care, as it spoils them to get too well done, or not to be baked enough. Beat up the whites of 6 eggs to a stiff froth; add 8 ozs pulverized sugar; put in the strawberries and mix as gently as possible; fill the pie-plate with the mass and ornament the top with the meringue made as before; place the pies in the oven until they have a nice color, when they are ready for use. This is the best way of making pies of strawberries, because the crust being cooked before, they do not require any cooking after the berries are added, whereby the flavor is destroyed. The above makes an excellent shortcake by rolling the dough a little thicker and baking in a flat pan.

SWEET POTATO PIE.

Peel and cook as many sweet potatoes as desired; when cooked, press through a sieve or colander and season with spices. Make a custard, using 4 eggs to 1 quart milk and 8 ozs sugar; put the whole through a sieve again, and bake the same as pumpkin pie.

TRANSPARENT PIE.

¾ ℔ white sugar. 4 eggs.
¼ ℔ butter.

Beat the eggs very light; mix the ingredients, and bake in one lower crust; flavor to taste.

VANILLA CREAM PIE.

1 stick vanilla, pounded   ½ ℔ sugar.
   fine. 1 oz corn starch, dissolved
1 qt white wine. in cold water.
8 whole eggs.

Stir over a slow fire, removing immediately when it comes to a boil; finish as for custard pie.

VANILLA TARTS.

1 ℔ sugar. 1½ ℔s flour.
2½ doz eggs. Vanilla flavor.

Beat eggs; warm over the fire with the sugar; add flavor and flour, stirring well. Make the bottom out of short paste and place it in patty pans; put in the centre of each pan a little jelly; force the batter through a bag into the pans, or drop with a spoon; sift sugar over them and bake in a moderate oven.

WASHINGTON CREAM PIE.

1 ℔ sugar. ¼ ℔ citron, cut fine.
2 doz yolks of eggs. Cinnamon and allspice to
¼ ℔ bread crumbs. taste.
¼ ℔ grated chocolate.

Stir sugar and yolks together; beat up the whites stiff; mix altogether well; make the bottom of short paste, with a ridge around them; bake in a moderate oven.

CHAPTER VII.

PASTRY CAKES.

BREAD AND BUTTER PASTRY.

Roll out 1 ℔ puff paste $\frac{1}{4}$ inch thick; cut into bands 3 inches wide, and then into strips a little more than $\frac{1}{4}$ inch wide; place them (on the cut side) on a baking sheet in rows 2 inches apart, so as to allow them sufficient room to spread out; bake in a rather sharp oven, and just before they are done, glaze them, by shaking fine sugar over them and using the red-hot salamander. About 2 doz. of them are required for a dish; they must be spread with some kind of preserve and stuck together in pairs, to imitate bread and butter. Dish them up on a napkin, piled up in several circular rows, in a pyramid.

This kind of pastry may also be dished up with some stiffly whipped cream, seasoned with a glass of liqueur in the centre.

CHEESE-CAKES, (1.)

1 ℔ pressed curd.	1 doz. yolks of eggs.
$\frac{1}{4}$ ℔ ratafias.	Zest of 4 oranges or lemons

¾ ℔ sugar.   Pinch salt.
¼ ℔ butter.   Nutmeg to taste.

Press the curd in a napkin to absorb the superfluous moisture; pound it thoroughly in a mortar, and mix in the above ingredients; when the whole is incorporated together into a kind of soft paste, take this up in a basin. Line four dozen or more tart pans with some well-worked trimmings of puff paste; garnish them with the cheese curd; place a strip of candied peel on the top of each; put them on a baking sheet, and set them in the oven, at a moderate heat, to be baked of a very light brown color; when done, sift a very little sifted sugar over them, serving them quite hot.

Currants, dried cherries, sultanas or citron, etc., may be used instead of the candied peel.

CHEESE-CAKES, (2.)

Four eggs well beaten, stirred into one pint of boiling milk; put pan containing the milk and eggs over the fire and stir until it curdles; strain off the whey, and let the curd cool; grate six ounces of stale sponge cake and mix the cold curd; stir half a pound of butter and the same of pulverized sugar to a cream, add a wine glass of brandy and Madeira mixed, a little rose water and powdered cinnamon; mix all these ingredients together. Have ready a nice puff paste, roll it out very thin, and cut it into squares about four or five inches wide; place a large spoonful of the cheese mixture in the centre of each square, spread it a little and fold the edges of the paste partly over it, press and pinch down the corners. This forms a flat square tart. Sprinkle a few Zante currants in the centre on the uncovered portion of the cheese; place them on baking tins and bake in a moderate oven.

CHEESE-CAKES, (3).

See under Baked Puddings, Part II, Chapter 5:
    Almond Cheese Curd Pudding;
    Cheese Curd Pudding;
    Egg Cheese Curd Pudding;
    Lemon Cheese Curd Pudding;
    Orange Cheese Curd Pudding;
    Potato Cheese Curd Pudding;
Also under Cold Puddings, Part II, Chapter 9:
    Dorothy's Curd Pudding.

CONDE CAKES.

Chop ¾ ℔ of Jordan Almonds as fine as possible; mix them with ½ ℔ sifted sugar, some lemon zest and the whites of two eggs; the whole should present the appearance of a rather firm paste. Roll out 1 ℔ puff paste 1-8 inch thick, and with a tin cutter of an oval, circular, cresent, diamond, or any other fancy shape, stamp out about 3 doz. Condes, and place them on a baking sheet, previously wetted over with a paste brush. Spread a coating of the prepared chopped almonds on the surface of each; shake some fine sugar over them, and bake of a very light-fawn color.

DARIOLES.

1 ℔ puff paste trimmings.	2 eggs and 1 doz. yolks.
2 ozs flour.	2 ozs candied orange
4 ozs pounded sugar.	flowers.
2 ozs ratafias.	2 ozs butter
6 gills cream.	Pinch salt.

Place the sugar, flour, bruised ratafias and the eggs,

in a spouted basin; work the whole well together, and add the cream, salt and a tablespoon of orange-flower water. Line 2 dozen dariole-moulds with some trimmings of puff paste; place them on a baking sheet; put a very small piece of butter at the bottom of each dariole, and then after stirring the batter well together, pour it into the moulds; strew the candied flowers on the top of each, and set them in the oven (at moderate heat) to bake. When done, the darioles should be slightly raised in the centre, and of a light color; take them out of the moulds without breaking them; shake some finely sifted sugar over them, and serve them hot.

Darioles may also be flavored with vanilla, lemon, orange, coffee, chocolate, etc.

D'ARTOIS CAKES.

Make 1 ℔ puff paste, giving it seven turns or foldings; take one-third of it, and after kneading this well together, roll it out to the size of a square baking sheet about 14x12 inches, and lay the paste upon it; spread a rather thick layer of apricot or other jam over the paste to within about an inch of the edges. Roll out the remainder of the puff paste to the size of the baking sheet, and place it neatly over the surface of the jam; fasten it round by pressing upon the edges with the thumb, and trim the edges by cutting away the superfluous paste from the sides with a knife.

The D'Artois must now be marked out in small oblong shapes with the back part of a knife; and after the whole surface has been egged over, score them very neatly, forming a kind of feather-pattern on each cake. Bake them of a bright, light-brown color; and when they are done, shake some finely-sifted sugar over them;

5

put them back again into the oven for a minute or two
to melt the sugar, and then pass the red-hot salamander
over them to give the pastry a bright, glossy appearance.   When the D'Artois have become sufficiently cold,
cut them up, and serve them, dished up in circular rows
piled on a napkin.

This kind of pastry may also be garnished with Pethivier's cream, pastry cream, apple marmalade, or any
other kind of preserve.

Puff-paste or large D'Artois cakes may also be garnished with mince-meat, etc.   In this case, however,
where the cake has been covered in with the puff paste,
previously to marking out the design on its surface, it
must be egged over with a paste brush; when it has
been baked of a bright yellow color, shake some finely
sifted sugar over it and proceed as directed above.

ECCLES CAKE (1.)

Roll out a sheet of paste sufficiently large to cover the
baking plate, about $\frac{1}{4}$ inch thick; roll out another sheet
the same size but rather thicker; spread some Banbury
meat (see Banbury Puffs) on the first sheet, $\frac{1}{4}$ inch
thick; cover it with the second sheet; trim it, and mark
the top sheet into squares; bake in a moderate oven;
when done dredge the top with powdered sugar.

ECCLES CAKE (2.)

Have ready some tins 1 foot long by 6 or 9 inches
wide.   Roll out a sheet of puff paste rather more than
$\frac{1}{8}$ inch thick, and sufficiently large to line the tin; put
on a layer of Banbury meat $\frac{1}{2}$ inch thick; cover with a
sheet of paste as thick again as the bottom crust; trim
the paste from the sides, and divide the top into small

squares; bake in a moderate oven; as soon as it is done, dust the top with powdered loaf sugar.

The thickness of the Banbury meat, as well as the size of the squares, should be regulated by the price at which they are to be sold.

ECCLES CAKE (3.)

Make a $\frac{3}{4}$ paste, or use scraps of paste; roll it out $\frac{1}{8}$ inch thick and cut in 3-inch squares; prepare a mixture of equal quantities of moist sugar and clean currants; add a little finely-chopped lemon peel, also a little lemon flavor; add a good flavoring of ground cinnamon and ginger. Mix the whole together, just wetting it with water; place a tablespoonful of this in the centre of each piece of paste, and draw the paste over it so as to cover it, making it round in form; roll them out 4 inches in diameter and pan the folded part down; wash with eggs and milk, and dust with sugar; with a knife give them a few cuts across each other on the surface, and bake in a solid oven a nice brown.

If a poorer quality is desired, add a few cake or cracker crumbs.

FANCY PASTRY CAKES (1.)

Puff paste, turned or folded eight times, rolled out $\frac{1}{8}$ inch thick, and stamped with appropriate fancy-shaped tin cutters—either in the form of crescents, leaves, trefoil or shamrock, stars, etc. It should be baked as directed for rings and wreaths, and decorated in the same manner, a paper cornet being used for this purpose.

FANCY PASTRY CAKES (2.)

Roll out puff paste thin; cut it into small pieces with

a round scolloped cutter, or into square pieces with a knife; or make them in any form desired with tin cutters; place the cakes on a clean tin, and bake them in a moderate oven; put jam or jelly on the top of each, and arrange them tastefully in a nougat or other basket, or in a dish on a folded napkin.

FRENCH PASTE.

See Raspberry Sandwich.

GERMAN TOURTE OF APRICOTS, ETC.

Cut 1 doz ripe apricots into quarters, and put them, with the kernels extracted from the stones, into a small sugar boiler or stewpan, with 4 ozs pounded sugar and a spoonful of water; stir over the fire until the fruit has dissolved into a jam, and then remove.

Roll out some puff-paste trimmings, or about $\frac{1}{2}$ lb short paste, to the diameter of 8 inches; place this on a circular baking sheet, and with the forefinger and thumb of the right hand, twist the paste round the edges, so as to raise it in imitation of cording; cut up 1 doz ripe apricots into quarters, and place these in close circular rows on the paste; shake sifted sugar (mixed with lemon zest) over the apricots, and bake the tourte at a moderate heat. When it is done, pour the marmalade of apricots over the others; shake sifted sugar mixed with cinnamon powder over the surface; dish the tourte on a napkin, and serve it either hot or cold.

This kind of tourte may be made of every kind of fruit, following in each case the above directions.

GENOISE PASTRY.

Take a $\frac{1}{4}$ lb of fresh butter, put it into a bowl, and warm it until it can be beaten with a spoon; add 4 ozs of powdered loaf sugar, and beat the two together until a smooth white cream is obtained; then add one egg, and keep on beating the mixture till it is smooth again, then add three more eggs in the same manner. Lastly, incorporate quickly with the mixture $\frac{1}{4}$ lb of the finest flour, and as soon as it is smooth pour it out to the thickness of $\frac{1}{2}$ inch on a buttered tin, and put this into the oven at once. When done (in about 10 or 15 minutes) turn out the slab of Genoise and put it to cool, underside uppermost, on a sieve. When cold, spread a very thin layer of apricot jam over the top of the slab, then a coating of chocolate icing. Put it in the oven for a minute, then in a cold place till quite cold, when, with a sharp knife or cutter, the slab can be cut in a variety of shapes, to be served piled up on a napkin.

JAM SANDWICHES.

Mix the yolks of two eggs very smoothly with a tablespoonful of ground rice, add a very small pinch of salt, a tablespoonful of sugar, half a pint of thick cream, and a quarter of a pint of new milk. Beat the whites of the eggs to a firm froth, add them last of all, and beat the mixture for four or five minutes. Butter two large plates, put in the mixture, and bake in a quick oven until it is set and lightly browned. Spread a little jam over one of the cakes and lay the other upon it, the browned part uppermost. Sift a little sugar over it before serving. Jam sandwiches may be eaten either hot or cold. Time, twenty minutes to bake.

LOVER'S KNOTS.

Roll out a piece of puff paste into a thin sheet; cut it into pieces 3 or 4 inches square; fold each corner over

into the centre, and cut a piece out from each side, leaving it in the form of a true lover's knot; put them on a
tin, and bake in a moderate oven; when they are done,
place some jam or preserve on each point, and some in
the centre.

MARIGOLDS.

Roll out 1 ℔ puff paste 1-6 inch thick; stamp out 40
flats with a circular fluted tin cutter, about 1¾ inches in
diameter, and place them on a wetted baking sheet;
roll out the trimmings rather thin, and with two smaller
cutters stamp out as many rings, about ¾ inch in diameter, as there are cakes, placing one of these on the centre
of each marigold, previously wetted all over the surface.
Place some almonds split into four strips lengthwise
closely around the rings, in a somewhat slanting direction; these must be slightly pressed in the paste to make
them hold on, and should be so arranged as to give to
the cake as much as possible the appearance of the
flower they are meant to resemble. When they are all
completed, shake sugar over them, and bake of a light
color. When done, insert some very narrow strips of
bright, firm, red currant or apple jelly, between each
piece of almond, and place a piece of apricot or greengage jam in the ring.

MINCE CAKES.

See Eccles Cakes.

MIRLITONS.

1 doz. eggs.	¼ ℔ butter.
¾ ℔ sugar.	Pinch salt.
¼ ℔ ratafias.	Puff paste trimmings.
2 ozs candied orange flowers.	

Put the above into a basin having a spout. The ratafias and orange flowers must be bruised, and the butter merely melted. Work the whole well together with a wooden spoon, until the batter presents the appearance of a rich, creamy-looking substance; it must then be instantly poured into about 8 dozen small, deep tartlet-pans lined with puff paste trimmings; shake a rather thick coating of sifted sugar over the Mirlitons, and when it has nearly melted on their surface, put them in the oven (at very moderate heat) and bake them of a light fawn color. When the Mirlitons are done, the centre should rise out from the tartlets to the height of about $\frac{1}{2}$ inch, resembling the crown of a boy's cap.

These cakes may also be flavored with grated chocolate, or with pounded pistachios or almonds. They may also be flavored with extract of vanilla, lemon, etc. Previously to pouring the batter into the tartlets, a spoonful of apricot or pineapple jam may be placed in them.

PARISIAN LOAVES.

Prepare some small slender finger-biscuits; spread them with apricot or greengage jam, and stick two of them together; hold one at a time on a fork and mask them over slightly with meringue paste; then with a paper cornet filled with some of the same paste, draw parallel lines across the cakes in a slanting direction; when they are all completed, shake sugar over them, and put them into the oven to be baked, or rather dried of a very light fawn color. When done, insert some narrow strips of currant jelly, greengage jam, or apple jelly, between the bars of decoration.

PARISIAN TURNOVER OF APPLES, ETC.

Peel about 1 doz apples; cut them in quarters and

take out the cores; after which, put them into a stewpan with 8 ozs sugar, 2 ozs butter, the zest of a lemon,
and two tablespoons of water; toss the apples over a
slow fire until they are about half done, when remove.
While the apples are being prepared, roll out a piece of
short paste in a circular form, ⅛ inch thick, and about
the size of a dinner plate; wet this round the edge;
fasten a rolled cord of paste, the thickness of the small
finger, within an inch of the edge, and pile the prepared apples up in the centre in the form of a dome.
Spread apricot marmalade over the surface, and cover
the whole in with a circular piece of puff-paste; press
them together round the edges, wet the extremities, and
with the forefinger and thumb of the right hand, turn
or fold the edges over in the form of a cord. Let the
turn-over be now egged all over with a soft paste-brush
dipped in some beaten white of egg; strew rough granite
sugar over the entire surface, and bake of a light color.

These turnovers may also be made of all kinds of
plums, the only difference in their mode of preparation
being that they need not undergo any dressing previously to placing them in the paste, except that the
stones should be removed. The plums, peaches, or
apricots, must be piled up in several rows forming a
dome, with pounded sugar between each layer; and
some of the same kind of fruit the turn-over is made of
should be first boiled down to a jam, for the purpose of
masking the fruit with, preparatory to its being covered
in.

PASTRY PYRAMIDS.

Roll out some puff-paste into a sheet ½ inch thick;
cut it out, either with round or oval cutters, into pieces

each a size or two smaller than the other; bake in a moderate oven; spread jam or marmalade over each piece, being careful not to put in enough to run down the sides and disfigure them; put the pieces one on the other in the shape of a pyramid. Each slice or piece may be spread with a different sort or colored preserve.

PETHIVIER'S CAKE.

1 ℔ almonds or nuts.   8 yolks of eggs.
¾ ℔ sugar.   A pinch of salt.
½ ℔ butter.   2 spoonsful orange flower
¼ ℔ ratafias.   water.

Blanch and pound the almonds or nuts with a little white of an egg until they become pulverized; add the remainder of the ingredients and pound the whole well together until thoroughly incorporated, when it should present the appearance of a rather soft creamy paste; take this up in a basin.

Have ready 1 ℔ puff-paste; take about ⅔ of this and knead or rather fold it, by twisting over the corners, so as to form it into a cushion; knead the other piece in a similar manner; roll them both out in a circular or oval form, to the size of a small dish or dessert plate; place the thinest piece on a baking sheet; wet around the edges with a paste-brush dipped in water; fill the whole of the centre with the layer of Pethivier's cream, about an inch thick, placing the other piece of puff-paste over the top of this; press it all round the edge by bearing on it with the thumb of the right hand; trim the edges round neatly, and with the point of a knife, handling lightly and freely, sketch or mark out some neat or elegant design, such as a lyre, a vase of flowers, a helmet with flowing mane or feathers, a wreath, star, etc.

Shake finely sifted sugar over the cake, and bake of the lightest possible color; indeed, it should be free from any color, the characteristic appearance of this kind of pastry being its whiteness. Pethivier's cake should be eaten cold.

These cakes may also be made in tart moulds, thinly lined with puff-paste, and after being neatly filled with the Pethivier's cream (the edges being previously wetted round) the mould must be covered in with circular pieces of puff paste, stamped out with a cutter to fit them; they should then be fastened down by pressing the two pieces of paste together with the forefinger and thumb of the right hand, and finished and baked as directed above.

PLAITS.

Roll out 1 ℔ puff-paste ⅛ inch thick; cut this into bands about 5 inches in width, and divide these into narrow strips ¼ inch wide. Take four of these strips, and after fastening them together at one end, with a little egg or water, plait them neatly but rather loosely together, and when finished, fasten the ends. As each plait is completed, place it on a baking sheet, and when they are all ready, egg them over and bake them of a light color; when done, let them be glazed as usual. Just before sending these cakes to the table, decorate them by placing in the small cavities some dots of bright currant or apple jelly, and some greengage jam.

POLISH CAKES.

Roll out 1 ℔ puff paste about 1·6 inch thick; cut it up into square pieces of 2 inches each; wet these in the centre, folding down the corners so as to make them

all meet in the middle of the piece of paste; place a dot
of paste in the centre of each, pressing it down with the
end of the finger; egg over, and bake in a rather sharp
oven, of a fine, bright, light color; just before they are
done, shake finely sifted sugar over them; put them back
in the oven to melt the sugar, and pass the red-hot salamander over them to give them a glossy appearance.
Decorate this kind of pastry with red-currant or apple
jelly.

PUITS D'AMOUR.

Roll out puff paste as for patty cases; cut out as many
pieces as required with an oval scolloped cutter about 2
or 3 inches long; cut the top of the paste with a sharp-
pointed knife half through at each end of the oval;
brush the tops over with egg, place them on a tin and
bake in a moderate oven. Roll out pieces of tart paste
into a small roll; twist them and make them into semi-
circles, to form handles; place in a tin and bake them.
Take out the paste from the centre of the ovals where it
was marked with a knife, and fill with any sort of preserve or cream; or a fine strawberry, grape or gooseberry may be put on each; fix the handle over the centre with a little barley sugar or icing.

These cakes may be made round instead of oval, and
the edges may be strewn with blanched and chopped
sweet almonds or pistachios, and the sides piped with
any sort of jam or jelly. These cakes form a pretty
dish for a second course.

RASPBERRY SANDWICH.

Roll out puff paste· ½ inch thick; cut into strips 3
inches long and ½ inch wide; lay them on a baking plate
with the cut side uppermost, placing them about 3

inches apart. Bake in a moderately quick oven. While they are baking, instead of rising they will spread out like a fan; take them out and dust over them some fine powdered sugar; put them again into the oven one minute to melt the sugar, and they will be glazed. When done, form a sandwich by spreading some raspberry jam between two pieces.

By varying the jam used, quite a variety may be made from this recipe. Another name for the above is French or Swiss Paste.

RINGS OR WREATHS.

Roll out 1 ℔ puff paste 1-6 inch thick; stamp out 40 circular pieces with a fluted tin cutter, about 1¾ inches in diameter; stamp out the centre of these with a plain, circular cutter ¾ inch in diameter; place the rings on a wet baking sheet; shake some fine sugar over them, and bake in a moderate oven of a very light color. When they are done, decorate them with the whipped white of egg and sugar, over which strew some coarse sugar; put them in a screen to dry; finish decorating them by placing or inserting some strips of currant or apple jelly between the folds or dots of the decoration.

ROYALS.

Mix the whites of 4 eggs with as much finely sifted sugar as they will absorb, so as to form a soft paste; mix as lightly as possible and flavor to taste. Roll out 1 ℔ puff paste and finish as for Conde Cakes.

SANDWICHES.

Roll out puff paste into a thin sheet; spread raspberry or other jam over it; roll out another piece the same size and thickness as the former, and put it over it; cut the whole with cutters into rings, crescents, or other forms; or with a knife into diamonds, squares, triangles or fingers; glaze as for Raspberry Sandwiches; or they may be iced with the white of an egg that has been whisked to a froth, and dusted with fine powdered sugar, and sprinkled with just enough water to soften the sugar.

SHORTCAKES.

See Fancy Pastry Cakes, Sandwiches, etc.

SWISS PASTE.

See Raspberry Sandwich.

TALMOUSES.

1 pt. milk,	$\frac{3}{4}$ ℔ cream curd,
$\frac{1}{2}$ ℔ flour,	Zest of two oranges,
$\frac{1}{4}$ ℔ sugar,	1 doz. yolks of eggs,
$\frac{1}{4}$ ℔ butter,	Pinch salt.

Put the milk, butter, sugar and salt into a stew-pan on the fire, and as soon as they begin to simmer, fill in the flour by stirring the whole with a wooden spoon for 2 or 3 minutes; add the curd (from which all superfluous moisture must be extracted by pressing it with a napkin,) and work in the eggs one after the other, remembering that this paste must be kept to about the same substance as for Petits-choux.

Roll out 1 ℔ puff paste 1-8 inch thick; stamp out about 4 doz. circular pieces with a tin cutter 2 inches in diameter, placing them in neat order on a baking sheet, an inch apart; place a teaspoon of the above preparation in the centre of each; wet them round the edges, and turn up the sides so as to form each of them in the shape of a three-cornered hat; egg them over with a paste-brush; bake them of a light brown color, and when they are withdrawn from the oven, shake some fine sugar over them. These cakes may be served either hot or cold.

WALNUTS.

Roll out 1 ℔ puff paste 1-6 inch thick; stamp out 40 circular pieces with a fluted cutter, about 1½ inches in diameter; after wetting each of these with a paste-brush dipped in water, fold them up, at the same time pressing the two parts of paste slightly, so as to cause them to adhere closely together. They must then be placed on a baking-sheet in rows, egged over, and baked of a bright, light color; just before they are done, shake over them fine sugar, and put back in the oven for a little while to melt the sugar; pass the red-hot salamander over, and withdraw them. Previously to serving this kind of pastry, a broad strip of red-currant or apple jelly should be placed across the centre.

CHAPTER VIII.

PASTRY CREAMS—BLANC MANGE—CHARLOTTE RUSSE, ETC.

Bavarian Cream—Blanc Mange, (1)—Blanc Mange, (2)—Blanc Mange, Almond — Blanc Mange, American—Blanc Mange, Berry—Caramel Cream Celestine Cream—Charlotte Russe—Chocolate Cream—Coffee Cream—Fruit Creams—Italian Cream —Pastry Cream or Custard, (1)—Pastry Cream or Custard, (2) —Rock Cream—Russian Charlotte- Russia Cream —Tapioca Cream —Vanilla Cream, with fruit sauce—Whipped Cream, (1) —Whipped Cream, (2.)

BAVARIAN CREAM.

Whip 1 pt. double cream until it presents the appearance of a snow-like froth; be careful not to over-whip it for it would then produce butter. To the whipped cream add a glass of any kind of liqueur, 6 ozs. of sifted sugar and 2 ozs. clarified isinglass; mix lightly and thoroughly; use this to fill a mould imbedded in ice; when set firm, dip the mould in hot water, wipe it, and turn the cream out on its dish.

BLANC MANGE, (1).

2 qts. milk.
½ lb sugar.

½ pt. rose water.
4 ozs. isinglass.

Mix; let it come to a boil; flavor with almonds, etc.; allow it to stand until blood warm, and run in moulds.

BLANC MANGE, (2).

Pound in a mortar 4 ozs. of blanched sweet almonds

with ½ oz. bitter ones, moistening them gradually with orange flower water; mix this with 1 qt. fresh cream and 1 oz. clarified isinglass; put into a saucepan stirring constantly until it boils; pass through a fine sieve, pour into a mould and set on ice.

Blanc mange may be flavored with vanilla, Mocha coffee, maraschino, pistachios, etc.; in which case the bitter almonds should be left out.

BLANC MANGE—ALMOND.

Blanch and pound in a mortar 8 ozs. of sweet and 1 oz. of bitter almonds, with a little orange flower water to moisten them. Mix this with 2 ozs. isinglass and ½ gal. fresh cream; put it on the fire till it boils, stirring all the time; strain through a sieve; pour into moulds; which place on ice.

Blanc mange made according to this recipe may be flavored with coffee, strawberries, pistachios, maraschino, etc. If required in this case, use no bitter almonds.

BLANC MANGE—AMERICAN.

Peel and pound to a soft paste eight or ten Brazil nuts; add a gill of water while pounding; let this stand for two hours to extract the flavor. Beat four fresh eggs and mix them into five tablespoonfuls of corn starch; dissolve four ounces of loaf sugar in a pint of new milk; add the nuts, simmer for five minutes, let it stand off the fire for five minutes, then strain it into the eggs, stirring them quickly as the milk is added; stir over a slow fire till it thickens. Pour the mixture into a mould, and let it remain in a cool place till firmly set.

Turn out carefully, and garnish with preserved mango, guava jelly, or preserved ginger.

BLANC MANGE—BERRY.

Stew ripe strawberries or raspberries, strain off the juice and sweeten to taste; place over the fire, and when it boils stir in corn starch wet in cold water, allowing two tablespoons of corn starch for each pint of juice; continue stirring until sufficiently cooked, pour into moulds wet in cold water and set away to cool; serve with cream and sugar, and fresh berries if desired. This makes a pretty and delicious dessert.

CARAMEL CREAM.

Put 4 ozs. of sugar with a bruised stick of cinnamon, the peel of a lemon and ½ gill of water, into a stewpan on the fire, to boil until it is of a light brown; it must then be stirred a little while longer on the fire, without allowing it to gain too dark a hue; pour in ½ gill water to dissolve it, and add 8 yolks of eggs, 1 pt. milk, and 6 ozs. sugar; stir the cream on the fire until it thickens; run it through a sieve into a basin, add ½ pt. whipped cream, and 2 ozs. dissolved gelatine; mix, and fill a mould imbedded in ice.

CELESTINE CREAM.

Imbed a plain mould in some rough ice; line the bottom and sides of the mould with picked strawberries, taking care to dip each strawberry in dissolved thin isinglass, in which there has been mixed some maraschino, as they are built round the mould; when the mould is thus completely lined inside, fill the interior with any pastry cream.

6

CHARLOTTE RUSSE.

1 pt. sweet cream. 1 oz. isinglass.
½ pt. new milk. 1 doz. eggs.
2 glasses Madeira.

Form a custard with the yolks of the eggs and the milk; sweeten to taste; dissolve the isinglass in 1 pt. water, and add it to the custard; put the whole on the fire until it gets thick and creamy, keep stirring and add the wine. Whip the cream; sweeten it and mix with the custard; pour the mixture into moulds previously lined with sponge cake, and set on ice.

The custard must be allowed to cool before adding the whipped cream. Any flavor desired may be added in place of the Madeira wine.

CHOCOLATE CREAM.

Grate 6 ozs. chocolate and put it into a stewpan with 1 pt. boiled milk, 6 ozs. sugar, and 8 yolks of eggs; stir the cream over the fire until it thickens; run it through a hair sieve into a basin; add 2 ozs. dissolved gelatine; mix, and set the cream in a mould imbedded in rough ice.

COFFEE CREAM.

Put a breakfast cupful of Mocha coffee into a stewpan with rather better than ½ pt. boiled milk; add 8 yolks of eggs, a pinch of salt, and ½ ℔ sugar; stir the cream briskly on the fire until it begins to thickens; stir for a minute longer, and then run it through a sieve into a basin; add 2 ozs. dissolved gelatine; mix, and set the cream in a mould imbedded in rough ice.

FRUIT CREAMS.

These are made by adding a sufficient quantity of

any kind of fruit, pureed (see Part 2, Chapter 1), to 1 pt whipped cream and 2 ozs clarified isinglass; mix and with this fill a mould imbedded in rough ice; finish as for Bavarian Cream.

ITALIAN CREAM.

Put 4 ozs of ratafias into a stewpan with 8 yolks of eggs, a glass of curacoa, a bruised stick of cinnamon, some orange rind, 1 pt boiled milk, and 6 ozs sugar; stir the cream on the fire until it thickens; rub it through a hair sieve into a basin; add 2 ozs dissolved gelatine, ½ pt whipped cream and 2 ozs each of preserved ginger, dried cherries and candied peel—all cut small; mix, and fill a mould imbedded in ice.

PASTRY CREAM OR CUSTARD (1.)

Boil ½ pt each of milk and cream with the peel of a lemon and some sugar; put this into a stewpan with the yolks of ½ doz eggs and two spoonfuls of flour; mix this with a wooden spoon and dilute with the above; stir this over the fire till it boils, working it well for five or six minutes; mix in ¼ ℔ clarified butter with the paste; put into a basin and stir until cold; if it is too thick, add a little cream.

PASTRY CREAM OR CUSTARD (2.)

8 ozs flour.	1 qt cream or milk.
8 ozs sugar.	2 spoonfuls orange flower
4 ozs butter.	water.
2 ozs ratafias.	Pinch salt.
12 yolks of eggs.	

Mix the flour, sugar, and salt with two whole eggs, in a stewpan with a wooden spoon; add the cream and the batter, stirring the whole over the fire till it boils;

it must then be well worked together to make it smooth. Withdraw the spoon, and after putting the lid on the stewpan, place the cream in the oven, or over a slow fire, to simmer gently for about 20 minutes; the cream must then be put into a basin and the bruised ratafias, the yolks of eggs and the orange flower water added. Put 8 ozs of butter into a small stewpan on the fire, and as soon as it begins to brown, add to the cream, and mix the whole thoroughly.

The above cream is used to garnish various kinds of pastry.

ROCK CREAM.

Steam one cup of rice in new milk until tender; sweeten with white sugar and heap on a dish; lay over it small slices of jelly, or any preserved fruit; beat the whites of eggs to a froth with a little white sugar, and flavor with vanilla; add one tablespoonful of rich sweet cream and lay over the rice with a spoon, giving the form of a rock of snow. It is both ornamental and delicious.

RUSSIAN CHARLOTTE.

Trim about 6 ozs finger biscuits perfectly straight, so as to make them fit closely to one another, and line the bottom and sides of a plain mould with them; imbed the mould in rough ice; fill in with any fruit or other cream (to which add ½ pt whipped cream); when set turn it out on its dish.

RUSSIA CREAM.

Four eggs, ¼ lb sugar, one qt milk, 2 ozs gelatine dissolved in one-half pt of warm water. Beat the yolks of the eggs and sugar together, and cook with the milk like custard. Take off the stove and add the well-beaten whites of the eggs, stirring rapidly for a few moments; add the gelatine, and then a teaspoonful of vanilla. Pour it into a pretty-shaped dish to harden, and turn it out on a platter and cut off in blocks, as ice cream. Make this the day before it is to be used.

TAPIOCA CREAM.

After soaking three tablespoonfuls of tapioca in water for an hour, put it in a quart of milk, setting it in a kettle of boiling water, and cooking until soft, stirring often. Beat the yolks of four eggs with 2 or 3 ozs of white sugar; stir it into the milk with a little salt; divide the four whites, beat them to a stiff froth; have two of them ready to stir into the tapioca as soon as done, taking from the fire before stirring them in, and flavor with vanilla. Beat the two remaining whites to a stiff froth, and place them over boiling water, letting them stand until hard, and then spread over the top. Eaten cold.

VANILLA CREAM WITH FRUIT SAUCE.

Make a custard with a pint of rich milk and the yolks of 5 eggs, about $\frac{1}{4}$ lb sugar, and vanilla to taste. When this custard thickens take it off the fire, and add, while still hot, about 2 ozs of gelatine previously dissolved in cold water. Wet a mould, pour in the cream, and set on ice. When set turn it out on a deep dish, arrange a bunch of fine candied cherries on top, and pour around it a sauce made of red cherries stewed, sweetened, strained and slightly thickened with corn starch.

VELVET CREAM.

Put into a pan 1 oz isinglass, ½ pt sherry, the juice of a lemon and half the rind, with two or three ounces of sugar. Let it boil gently until the isinglass is melted, and strain through a piece of muslin into a pint and a half of cream. Keep stirring until nearly cold, and put into moulds, first wet with clear water.

WHIPPED CREAM (1.)

Whip 1 pt or more of double cream with a whisk until stiff; sweeten very slightly and flavor to taste. Care must be taken not to over-whip the cream, as it would then produce butter.

WHIPPED CREAM (2.)

12 eggs.	10 drops each of essence
1 qt cream.	lemon, orange and
½ pt pale sherry.	musk, to flavor.

Whisk to a froth; remove the latter onto a sieve; fill glasses with the cream; pile the froth on top of them.

CHAPTER IX.

PUFFS.

Apple Pasty—Banbury Puffs (1)—Banbury Puffs (2) Claires—Coventry Puffs—Cream Puffs—French Puffs—Fried Pies—Petits Choux—Petits Choux a la Creme—Potato Puffs—Raspberry Puffs - Spanish Puffs—Three Cornered Puffs—Turn-over Puffs.

APPLE PASTY, OR TURNOVER.

Make a short crust with half a pound of flour, two ounces of butter, two ounces of lard, and a little salt. Rub the butter thoroughly into the flour, mix it with very little water, and roll it out thin on the pastry board. Stamp out with a small cutter as many rounds as there are pasties to be made. Moisten the inside of the round; lay stewed apples, sweetened and flavored, on one half, and lift the other half right over it. Press the edges, and bake in a quick oven. A plain and very nice crust may be made with good beef drippings and a little baking powder. Time to bake, a quarter of an hour. Make a dozen pasties.

BANBURY PUFFS (1.)

Roll out the puff paste and cut it the sizes required, with a cake cutter; form an oval puff with the hand; put some meat in the middle; turn them over and lay them together; dust over them some powdered sugar, and bake in a moderate oven.

The meat for Banbury Puffs is made according to requirements and ingredients at command. The following will make a good mixture for this purpose: Chopped apples, candied peel cut fine, bruised currants, and crumbled stale sweet cake; mix the whole with a little molasses or moist sugar; shake mixed spice over the lot.

BANBURY PUFFS (2.)

Cut the paste as directed for Coventry Puffs, without rolling it thin; lay some Banbury meat in the middle, and fold up the edges of the paste, so as to form an oval puff; this is done by pressing more of the paste together at the ends than in the centre; turn them and dust the tops well with loaf sugar dust; bake in a moderate oven.

Banbury Meat (1.)—Cream, ½ ℔ butter, and mix with 1 ℔ moist sugar, ¾ ℔ flour, and ¼ ℔ of candied orange and lemon peels, cut up fine, 2 ℔s chopped currants and ½ oz mixed spices; keep in a jar for use.

Banbury Meat (2.)—Crumble together stale Savoy pound cake, or sweet biscuits; mix with chopped apples, currants, candied peels (cut fine), mixed spices, a little butter, sugar and lemon zest; moisten the whole with thin raspberry jam or molasses; mix according to taste, making it richer or poorer according to judgment; press the whole into a jar and keep for use.

CLAIRES.

Prepare the batter as for Cream Puffs; then with a spoon lay out the "Claires" on pans, about five inches in length, and about the thickness of the thumb, and bake them. These require no washing, as they are covered with icing of some kind. When baked, cut them open lengthwise, the same as for Cream Puffs, and fill them with cream. The neatest way of filling them is to fill a bag, with a tube to it, with the cream, then insert the end of the tube into the "Claires," and fill in that way. When filled, proceed to ice them. They are generally covered with a thick coating of chocolate.

COVENTRY PUFFS.

Roll out the paste about ½ inch thick and cut in square pieces of any desired size; roll out rather thin; put some raspberry jam in the centre and fold up the sides to form a three-cornered puff; turn it over, notch the edges with a knife, and ice them, by first washing them over with the white of an egg, that has been whisked to a froth; dust them well with finely powdered loaf sugar, and with a brush sprinkle them with clean water, just sufficiently to moisten the sugar. If sprinkled too much, they will appear as if not iced at all, as it washes the sugar off again.

CREAM PUFFS.

1½ lbs flour.	1 lb lard or butter.
1 qt water or milk.	26 eggs.

Boil the water and lard a couple of minutes; stir the flour in quickly; take it from the fire and mix in the eggs, three or four at a time; butter the pans well, and drop with a spoon the size wanted; bake in a hot oven. When baked, they will be hollow inside; cut them open and fill with pastry cream.

FRENCH PUFFS.

Use same batter as for Cream Puffs and flavor with vanilla; drop with a spoon, pieces the size of a walnut, in a kettle of hot lard; when done, take out with a skimmer; let them drain; split them in the middle with a sharp knife; put currant jelly inside, and sugar them over the top; to be eaten warm.

FRIED PIES.

Take ordinary doughnut dough; roll out thin pieces about the size of a walnut; wet round the edges: put stewed apples or other fruit in the centre; double over; press the edges down and trim with a cutter to desired size; fry in hot lard.

PETITS CHOUX.

6 ozs butter.   ½ pt water.
2 ozs white sugar.   Pinch salt.
½ stick vanilla.

Put into a stewpan over the fire and when it begins to boil, stir in 3 tablespoons of flour; continue stirring it over the fire, keeping it cleared from the bottom of the stewpan until it becomes a tough paste; take it from the fire and stir in gradually 7 or 8 eggs; work well into the paste; butter a baking sheet, and lay the paste upon it in pieces the size of an English walnut; egg them over; sugar them and bake them in a moderate oven; when baked and cold, open a lid at the top of each, and fill it with jam or marmalade; replace the lid and serve upon a napkin.

PETITS CHOUX A LA CREME.

Put about 1 pt of water into a saucepan with a few grains of salt, a pat of butter, sugar to taste, with plenty of grated lemon peel. When the water boils, throw into it gradually flour enough to form a thick paste; take it off the fire, let it remain ten minutes, and work into it three or four eggs. Butter a baking sheet and lay the paste upon it in neat little heaps, about one teaspoon to each. Bake a nice color in a moderate oven; take them out, sprinkle powdered sugar over them, and put them in again for a few minutes. Make an incision in the under side of each, and insert a small piece of jam or jelly, or some pastry cream or custard.

POTATO PUFFS.

Two large cups of cold, mashed potato, two spoonfuls of melted butter, two well-beaten eggs, a cup of milk, and salt to taste. Mix the butter with the potato and beat smooth. Then add the other ingredients, beat well; put into a deep dish and brown in a quick oven. Serve at once.

RASPBERRY PUFFS.

Proceed precisely the same as for open tarts, rolling them out thin, about six inches in diameter; place a teaspoonful of raspberry preserves on each, a little from the centre, spread it a little, and then bring the back part over on the preserve, keeping it back a little from the front edge, for if it laps over, the bottom edge is prevented from raising. It is best to allow the top edge to lie back from the front edge at least one-fourth of an inch. This folding forms a half circle. This being done, wash them with water, or egg and water, and dust them with powdered sugar. Also cut a few deep but short cuts across the top—over where the preserve lays—when baked the preserve shows through.

SPANISH PUFFS.

Make some paste as for Petits Choux a la Creme, and with the fingers or with a teaspoon lay this out in the form of round balls, the size of walnuts, on sheets of buttered paper; these being held at one end, must be immersed in hot frying fat, to be gently shaken off. As they are frying, they are to be carefully moved about

with a draining spoon, until they are done of a light
color, and have increased four times their original size;
they must then be drained on a wire sieve, dished up on a
napkin, some sugar dredged over them, and served immediately.

THREE-CORNERED PUFFS.

Roll out a thin sheet of paste and cut it with a cake
docker, according to the size the puffs are to be made;
put a tablespoon of thin raspberry or other jam in the
middle; turn up the sides in three places, forming a
peak at the top; turn them over, and place them on the
board, side by side, fitting in closely to each other;
whisk the white of an egg and wash the puffs all over
with it, laying it on with a brush; dredge them all over
with powdered sugar; just before putting them into the
oven sprinkle them over with water.

TURN-OVER PUFFS.

Roll out some puff paste $\frac{1}{4}$ inch thick; cut into pieces
with a round-scolloped cutter, or into square pieces with
a knife; put a little jam or preserve into the centre of
each; fold or double them over; press down the thumb
a little on each side of the jam to close them; ice as
directed for Coventry Puffs, and bake in a moderate oven.

CHAPTER X.

CUSTARDS.

General Directions—Almond Custard—Baked Custard—Discolorations on Custard Cups—Boiled Custard, (1)—Boiled Custard, (2)—Burnt Custard—Cake Custards—Caramel Custards—Chocolate Custards—Chocolate Custard, Baked—Chocolate Custards, Boiled—Oatmeal Custard—Rice Custard—Strawberry Custard—Sweet Potato Custard—Tapioca Custard.

For several good ways of making custards see the second part of this work under the chapters treating of steamed, boiled and baked puddings. See also this part under Pie and Tart Fillings. A few special recipes are, however, given below.

For custards use only perfectly fresh eggs. Custards should not be allowed to boil.

ALMOND CUSTARD.

Blanch and beat fine 8 ozs. almonds with a spoonful of water. Beat 1 qt. of cream with a little rose-water and put to the yolks of 8 eggs; sweeten to taste and add the almonds; stir over a slow fire till it is of a proper thickness; do not let it boil; pour it into cups.

BAKED CUSTARD;

Made with a pint of milk, two or three eggs, two tablespoonfuls of sugar, a pinch of salt, a teaspoonful of flavoring, and a grating of nutmeg, baked in cups set in a pan of water and served in the same cups, accompanied by plain cake, is as good as it is simple. The excellence depends on the baking, which should be done slowly. Three eggs make the best custard, but two will answer.

DISCOLORATIONS ON CUSTARD CUPS.

To take the brown discolorations off of cups in which custards are baked, rub with damp flannel dipped in best whiting. Scouring-sand or sand-soap will answer the purpose.

BOILED CUSTARD, (1).

Boil a quart of new milk with sugar, a piece of cinnamon and lemon-peel, and a bay-leaf. Mix a tablespoonful of ground rice with a little cold milk, and the beat yolks of four or six eggs. Stir the whole gradually into the boiling milk in a basin, then put it in a saucepan and thicken over the fire, but not boil. Pour it into a cold dish and stir one way till cool.

BOILED CUSTARD, (2).

1 qt. milk,	Pinch salt,
3 eggs well beaten,	2 tablespoons corn starch.

Heat the milk nearly to boiling; add the starch previously dissolved, the eggs, and sugar to taste; let it boil up once or twice, stirring briskly; flavor to taste.

BURNT CUSTARD.

1 quart of milk, 5 eggs, 3 tablespoonfuls of sugar, nutmeg and flavoring extract to taste. Scald the milk, but not to boiling; beat eggs light with the sugar, and pour upon them the hot milk. Mix well, and bake in a well-buttered dish; turn out when cold; strew very thickly with white sugar. Set the plate containing the custard upon the upper grating of a hot oven. The sugar

will melt, and run in brown streams all over the moulded pudding. Slip carefully to a dish, and eat cold.

CAKE CUSTARDS

Moisten two cupfuls of stale cake with a custard made of one pint of milk, four eggs, and two tablespoonfuls of sugar; put into buttered cups, set them in a pan with enough hot water to reach half way to the brim, and bake in a moderate oven until the custard is firm. They may be served in the cups or may be turned out and dusted with powdered sugar; any kind of pudding sauce preferred may be served with them.

CARAMEL CUSTARDS.

Put a handful of loaf-sugar in a sauce-pan with a little water, and set it on the fire until it becomes a dark-brown caramel: then add more water (boiling), to produce a dark liquor like strong coffee. Beat up the yolks of six eggs with a little milk; strain, add one pint of milk (sugar to taste) and as much caramel liquor (cold) as will give the mixture the desired color. Pour it into a well-buttered mould, put this in a *bain marie* with cold water, then place the apparatus on a gentle fire, taking care that the water does not boil. Half an hour's steaming will set the custard, which then turn out and serve. By using the white of one or two eggs in addition to the six yolks, the chances of the custard not breaking are made more certain.

CHOCOLATE CUSTARDS.

One quart of milk; one ounce of best French chocolate; eight eggs; two teaspoonfuls of vanilla; sugar to taste. Beat the eight yolks and the two whites of the eggs until they are light. Boil the milk; when boiling stir the chocolate and the sugar into it, and then put it into a clean pitcher. Place this in a pot of boiling water; stir one way gently all the time until it becomes a thick cream; when cold strain it and add the vanilla; place it in cups; beat the whites of the eggs to a stiff froth, and add the sugar to them; beat well, and place some of this frosting on the top of each custard.

CHOCOLATE CUSTARD—BAKED.

1 qt. milk,	1 oz. grated French choc-
½ doz. eggs, yolks & whites	olate,
separated,	Vanilla flavoring.

Scald the milk; stir in the chocolate and simmer two minutes, to dissolve and incorporate well with the milk. Beat up the yolks with the sugar and put into the hot mixture. Stir for one minute before seasoning and pouring into the cups, which should be set ready in a pan of boiling water. They should be half submerged, that the water may not bubble over the tops. Cook slowly about twenty minutes, or until the custards are firm. When cold, whip the whites of the eggs to a *meringue* with a very little powdered sugar (most *meringues* are too sweet) and pile some upon the top of each cup. Put a piece of red jelly on the *meringue*.

CHOCOLATE CUSTARDS—BOILED

One quart of milk; six eggs, whites and yolks separately beaten; ¼ ℔ sugar; 1 oz grated chocolate; vanilla to taste, a teaspoonful to the pint being a good rule. Scald the milk, stir in sugar and chocolate. Boil gently five minutes, and add the yolks. Cook five minutes more, or until it begins to thicken up well, stirring all the time. When nearly cold beat in the flavoring, and whisk all briskly for a minute before pouring into the custard cups. Whip up the whites with a little powdered sugar, or what is better, half a cup of currant or cranberry jelly, and heap upon the custards.

OATMEAL CUSTARD.

Take two tablespoonfuls of the finest Scotch oatmeal, beat up in sufficient cold water to run freely, add the beaten yolk of a fresh egg; have a pint of scalding new milk on the fire. Pour the mixture into it, stirring thoroughly; add sugar to taste, and a glass of sherry with a little grated nutmeg: Pour out in dish and take warm in bed. It will be found very grateful in colds and chills.

RICE CUSTARD,

Is made of one quart of sweet milk, two-thirds of a cup of uncooked rice, and a little salt. Put this in tea or coffee cups, set them in the steamer over a kettle of boiling water. Let it cook until the rice is almost like jelly. When cold turn it out of the cup. Serve with sugar and cream or with pudding sauce.

STRAWBERRY CUSTARD.

Make boiled custard of a quart of milk and the yolks of five eggs properly sweetened. Boil till it thickens to the right consistency, take it off the fire, and put in the flavoring. Take a gill of sugar and a pint of ripe strawberries; crush them together and pass through a fine strainer. Take the whites of four of the eggs, and while beating them to a stiff froth add a gill of sugar, a little at a time. Then to the sugar and eggs add the sweet-

7

ened strawberry juice, beating all the while to keep it stiff. This makes a beautiful pink float, which is to be placed on top of the custard.

SWEET POTATO CUSTARD.

Boil 8 ℔s prime sweet potatoes; peel them, and force them through a sieve; add ½ lb butter, 1 gal. milk, 1 ℔ sugar, and 1½ doz. eggs; flavor with cinnamon; beat the whole for a few minutes and bake in deep dish lined with paste.

TAPIOCA CUSTARD.

One teacupful of tapioca dissolved in water over night. Beat 3 eggs and ¼ ℔ of sugar together, and stir into the tapioca; add 1 quart of sweet milk; stir well; bake in a pudding dish until the custard thickens.

APPENDIX.

ALMOND CHEESE CURD PUDDING.

Blanch and pound ¼ ℔ sweet almonds and 8 bitter ones, with one glass of orange-flower water; add ¼ ℔ sugar, ¼ pt. cream, and the whites of two eggs beat stiff; bake as for cheese curd pudding.

CHEESE CURD PUDDING OR CHEESECAKE.

Mix with the dry beat curd of 3 pts. milk, 6 ozs. of well washed and picked currants, sugar to taste, a little lemon zest, and the yolks of 4 eggs beat in ½ pt. scalded cream, and 1 glass of brandy; mix well and put into a tourte tin lined with puff paste; bake, and serve with a dust of sugar.

To make the curd, put new milk into a clean pan and set it by the side of the fire so that it will keep blood warm; put a spoonful of rennet into it, not too much, or it will make the curd hard and the whey very salt; in a short time it will separate into curd and whey; cut the former into small pieces with a knife.

A large variety of cheesecakes may be made from the above recipe by the addition of proper flavors and materials.

DOROTHY'S CURD PUDDING.

Boil with lemon peel and cinnamon, 1 qt. of milk or cream; add to it 8 eggs; sweeten and flavor with rum;

stir and let it boil until it curdles, and until the whey is completely separated; then drain it on a sieve, and put into a mould with holes in it, to let the whey drain wholly off; when firm, turn it out, and serve with cold sauce.

EGG CHEESE CURD PUDDING.

Boil with lemon peel and cinnamon, 1 qt. milk or cream; add 8 eggs well beat and a little salt; sweeten and flavor with two glasses of rum; stir and let this boil until it curdles, and the whey is completely separated; drain it well on a sieve, add ¼ ℔ butter, put into a dish lined with puff paste, and bake.

LEMON CHEESE CURD PUDDING.

Cut into slices four sponge biscuits, and soak them in a gill of cream; add the zest and juice of three lemons, with ¼ ℔ each of butter and sugar, a little mixed spice and three eggs; bake as for Cheese Curd pudding, decorating with candied lemon peel.

ORANGE CHEESE CURD PUDDING.

Proceed with oranges as for Lemon Cheese Curd Pudding; decorate with candied orange peel.

POTATO CHEESE CURD PUDDING.

Boil or roast ½ ℔ good mealy potatoes; take off their skins and press them fine; then reduce ¼ ℔ good butter to a cream; mix this with the yolks of 3 eggs, 3 ozs. powdered loaf sugar, a piece of stale savoy or pound cake crumbled, and a little essence of lemon; mix as for pound cake, adding the potato pulp after the butter and sugar, using a few currants if desirable.

CUSTARD PUDDING—BAKED.

Put 1 pt. milk into a stewpan with half a stick of cinnamon, the rind of a lemon, and three cloves; bring this to a boil, and strain it over 4 yolks and 4 whole eggs beat; mix well with the whisk, adding one glass each of brandy, rum and noyeau, and a little pineapple syrup; bake slowly in a buttered dish, and serve with whipt cream in a boat.

CUSTARD PUDDING—STEAMED.

Beat fifteen yolks of eggs; add this to 1 pt. cream, ½ pt. milk, a little sugar, and a pinch of salt; put into a prepared mould; place in a stewpan with a little boiling water; cover, and steam at the corner of the stove until set, but by no means allow the water to boil.

TO BLANCH ALMONDS, PISTACHIOS, ETC.

Boil over the fire some water, with a pinch of salt; when boiling, throw in the almonds, pistachios, etc.; in a little more than a minute the skins if tried will come off freely; remove from the fire, throw on a sieve, pour cold water over them, and skin or blanch.

PUREES.

A puree of fruits is fruit cooked according to recipe, and passed through a sieve; and sometimes, as for ripe, fleshy fruits, such as ripe apricots, strawberries, etc., passed through raw. The term puree applies also to nuts, meat or fish; but these are not generally passed through raw.

USE OF THE SALAMANDER.

This is a thick and heavy piece of iron with a long

handle; it is made red hot in the fire, and is used to brown the tops of cakes, puddings, etc., when so directed; if sweet, the cake, pudding, etc., must be dusted with sugar, and if a cheese pudding, it must be sprinkled with grated Parmesan cheese, bread crumbs, or a few bits of butter, before the salamander is applied.

ENGLISH MINCE MEAT.

25 ℔s. beef.	¼ ℔ ground nutmeg.
8 ℔s. suet.	2 ozs. " mace.
¾ bbl. apples.	1½ gals. molasses.
6 ℔s. muscatel raisins.	1 gal. brandy.
4 ℔s. seedless "	1 " Maderia wine.
7 ℔s. currants.	2 gals. boiled cider.
4 lbs. citron.	6 lemon rinds, peeled thin
½ ℔ ground cloves.	and chopped fine.

Chop the beef, suet and apples very fine; mix all well together, and let stand two weeks before using.

END OF PART I.

THE COMPLETE

Practical Pastry Cook,

— IN —

THREE PARTS.

PART II.

Sweet Sauces and Puddings.

CHICAGO:

J. THOMPSON GILL, MANAGER CONFECTIONER AND BAKER PUBLISHING CO.

1888.

CONTENTS.

CHAPTER I.

Moulds, Flavors, and Other Materials Used for Sweet Puddings.

MOULDS AND DISHES.

Plain pudding moulds are made of copper, tinned on the inside, or of plain tin, either round or oval.

Plain dariole moulds are miniature ones of the same class.

Boudin moulds are a kind of oblong, plain copper mould, tinned inside, or of plain tin, with or without flutes.

A souffle dish consists of a silver case, with an interior lining; the souffle is baked or iced in the prepared lining, being served in the silver case.

Special pudding tins, pudding basins, earthenware pudding moulds and dishes, etc., need only to be mentioned.

TO PREPARE A PLAIN MOULD FOR PUDDINGS.

Butter the interior of a round or oval plain mould; cut a piece of foolscap paper to fit it at the bottom; butter this; decorate the interior, if approved, with fruits, etc., and use for baked, boiled or stewed puddings, as directed.

TO PREPARE SOUFFLE CASES FOR HOT OR COLD SOUFFLES.

Butter the interior of the souffle lining; tie and pin

round it a double band of buttered paper, about 7 or 8 inches in height; when ready to serve, remove the paper and put the lining into the silver dish.

USE OF THE SALAMANDER FOR PUDDINGS.

This is a thick and heavy piece of iron with a long handle; is made red hot in the fire, and is used to brown the tops of puddings, etc., when so directed; if sweet, the pudding must be dusted with sugar, and if a cheese pudding, it must be sprinkled with grated Parmesan cheese, bread crumbs, or a few bits of butter, before the salamander is applied.

HINTS ON PUDDING CONDIMENTS, FLAVORS, ETC.

As a general rule, a little salt should be added to all sweet puddings, and in most cases a little sugar to all savory ones; essences are good and useful, but should be used carefully; flour should be sifted before it is used; when not otherwise mentioned in the recipe the sugar should be the best loaf, pounded and passed through a hair seive; fresh butter is the best, particularly for the more delicate sort of puddings. Great care should be taken in using eggs, as a single musty one will spoil any of the puddings.

SAVARIN FOR PUDDINGS.

Weigh 1 lb flour; mix 1 oz. German yeast in a basin with a little luke-warm water and a little flour, to the consistency of cream; put it in a warm place to rise; melt 10 ozs. of butter to a sort of cream, beat this to a smooth paste with the flour, with ½ doz. whole eggs and 4 yolks, 2 ozs. sugar and a little salt; then beat in the sponge; cover over with a cloth, and let this rise; when

well risen put into a plain mould prepared as for souffle;
put onto a baking sheet with a bed of salt under the
mould to prevent the bottom from burning; bake in a
moderately quick oven.

SAVOY CAKE FOR PUDDINGS.

1 lb sugar,   ¾ lb flour,

10 eggs,   Zest of a lemon.

Beat together the sugar, eggs and zest; stir in the
flour lightly with a wooden spoon; put the mixture into
a mould, the interior of which has been brushed over
with clarified butter mixed with a very little flour; the
mould is then dusted with fine sugar, and a buttered
double paper band fastened round the top; bake in a
moderate oven.

GENOISE FOR PUDDINGS.

Cream 1 lb. butter with a wooden spoon; stir in 1 lb
sugar and 10 eggs, (one at a time); thoroughly mix in
1¼ lbs flour and a little lemon zest, or other flavors;
spread this batter on a baking sheet with a turned up
edge, which has been previously buttered, papered, re-
buttered and floured; bake in a moderate oven and use
as directed.

MERINGUE FOR PUDDINGS.

Beat up very fine the fresh whites of ½ doz. eggs; stir
in ¾ lb sugar, lightly; make this into spoon meringues, or
any other form according to recipe.

PETITS CHOUX FOR PUDDINGS.

Put ¼ pt. water into a stewpan with a pat of butter;
add to this while boiling, ¼ lb flour, and stir with a

wooden spoon until it detaches from the sides of the stewpan; then remove from the fire and stir in 3 or 4 eggs, one at a time; flavor or season according to recipe.

PASTRY CREAM FOR PUDDINGS.

Boil ½ pt. of cream and the same of milk with the peel of a lemon and some sugar; put this into a stewpan with the yolks of ½ doz. eggs, and two spoonsful of flour; mix this with a wooden spoon, and dilute with the above; stir this over the fire until it boils, and work it well for five or six minutes; then mix in ¼ lb clarified butter with the paste; put it into a basin and stir until cold; if it is too thick add a little cream.

CARAMEL SUGAR FOR PUDDINGS.

Put into a copper sugar boiler about 1½ lbs broken sugar, adding sufficient water to soak it; when dissolved put it on a quick fire with a cover over it, and boil down very rapidly; have ready a small basin of water with a lump of ice in it, and half a lemon and an iron spoon by the side; and as it reduces, try it by dipping the handle of the spoon into the sugar, from thence into the water and ice; when near the crack (which is the case when it breaks with a snap between the fingers), put in half a teaspoon of lemon juice; try it again quickly, remove from the fire and it is ready for use.

VANILLA SUGAR FOR PUDDINGS.

Cut up three sticks of vanilla into small pieces; pound in a mortar with ¼ lb lump sugar; pass it through a hair seive; then beat the dregs with another ¼ lb lump sugar which pass as before; put into a canister for use.

ZEST OF ORANGE OR LEMON FOR PUDDINGS.

Rub an orange equally all over on the rough part of a rather large lump of loaf sugar; scrape this off with a knife, and use for puddings as directed. Proceed in the same manner for lemon zest.

TO CUT ORANGE AND LEMON PEEL FOR PUDDINGS.

When orange or lemon peel is required, care should be taken to cut it very thin with a sharp knife; the zest of the rind is contained in a number of very small cells all over the surface, to liberate which, for the sake of its flavor, it is necessary to cut the peel thin, so as to divide or open these cells, and thus obtain their essence; therefore peel cut thick is not of the slightest use for culinary purposes.

TO BLANCH ALMONDS, PISTACHIOS, ETC.

Boil over the fire some water, with a pinch of salt; when boiling, throw in the almonds, pistachios, etc.; in a little more than a minute the skins if tried will come off freely; remove from the fire, throw on a seive, pour cold water over them, and skin and blanch.

PUREES.

A puree of fruits is fruit cooked according to recipe and passed through a sieve; and sometimes, as for ripe, fleshy fruits, such as ripe apricots, strawberries, etc., passed through raw. The term puree applies also to nuts, meat or fish; but these are not generally passed through raw.

COMPOTE OF ORANGES FOR VARIOUS PUDDINGS.

Cut up with a sharp knife six or eight oranges with the skin on, each one into six divisions; cut away the skin and white part with one cut; make one cut across the edge, cut away the pips; trim the pieces slightly, and put them into a basin with pounded sugar for an hour or two.

COMPOTE OF CHERRIES FOR VARIOUS PUDDINGS.

Stone the cherries, put them in a copper pan with pounded sugar, and boil for about five minutes; take the cherries out and put them into a flat dish; put the juice on the fire again, adding a glass of noyeau and a little lemon juice; color with cochineal; when it comes to a boil thicken with arrowroot; pour it over the cherries and let it cool for use.

GOOSEBERRY AND RHUBARB FOOL FOR PUDDINGS.

Put 3 pts. green gooseberries into a copper preserving pan with cold water, and a tablespoon of salt to preserve the color; set them over a slow fire to simmer until tender; strain and puree them; put the puree over the fire with about $\frac{3}{4}$ lb sugar; put this into a basin, and then reduce the consistency with cream. Proceed in the same manner for rhubarb.

CARAMEL FRUITS FOR PUDDINGS.

To caramel fruits they must be very dry, such as cherries, grapes, etc.; cut the stalks short, just leaving room enough to hold them by; dip them in caramel sugar, strain at the side of the sugar boiler, and place each one carefully on an oiled slab or baking sheet; when cold, cut off the stalks, and build them in a plain mould slightly oiled, sticking them with the caramel sugar.

CARAMEL ORANGES FOR PUDDINGS.

Take the peel and white part off 1 doz. dividing oranges; carefully divide them with the fingers, and put them in a sieve; dip each piece in melted caramel sugar; put on an oiled slab or baking sheet; when cold, build them in an oiled mould with caramel sugar. The divisions of orange should be left on the sieve for three or four hours to dry before they are used.

CHAPTER II.

Sweet Sauces for Puddings.

There is a great variety of ways of making sauces for puddings, but the general principles may be briefly illustrated as follows:

Take, say 2 qts. of water; boil in a saucepan, one stick of whole cinnamon, and one sliced lemon; let it boil for three or four minutes; take ¼ ℔ butter, ¼ ℔ or more brown sugar (beat together as for cake); add to this 2 ozs. flour or corn starch; put it into the water and stir briskly for one minute, until it becomes of the consistency of thick cream, taking care that it does not burn. If the cinnamon is left out it will be lemon sauce; or leave out the lemon and it is cinnamon sauce; leave out both and flavor with brandy, wine, rum, etc., for brandy, wine and rum sauce, etc.

The above sauce, owing to the presence of the butter, is too rich for many persons, and the following sauce is one which will give more general satisfaction: Take one sliced lemon and 2 qts. water (boil from three to five minutes), ½ ℔ brown sugar, sifted with two ozs. of corn starch; stir into the boiling water until it colors or thickens, when it is ready for use.

This latter sauce can be made into any kind of wine or brandy, or lemon sauce, that suits; or it can be made strong with liquor; or if there are temperance people who object to the use of liquor, the spirits can be dispensed with in a part or the whole sauce. For brandy sauce, use a little caramel for coloring; for rum, use no color; for sherry wine, a little caramel; cochineal is appropriate for port or claret; for champagne sauce, in place of brown sugar, use granulated with more lemons to give it the required color.

ALMOND AND RAISIN SAUCE.

Soak 3 ozs. of the best dried raisins in brandy for four hours; cut up in fillets, or chop, 2 ozs. of blanched almonds; throw these into an arrowroot sauce.

ALMOND SAUCE.

Blance and pound to a paste in a little milk 2 ozs. almonds; add this during the process of making to a custard of ¼ pt. cream, 3 yolks of eggs, and ⅓ glass of noyeau; sweeten to taste.

APPLE JELLY SAUCE.

Melt a pot of apple jelly with two glasses of sherry; add lemon juice and syrup to taste.

APPLE SAUCE.

Add a little lemon zest in the making of a puree of six apples; dilute this with cream.

APRICOT JAM SAUCE.

Pass a pot of apricot jam through a sieve; add the juice of a lemon, two glasses of sherry, and a little syrup; make this hot and serve.

APRICOT SAUCE.

Pass six apricots through a sieve; mix with some syrup, half a glass of brandy, and a little lemon juice; stir altogether over the fire for a few minutes.

ARROWROOT SAUCE.

Mix some Bermuda arrowroot in a little cold water; add this according to judgment to any boiling liquid which requires thickening with arrowroot.

BLACK CHERRY SAUCE (1).

Proceed as for red cherry sauce, using black-heart cherries, and omitting the cochineal.

BLACK CHERRY SAUCE (2).

Proceed as for red cherry sauce, with ½ ℔ black-heart cherries, adding the juice of half a lemon.

BLACK CHERRY ARROWROOT SAUCE.

Proceed as for red cherry arrowroot sauce, using black-heart cherries, and omitting the cochineal.

BLACK CURRANT SAUCE.

Stew 1 pint black currants with 6 ozs. sugar, 1 glass of sherry, and a little lemon, for five or six minutes over the fire.

BLACK CURRANT JELLY SAUCE.

Proceed with black currants as for red currant jelly sauce, using a glass of port wine.

BLACK GRAPE SAUCE.

Proceed as for white grape sauce, substituting black grapes and a glass of port wine instead of sherry.

BLOOD ORANGE SAUCE.

Port wine arrowroot sauce with cochineal, and just before serving throw in a compote of six blood oranges.

BRANDY ARROWROOT SAUCE.

Proceed as for wine arrowroot sauce, using a glass of brandy and the juice of half a lemon.

BRANDY PLUM PUDDING SAUCE.

Make some good melted butter with milk; sweeten to taste, and add two glasses of brandy.

BROWN BREAD PUDDING SAUCE.

Melt a little red currant jelly with three glasses of port wine and two of claret; sweeten to taste.

CHOCOLATE SAUCE.

Scrape a fillet of chocolate; melt it in a little weak syrup; add half a glass of brandy, and sufficient arrowroot to make it the consistency of double cream.

CIDER SAUCE.

Simmer ½ pt. cider with ¼ lb sugar for about ten minutes; add 2 ozs. butter and slightly thicken with arrowroot.

COCOANUT SAUCE.

Work a grated cocoanut over the fire with 3 yolks of eggs, ½ pt. cream, 1 oz. sugar, and then a glass of maraschino; when set, serve in a boat.

COLD SAUCE.

Work ¼ lb butter with a wooden spoon to a cream, adding first ¼ lb sugar, and then a glass of sherry, and the same of brandy by degrees.

COFFEE SAUCE.

Simmer ¼ lb of whole coffee in ¾ pt. cream, for about ten minutes; add half a glass of brandy, 5 yolks of eggs, and sugar to taste, pass through a metal sieve and serve.

DAMSON SAUCE.

Stone and stew 1 pt. damsons in weak syrup until tender; puree them, with the juice of a lemon.

DUNDEE SAUCE.

Melt a pot of orange marmalade with one glass of sherry and one of curacoa.

EGG SAUCE.

Add to smooth custard sauce one glass of brandy and two hard boiled eggs cut into small dice, just at the last.

EVA'S CREAM SAUCE.

Put ½ pt. cream and two glasses of maraschino, on the fire; when it has come to a boil, thicken to the consistency of double cream, with a little arrowroot.

GERMAN SAUCE.

Put three glasses of sherry into a stewpan, with the juice of a lemon, a little syrup, and 4 yolks of eggs; whisk sharply over a not too quick fire for four or five minutes until done.

GINGER SAUCE.

Chop up ¼ ℔ preserved ginger; add this with a little of the syrup, to ½ pt. cream, and two yolks of eggs; stir this over the fire until set.

GREENGAGE JAM SAUCE.

Proceed with a pot of greengage jam, as for apricot jam sauce, adding a glass of brandy.

GROUND RICE SAUCE.

Boil some ground rice in single cream, stirring all the

while until it comes to the consistency of double cream; flavor with maraschino or noyeau.

HARD SAUCE.

Take ½ lb table butter, and 1 lb powdered sugar; beat them up until very light in a wooden bowl or earthen dish; add the white of one egg and flavor with brandy, lemon, etc. (or whatever flavor there is in the pudding); place in ice till ready to use; one teaspoonful is sufficient for each order.

KIRSCHWASSER SAUCE.

Thicken ¼ pt. kirschwasser over the fire with the yolks of four eggs and one gill cream; sweeten to taste.

LEMON ARROWROOT SAUCE.

Proceed as for orange arrowroot sauce, with the zest and juice of one lemon.

LIQUEUR ARROWROOT SAUCE.

Make a clear arrowroot sauce with very weak syrup, adding a glass and a half of any of the liqueurs, and the juice of half a lemon.

MACARONI SAUCE.

Cut some boiled macaroni into very small lengths, and add arrowroot sauce.

MARROW PUDDING SAUCE.

Work the yolks of four eggs over the fire, with a spoonful of flour, 2 ozs. of sugar, 2 ozs. of butter, 3 glasses of Madeira, and the juice of half a lemon; when up to the boil pass it through a metel sieve and serve.

MELTED BUTTER SAUCE.

Make some melted butter with milk; stir in one glass

2

of sherry, half a glass of rum, the zest of a lemon, and powdered sugar to taste; serve in a boat with grated nutmeg on top.

MIXED SPICE SAUCE.

Make a melted butter sauce; add to this half a teaspoon of ground ginger, and the same of mixed spice.

NECTARINE SAUCE.

Pass ½ doz. nectarines through a sieve, and finish as for apricot sauce.

NOUILLE SAUCE.

Make some nouilles; add them just at the last to smooth custard sauce, flavored with a little rum.

ORANGE ARROWROOT SAUCE.

Boil with the weak syrup arrowroot sauce, the zest of an orange; add the juice of two oranges and half a lemon.

ORANGE FLOWER SAUCE (1).

Add two glasses of orange flower water to the weak syrup arrowroot sauce.

ORANGE FLOWER SAUCE (2).

Add orange flower water to taste, to smooth custard sauce.

ORANGE SAUCE.

Cut ½ doz. oranges as for compotes; throw them into wine arrowroot sauce just before serving.

PEACH SAUCE.

Proceed as for apricot sauce with ½ doz. peaches, adding a few drops of essence of almonds, and omitting the brandy.

PEAR SAUCE.

Make a puree of ½ doz. mellow pears and ¼ lb sugar; dilute this with cream.

PINEAPPLE JAM SAUCE.

Put about ½ lb pineapple jam into a stewpan over the fire, with the yolks of three eggs, ½ pt. cream, and the juice of half a lemon; stir over the fire and pass through a sieve.

PINEAPPLE SAUCE.

Peel and cut a small pineapple into slices; take out the core; cut into small dice; stew them in a weak syrup; when done, add the juice of one lemon and a half; thicken with arrowroot.

PISTACHIO SAUCE.

Chop 3 ozs. of blanched and dried pistachios very fine; throw them into a very clear arrowroot sauce, flavored with brandy.

PORT ARROWROOT SAUCE.

Make a clear weak arrowroot sauce with very weak syrup, adding two glasses of port wine and the juice of half a lemon.

PUNCH ARROWROOT SAUCE.

Add to a weak syrup arrowroot sauce, a little decoction of green tea, two glasses of rum, and the juice of half a lemon.

PUNCH STORE SAUCE.

Mix together 1 pt. sherry, ½ pt. rum, ½ pt. brandy, ¼ pt curacoa, ½ oz. lemon peel, and ½ oz. Seville orange peel;

infuse this for ten days, shaking the bottle every day; strain, and add ½ pt. rich syrup, and bottle for use.

RASPBERRY AND CURRANT SAUCE.

Stew ½ pt. each of red currants and raspberries in 6 ozs. sugar; if too liquid, add a little arrowroot; serve hot or cold.

RASPBERRY SAUCE.

Proceed with ¼ lb fine raspberries as for strawberry sauce.

RASPBERRY JAM SAUCE.

Proceed with raspberry jam as for strawberry sauce.

RATAFIA SAUCE.

Stir ½ pt. cream, the yolks of three eggs, and 3 ozs. of very finely bruised ratafias, over the fire until set.

RED AND WHITE CURRANT SAUCE.

Stew for five minutes in a stewpan, with 6 ozs. sugar, half a glass of brandy, and ½ pt. each of red and white currants; serve hot or cold.

RED CURRANT JELLY SAUCE.

Melt about 1 lb of red currant jelly with a glass of brandy; add syrup to taste.

RED CHERRY ARROWROOT SAUCE.

' Stone and pass ½ lb red cherries through a sieve; boil a little syrup down strong; add the cherries, a few drops of cochineal and some lemon juice: thicken slightly with arrowroot, and serve.

RED CHERRY SAUCE (1).

Use a compote of red cherries with sufficient arrow-root.

RED CHERRY SAUCE (2).

Stew ¾.lb stoned red cherries in a little syrup; pass them through a sieve, and add one glass of port wine, and some royal white sweet garnish pudding; cut into rather small dice and throw in at the last.

REDUCED WINE SAUCE.

Reduce on the fire ¼ pt. port wine and ½ pt. sherry, mixed together, till half the original quantity; add a little sugar and lemon juice.

RED GOOSEBERRY JAM SAUCE.

Pass gooseberry jam through a sieve with two glasses of sherry; make hot and serve.

SEVILLE ORANGE ARROWROOT SAUCE.

Add the zest and juice of two Seville oranges and half a glass of brandy, to a weak syrup arrowroot sauce.

STRAWBERRY JAM SAUCE.

Proceed with strawberry jam as for aprocot jam; substituting two glasses of claret for the sherry.

STRAWBERRY SAUCE.

Throw three dozen fine strawberries into wine arrowroot sauce before serving.

SHRUB ARROWROOT SAUCE.

Thicken three glasses of shrub over the fire with a little arrowroot; add syrup to taste.

SMOOTH CUSTARD SAUCE.

Stir ¾ pt. cream over the fire until it boils; add three yolks of eggs mixed with a little milk; sweeten and flavor to taste.

TEA SAUCE.

Add a custard of four yolks of eggs and ½ pt. of cream to some strong decoction of tea, and half a glass of brandy; sweeten to taste,

TRAFALGAR SAUCE.

Melt three glasses of jelly in a stewpan; add one glass of sherry, one of curacoa, and a little lemon; thicken slightly with arrowroot.

UNCLE TOM'S CAROLINA SAUCE.

Boil a little Carolina rice; dry it; put into arrowroot sauce, flavored with a glass of rum.

VANILLA SAUCE.

Sweeten smooth custard sauce with vanilla sugar.

VERMICELLI SAUCE.

Proceed as for nouille sauce, with some vermicelli broken and blanched in milk.

WALNUT SAUCE.

Prodeed with 1 doz. blanched walnuts as for almond sauce.

WHITE CHERRY ARROWROOT SAUCE,

Proceed as for red cherry arrowroot sauce, using white cherries, adding a glass of white noyeau, and omitting cochineal.

WHITE CHERRY SAUCE (1).

Proceed as for red cherry sauce (1) using white-heart cherries, stewing them longer and omitting the cochineal.

WHITE CHERRY SAUCE (2),

Proceed as for red cherry sauce (2) with ½ lb white-heart cherries and two glasses of sherry.

WHITE GRAPE SAUCE.

Make an arrowroot sauce with a weak syrup: add the juice of half a lemon, a glass of sherry, and half a glass of elder flower water; throw in 3 doz. small white grapes just before serving.

WHIPT CREAM GARNISH FOR PUDDINGS.

Whip ½ pt. or more of double cream with a whisk until stiff; sweeten very slightly and flavor to taste; care must be taken not to over-whip the cream as it would then produce butter; if required to pour round a pudding it should only be half whipt.

WINE ARROWROOT SAUCE.

Make a clear arrowroot sauce with very weak syrup; add a couple of glasses of sherry or any other wine.

YANKEE SAUCE.

Put ¼ lb molasses into a stewpan with a glass of rum, one of brandy, one of sherry, and the juice of half a lemon; serve very hot.

CHAPTER III.
STEAMED PUDDINGS.

ALBERT PUDDING.

Take the crumb of two French rolls; soak it in $\frac{1}{2}$ pt. boiling milk; when cold, add 5 eggs (leaving out the whites of two), 6 ozs of butter, 1 glass each of port wine and brandy, and $\frac{1}{2}$ teaspoon of ground ginger; sweeten to taste; put into a mould and steam for one hour; serve with German sauce.

AMERICAN PUDDING.

Cut some thin slices of superior gingerbread; make a cold custard of 4 eggs and $\frac{3}{4}$ pt of milk, flavored with a little preserved ginger syrup; soak the slices in a little of the custard; place them in the mould and fill up with the remainder; steam and serve with Yankee sauce.

BISCUIT PUDDING.

Pour 1 pt boiling cream over $\frac{3}{4}$ lb broken Savoy cake; let it steep five minutes; add $\frac{1}{4}$ lb sugar, essence of vanilla to taste, and a small pinch of salt; mix the whole with the yolks of six eggs and the whipped whites of two; put into a mould and steam for one hour; serve with vanilla sauce.

BLACK CAP PUDDINGS.

Butter eight dariole moulds; cover the bottom of each mould with washed and picked currants; fill them with Queen's custard (see Queen's custard pudding); steam and serve with shrub arrowroot sauce.

BLACK CHERRY PUDDING.

Proceed with black cherries as for red cherry pudding; serve with black cherry sauce (2).

BREAD PUDDING.

Put ¾ lb bread crumbs, 6 ozs of sugar, 2 ozs butter and the zest of a lemon into a basin; pour over this 1 pt of boiling milk letting it steep for ten minutes; then add 6 yolks of eggs and 2 whipped whites; mix all together; steam in a mould, serve with ratafia sauce.

BRIGHTON BISCUIT PUDDING.

Arrange lightly, about 2 doz Brighton biscuits in a mould; fill up with a cold custard of 4 eggs, and ¾ pt of milk; steam and serve with orange flower arrowroot sauce.

BROWN BREAD BISCUIT PUDDING.

Procure 1½ doz brown bread biscuits, (a light mixture made in square tins); cut in slices and place lightly in a mould; fill up with a cold custard; steam about ¾ hour, and serve with almond sauce.

BROWN BREAD PUDDING.

Take ¼ lb bread crumbs, ¼ lb unblanched almonds, chopped fine, ¼ lb brown sugar, ¼ lb mixed peel chopped, ¼ lb melted butter, 1 teaspoonful ground cinnamon, the zest of two lemons, and a glass of brandy; work in the yolks of 6 eggs; add the white, beat stiff; steam in mould and serve with brown bread pudding sauce.

CABINET PUDDING.

Decorate a mould with dried cherries, citron, etc, fill with sponge biscuits cut in slices, ratafias, and a little finely cut orange and lemon peels in layers; pour over this two glasses of brandy; fill up with a cold custard of 4 eggs and 1 pt of milk; flavor to taste, and serve with orange flower sauce.

CARAMEL PUDDING.

Put some powdered sugar into a plain copper pudding mould; melt it in the mould as for nougat, so that the inside will be perfectly masked over with the caramel; fill up with a cold custard of 10 yolks of eggs and 1 pt cream, flavored with a glass of rum, and sweetened to taste; steam gently for about 40 minutes, and serve without sauce.

CARRAWAY PUDDING.

The same as chocolate pudding, using carraway seeds in place of chocolate; serve with wine arrowroot sauce.

CHARCOAL PUDDING.

Pour 1 pt boiling milk over 2 doz charcoal biscuits; when thoroughly soaked, sweeten and flavor to taste; mix well with five beat eggs; steam in a mould, and serve with wine arrowroot sauce.

CHESTNUT PUDDING.

Peal and boil until tender 40 chestnuts (marrons); rub them through a sieve, and place in a stewpan with 1 pt cream, $\frac{1}{4}$ lb butter, $\frac{1}{4}$ lb sugar, a pinch of salt, and vanilla sugar to flavor; stir this over the fire until it thickens and detaches from the sides; remove from the fire and add 8 yolks and the whites of 6 eggs beat firm; mix the whole well together; put into a mould; steam for $1\frac{1}{2}$ hours, and serve with Eva's cream sauce.

CHOCOLATE PUDDING.

Make a petit chou mixture as for ginger pudding, using yolkes only at first, and adding the whites beat stiff, at the last; work in two sticks of chocolate, scraped, before the petit chou is put on the fire; put into a mould and serve with chocolate sauce.

COBURG PUDDING.

Cut up some Savarin cake in circular slices, about one inch less in diameter than the mould used, which should be previously decorated with cherries and citron; soak the slices of savarin in maraschino; spread them with apricot jam, placing them up the centre of the mould; fill up with a cold custard of 4 eggs, $\frac{3}{4}$ pt milk, and 2 ozs vanilla sugar; serve with liqueur arrowroot sauce.

CRUMPET PUDDING.

Proceed and finish as for muffin pudding.

CUSTARD PUDDING WITH FRUIT SAUCE.

Make a custard pudding; dish, and serve round it any of the fruit sauces.

CUSTARD PUDDING.

Beat fifteen yolks of eggs; add this to 1 pt cream, $\frac{1}{2}$ pt milk, a little sugar, and a pinch of salt; put into a prepared mould; place into a stewpan with a little boiling water; cover and steam at the corner of the stove until set, but by no means allow the water to boil.

DARIOLE CUSTARD PUDDING.

Fill eight buttered dariole moulds with custard as for custard pudding; steam; when set, dish, and pour over them smooth custard sauce.

EGGS A LA SURPRISE.

Make a small hole at each end of the eggs, so as to get the whole interior out without breaking or damaging the shell; stop up one end of the eggs with a small piece of stiff paste; fill the shells (by means of a very small funnel) with custard (see custard pudding) flavored to taste; stop up the aperture with paste; put them in a stewpan on the stove, simmering the water very gently until they are set; take off the paste at each end, and serve on a napkin with liqueur arrowroot sauce, in a boat.

FRENCH ROLL PUDDING.

Take two or three French rolls, pare off the crust and soak the crumb in 1½ pts boiling milk; flavor with ground cinnamon and a glass of shrub; add 5 yolks and 3 whites of eggs, and one oz sweet almonds; sweeten to taste; put in a decorated mould; steam and serve with red cherry arrowroot sauce.

GAUFFRE CUSTARD PUDDING.

Cut gauffres in quarters; trim and place them in a mould; fill up with a cold custard of 4 eggs, ¾ pt cream, a glass of rum, and sugar to taste; steam 40 minutes, and serve with punch store sauce.

GINGER PUDDING.

Put 1 pt cream into a stewpan with ¼ lb butter; place this on the fire to simmer; then mix in 6 ozs sifted flour, which work in the manner of *petits choux*; remove from the fire, stir in six eggs (one at a time), and add ½ lb preserved ginger, cut up small; mix all together; fill a mould; steam 1½ hours, and serve with ginger sauce.

GOOD FRIDAY PUDDING.

Cut ½ doz Good Friday buns in slices; place them in a mould and fill up with a cold custard of 4 eggs and 1 pt cream; sweeten to taste, steam, and serve with mixed spice sauce.

ITALIAN PASTE CUSTARD PUDDING.

Boil ¼ ℔ Italian paste, and drain on a sieve; make a custard of 8 yolks of eggs, 1 pt double cream, a desert-spoon of flour and a little butter, worked over the fire with a wooden spoon until it thickens; when cold add 2 yolks and 2 whole eggs; flavor to taste, and mix the paste in very lightly; put the whole in a prepared mould; steam 40 minutes, and serve with smooth custard sauce.

JUMBLE PUDDING.

Break about 1 doz jumbles into convenient pieces; place them lightly in a mould; fill up with a cold custard of 5 yolks and 2 whole eggs, 1 pt milk, and a little essence of ginger; steam and serve with ginger sauce.

LEED'S PUDDING.

Beat 9 eggs, adding 1 pt cream and a pinch of salt; steam in a prepared mould for about 20 minutes; serve with a cherry sauce, round the base, and hot sherry in a boat.

MACARONI PUDDING A LA SURPRISE.

Boil ¾ ℔ Naples macaroni in 3 pts milk and a little sugar; when tender drain it, cut and build it in a prepared mould as for timbale of macaroni; fill carefully with pastry cream, flavored to taste, and finished off with five extra yolks of eggs, introducing a small pot of apricot jam in the centre of the timbale; steam and serve with Eva's cream sauce.

MILK BISCUIT PUDDING.

Soak $\frac{1}{2}$ doz milk biscuits in 1 pt boiling milk; when cool, add 4 eggs, sweeten and flavor to taste; steam in a mould for $\frac{3}{4}$ hour, and serve with wine arrowroot sauce.

MONDAY PUDDING.

Line a mould with very thinly cut cold plum pudding; fill up with a cold custard of 12 yolks of eggs and 1 pt cream, sweetened to taste and flavored with a glass of brandy; steam gently and serve with German sauce.

MUFFIN PUDDING.

Take four fresh muffins; split and spread with apricot jam; close and cut them in quarters; lay them in a dish and soak them with a cold custard of 4 eggs, $\frac{1}{2}$ pt milk, $\frac{1}{2}$ pt cream, and flavor with a glass of brandy and one of maraschino; sweeten to taste; fill up the mould with the pieces and the remainder of the custard; steam and serve with vanilla sauce.

NEWCASTLE PUDDING.

Butter a half melon mould; line it with dried cherries; fill with bread and butter and a cold custard of 4 eggs, and $\frac{3}{4}$ pt milk; flavor to taste; steam 40 minutes, and serve with port arrowroot sauce.

NORFOLK CUSTARD PUDDING.

Make and boil some small suet dumplings of the size of marbles; fill the mould with these, filling up with a cold custard of 6 eggs and $\frac{3}{4}$ pt milk; steam and serve with mixed spiced sauce.

NOUILLE PUDDING.

Stir some nouilles lightly into a pastry cream, previously adding 4 yolks of eggs to it in a cold state; flavor with maraschino; steam in a mould, and serve with nouille sauce.

ORANGE FLOWER PUDDING.

Proceed with a handful of orange flowers as for chocolate pudding, omitting the chocolate; serve with orange flower arrowroot sauce.

ORANGE PRAWLING PUDDING.

Mix ½ lb orange prawlings in a pastry cream with four yolks and one whole egg added; steam one hour, and serve with Seville orange arrowroot sauce.

PALERMO PETITS CHOUX PUDDING.

Make some petits choux into small balls, and bake them; when cold, introduce some apricot jam into the centre of each; fill a mould with these, filling up with a cold custard of 4 eggs and ¾ pt milk; flavor to taste; steam a little more than half an hour, and serve with egg sauce.

PANCAKE PUDDING.

Mask some very thin pancakes with apricot jam; roll them up and cut across in slices; place these in miroton up the sides of a mould; fill the centre with sponge cake, and fill up with a cold custard of 4 yolks, 2 whole eggs, and 1 pt cream; sweeten and flavor with vanilla; steam and serve with vanilla sauce.

PICNIC PUDDING.

Pour 1 qt boiling milk over ¾ lb picnic biscuits; let

them stand on the corner of the stove for half an hour in a covered stewpan; remove from the fire, stir in five yolks of eggs, and the whites beat stiff; flavor to taste; steam in mould, and serve with strawberry jam sauce.

PINEAPPLE PUDDING.

Made in the same way as ginger pudding, substituting pineapple jam for the ginger; steam and serve with pineapple sauce.

QUEEN'S CUSTARD PUDDING.

Break 1 doz whites of eggs with the whisk; add 1 pt cream, half a glass of maraschino, and a small pinch of salt; steam in a prepared mould, being very careful not to let the water come to a boil; pour round it Eva's cream sauce.

RASPBERRY PUDDING.

Proceed with raspberries as for strawberry pudding, adding the juice of half a lemon to the mixture; serve with raspberry sauce.

RATAFIA PUDDING.

The same as cabinet pudding, using ratafias only, and omitting the orange and lemon peel; serve with ratafia sauce.

RED CHERRY PUDDING.

Beat ½ lb butter and ½ lb sugar till quite light, in a basin; add 8 yolks of eggs, and ¾ lb bread crumbs, which have been previously soaked in milk and passed through a sieve; add to this 1 lb whole red cherries, stoned, and 6 whites of eggs beat stiff; steam in mould for one hour; serve with red cherry sauce (2).

REGENCE PUDDING.

Add to ¼ ℔ butter 2 tablespoons flour, the zest of a lemon, and a teacup of milk; stir over the fire until it boils; add five yolks of eggs, and half a glass each of brandy and orange flower water; sweeten to taste; stir in the whites of the eggs beat; steam in mould and serve with punch store sauce.

ROYAL HEART PUDDING.

Cut 1 doz royal heart cakes in slices; place them round a prepared mould in alternate rows of brown and white parts; cover the bottom of the mould in the same manner; fill the centre with what is left of the cake; fill up with a custard of 4 eggs, 1 pt milk, and two glasses of noyeau; steam and serve with cocoanut sauce.

RUSK PUDDING.

Make a cold custard of 1 pt cream, ½ doz eggs, and 6 ozs sugar; line a mould all over with dried cherries; take some rusks, dip them in the custard, and place them in the mould with a little raspberry jam between each layer; fill up with the custard; steam and serve with punch store sauce.

SAGO PUDDING.

Proceed with sago as for tapioca pudding; steam and serve with punch arrowroot sauce.

STRAWBERRY PUDDING.

Proceed as for cherry pudding, using 1 ℔ strawberries for the purpose; serve with strawberry sauce.

TANSY PUDDING.

Half fill a mould with Savoy biscuit or sponge cake;

fill up with a cold custard of 1 pt cream, 5 eggs a few tansy leaves chopped fine, and 2 ozs finely chopped pistachios; sweeten to taste; steam and serve with port arrowroot sauce.

TAPIOCA PUDDING.

Take ½ ℔ tapioca, ¼ ℔ sugar, the zest of a lemon, and 2 ozs of butter; put the whole in a stewpan with 1 qt milk; stir over the fire until it boils; then cover and set at the corner of the stove for a quarter of an hour; remove it and stir in the yolks of 6 eggs, and the beat whites of 2; put into a mould or buttered basin; steam 1¼ hours, and serve with punch arrowroot sauce.

VANA PUDDING.

Make a custard with the yolks of 6 eggs, ½ pt milk and 2 tablespoons arrowroot ; when cold, add 4 whites of eggs, 3 tablespoons cream, 2 of brandy, 2 of marmalade, 1 of maraschino, 2 ozs muscatel raisins, 2 ozs ratafias, and 2 ozs chopped pistachios; decorate a mould with dried cherries; fill with the pudding; steam for 1½ hours, and serve with brandy arrowroot sauce.

VIENNOISE PUDDING.

Put into a large basin ¾ ℔ of bread, cut into small dice, the zest of 2 lemons, 2 ozs of sweet and ½ oz bitter almonds, chopped, and 6 ozs sultana raisins; pour over this two glasses of Madeira, adding enough burnt custard to fill a mould; decorate with citron; fill up with the mixture, and steam for 1½ hours; serve with walnut sauce. The burnt custard is made of 8 yolks of eggs, 1 pt cream, 2 ozs burnt and 6 ozs plain sugar.

WHITE AND BROWN BREAD PUDDING.

Cut some thin slices of white bread and butter, and an equal quantity of brown; cut these in large rounds with a circular cutter, one inch smaller in diameter than the prepared mould; decorate with dried cherries; stamp the middle of these with a two-inch circular cutter; spread the rings of brown bread and butter with raspberry jam, and the white with marmalade; place these alternately up the centre of the mould until it reaches the top; fill up with a cold custard of 4 eggs and 1 pt milk; sweeten and flavor with essence of almonds; steam and serve with Dundee sauce.

WHITE CHERRY PUDDING.

Proceed with white-heart cherries as for red cherry pudding; serve with white cherry sauce.

CHAPTER IV.
BOILED PUDDINGS.

SUET AND BUTTER PASTE FOR BOILED PUDDINGS.

6 ozs chopped suet.   Pinch of salt.

$\frac{3}{4}$ lb flour.

Mix together, and knead lightly with cold water, and roll it out; butter a pudding basin, line it with the paste, and fill the pudding with whatever required; wet the edge of the paste and cover the pudding with the top crust; tie over with a cloth, and it is then ready for boiling.

For butter paste, use 6 ozs of butter to $\frac{3}{4}$ lb flour.

In the following recipes where prepared pudding basin is mentioned, it is prepared as above.

ALEXANDRA PUDDING.

Fill a mould with equal quantities of bread crumbs, currants, and sultana raisins; add mixed spices and a couple of glasses of brandy; fill up with a cold custard of four eggs, and $\frac{3}{4}$ pt cream, sweetened and flavored to taste; tie the mould over with a cloth, as usual in boiled puddings; boil 2 hours, and serve with white cherry arrowroot sauce.

ALPHABETICAL CHRISTMAS PUDDING.

A.—Apples, chopped, 2 ozs.

B.—Butter, melted, $\frac{1}{4}$ lb.

C.—Currants, $\frac{1}{2}$ lb.

D.—Dried cherries, 2 ozs.

E.—Eggs, whole, ½ doz.

F.—Flour, 1½ ℔s.

G.—Greengages, dried, cut up and stoned, 2 ozs.

H.—Honey, 2 ozs.

I.—Imported figs, cut up, 2 ozs.

J.—Jam, apricot, ¼ ℔.

K.—Kirsch-wasser, half a glass.

L.—Lump sugar, pounded, ¼ ℔.

M —Milk, a very little, according to **judgment.**

N.—Nutmeg, grated, one.

O.—Orange peel, cut up, ¼ ℔.

P.—Port wine, one glass.

Q.—Quince jam, one tablespoonful.

R —Raisins, 1 lb.

S.—Salt, half a teaspoonful.

T.—Tamarinds, freed from the stones, 2 ozs.

U.—Uncut and unshelled whole walnut.

V.—Veal suet, ¾ ℔.

W.—White noyeau, half a glass.

X.—Excellent Jordan almonds, blanched and chopped, ¼ ℔.

Y.—Yolks of eggs, two.

Z.—Zest of one lemon.

&.—Pudding sauce; cold sauce.

This Christmas Pudding, the invention of Massey Bros., in spite of its whimsical method of treatment, is a very good and rich eating one. Much amusement will be caused (if the recipe is known) by some one getting the walnut in their share. Boil as a plum pudding.

APPLE PUDDING.

Pare, core and quarter about 1 doz apples; place them

in a prepared pudding basin, with about 6 ozs sugar, a little lemon zest, two or three cloves, and a pat of butter; boil about two hours.

APPLE AND CREAM PUDDING A LA CERES.

Take about 12 or 15 good apples; peel, core and quarter them, and place in a stew pan with ¼ ℔ fine sugar, the zest of an orange, and 4 ozs melted butter; cover the stew pan, and put into a moderate oven until the apples are tender; as soon as they are done, place them in a dish to cool; line a mould with butter paste; put a layer of apples on the bottom, and the remaining quarters up the sides; fill the centre with a pastry cream flavored with vanilla sugar; egg the edge of the pudding, covering it with a round piece of the paste; tie over tight with a cloth and boil 1¼ hours; when done, turn it out and mask lightly with apricot jam; strew with bruised macaroons, and serve with wine arrowroot sauce round the base.

APRICOT PUDDING.

Prepare a pudding basin; fill up with some apricots, peeled, stoned, and halved; add about ½ ℔ sugar; boil 1¼ hours.

APRICOT PUDDING A LA CERES.

Take 2 doz fine apricots; peel, divide, stone them; roll them in ¼ ℔ sugar; place them at the bottom and sides of the mould, and fill up with pastry cream; finish as for Apple and Cream Pudding a la Ceres; serve with wine arrowroot sauce.

APRICOT JAM ROLL PUDDING.

Spread the paste with apricot jam, adding a few drops of lemon juice; finish as for Marmalade Roll Pudding.

BALTIMORE PUDDING.

Proceed as for Princess Pudding, using ½ ℔ red cur_rant jelly (melted), and a few drops of lemon juice and cochineal; serve with raspberry and currant sauce.

BARBERRY PUDDING.

Stew enough barberries in a copper sugar boiler for five minutes, in weak syrup, to fill a prepared pudding basin; reduce the syrup, and add enough to sweeten the pudding; boil for 2 hours.

BATTER PUDDING.

Mix a little milk with ¼ ℔ flour; add to this 1½ pts. milk and a pat of butter; stir over the fire till it thickens; when cold add the beat yolks of 4 eggs and one whole one; boil in buttered basin for 2 hours; serve with melted butter sauce, in a boat, or plain.

BIRKENHEAD PUDDING.

¼ ℔ mashed potatoes.	2 ozs almonds, chopped.
¼ ℔ hard boiled eggs, chopped small.	2 eggs.
	1 glass brandy.
¼ ℔ mincemeat.	Sugar to taste.
2 ozs butter, melted.	

Mix well and boil in a mould for 2 hours; serve with a dust of sugar and egg sauce.

BLACK CURRANT PUDDING.

Fill a prepared pudding basin with black currants; add about ½ ℔ sugar; boil 1¾ hours; serve with double cream in a boat.

BLACK CURRANT PUDDING A LA CERES.

Roll 2 ℔s picked black currants in ½ ℔ sugar; finish as for Cherry Pudding a la Ceres; wine arrowroot sauce.

BLACK CURRANT JAM ROLL PUDDING.

Spread the paste with black currant jam; finish as for Marmalade Roll Pudding.

BLACKBERRY PUDDING.

Fill a prepared pudding basin with ripe blackberries and sliced apples; add a glass of cherry brandy, a few drops of lemon juice, and 10 ozs sugar; boil 2 hours.

BLACK HEART CHERRY PUDDING.

Fill a prepared pudding basin with black heart cherries; add $\frac{1}{2}$ ℔ sugar, and the juice of half a lemon; boil about 2 hours.

BLACK GRAPE PUDDING.

Half fill a prepared pudding basin with black grapes; put in the middle sufficient red currant jelly; fill up with grapes and $\frac{1}{4}$ ℔ sugar; boil $1\frac{1}{2}$ hours.

BLACK AND WHITE GRAPE PUDDING.

Proceed as for White Grape Pudding, using black and white grapes and double quantity of apricot jam in the centre.

BREAD PUDDING.

Put the crumb of three French rolls, cut in dice, into a basin, and cover with boiling milk; add a pat of butter and the zest of a lemon, a little grated nutmeg and a glass of brandy; when well plumped up, work it up with a wooden spoon, and beat in $\frac{1}{2}$ doz whole eggs; put it into a buttered basin; tie over with a cloth; boil nearly an hour, and be sure the water boils before the pudding is put in; serve with lemon arrowroot sauce.

BREAD AND BUTTER PUDDING.

Cut slices of French roll; butter them thinly on one side; put layers of the bread and butter and currants alternately up a mould; fill up with a cold custard of eight yolks of eggs and 1 pt milk, sweetened and flavored to taste; let it stand for ten minutes, then boil for $\frac{1}{2}$ hour; serve with Kirschwasser sauce.

BROWN BREAD PUDDING.

$\frac{1}{4}$ ℔ brown bread crumbs. Sugar and nutmeg to taste.
6 ozs beef suet. 4 eggs.
10 bitter almonds, blanch- One glass of brandy.
ed and beat. Two glasses of cream.

Put into a buttered basin; tie over with a cloth; boil 3 hours, and serve with Brown Bread Pudding sauce.

CAPE MAY PUDDING.

Proceed as for Princess Pudding, using 1 ℔ orange marmalade; serve with Seville orange arrowroot sauce.

CARROT PUDDING.

Mix $\frac{1}{2}$ ℔ of boiled carrots, pureed, with $\frac{1}{2}$ ℔ flour, 10 ozs currants, 6 ozs chopped suet; spices and sugar to taste; 3 eggs, and a little milk; boil for 3 hours in a basin, and serve with Seville orange arrowroot sauce.

CHERRY PUDDING A LA CERES.

Pick and stone $1\frac{1}{2}$ ℔s of cherries; shake them in a basin with the juice of a lemon, then roll them in $\frac{1}{2}$ ℔ sugar; pass them over the fire to extract the juice (which use for sauce); finish as for Apple and Cream Pudding a la Ceres; serve with wine arrowroot sauce.

CHERRY PUDDING.

Fill a prepared pudding basin with cherries, about $\frac{1}{2}$ ℔ sugar, and the juice of a lemon; boil for 2 hours.

CHESTNUT PUNCH MARROW PUDDING.

Skin about 40 or 50 chestnuts and make a puree with ¼ lb butter; add 6 ozs of rice flour, ½ lb veal suet, ¼ lb marrow, ¼ lb sugar, ¼ lb bruised macaroons, a little nutmeg, one glass of cream, 3 glasses of rum, one whole egg and eight yolks; boil in a cloth for 3 hours; serve with Marrow Pudding sauce.

CORN STARCH PUDDING.

Three tablespoons of corn starch to 1 qt milk; dissolve the corn in some of the milk, and mix with it three well beat eggs and a little salt; heat the remainder of the milk to *near* boiling, add the preparation, and boil four minutes, stirring briskly; put into buttered dish, grate nutmeg over the top, and serve with punch store sauce, in a boat.

CRANBERRY PUDDING.

Take 3 pts of cranberries out of the liquor; place them in a prepared pudding basin with 10 ozs sugar; boil about 2 hours.

CURRANT PUDDING.

1 lb chopped suet.	A little powdered cinnamon.
1 lb flour.	
¾ lb currants.	Pinch of salt.
4 eggs.	A teaspoon baking powder.

Beat the eggs, and add as much milk as will mix the whole together; tie in a cloth, boil about 3 hours, and serve with melted butter sauce, in a boat.

CURRANT MARROW PUDDING A LA FORTESCUE.

Mix ½ lb flour with 5 ozs of sugar, ¾ lb currants, ½ lb beef suet, ¼ lb marrow, the zest of a lemon, a little mixed spices, and 5 eggs; finish as for Marrow Pudding a la Fortescue, and serve with marrow pudding sauce.

DAMSON PUDDING.

Fill a prepared pudding basin with damsons and about ½ lb sugar; boil full two hours.

DATE PUDDING (1).

Mix 6 ozs of dates, stoned and cut in slices, with ½ doz sponge cakes soaked in cream, 3 eggs, a little lemon zest, a glass of brandy, and sugar to taste; boil in a basin for 1½ hours, and serve with port arrowroot sauce.

DATE PUDDING (2).

Proceed as for Barberry Pudding, adding a glass of brandy.

EVA'S CREAM PUDDING.

Mix 3 tablespoons of flour very smoothly with 6 yolks and two whole eggs; add 1 pt double cream and two glasses of white noyeau; put into a buttered basin, and tie over with a thickly-buttered and floured cloth; boil ¾ hour, and serve with Eva's cream sauce.

FRESH FRUIT ROLL PUDDING.

Almost any of the fresh fruit pudding sauces, stiffened with arrowroot, may be used for rolled puddings, of course excepting orange and a few others of the same nature.

GENOISE PUDDING.

Beat to a cream, with a wooden spoon, ½ lb butter; stir in ½ lb sugar, adding 5 eggs (one at a time), ½ lb flour, ¼ lb dried cherries, and the zest of a lemon; put into a mould; boil and serve with red and white currant sauce.

GREEN APRICOT PUDDING.

Fill a prepared pudding basin with green apricots, and about 10 ozs of sugar; boil for 2 hours.

GREEN CURRANT PUDDING.

Fill a prepared pudding basin with picked currants; add ½ ℔ sugar, and boil for 2½ hours.

GREEN GOOSEBERRY PUDDING.

Fill a prepared pudding basin with about 3 pts. picked gooseberries; add 10 ozs sugar, and boil 2½ hours.

GREEN FIG PUDDING.

Pick and halve about 1½ doz green figs; put them in a prepared pudding basin, with ½ ℔ loaf sugar, and the juice of a lemon; boil for 2 hours.

GREEN FIG PUDDING A LA CERES.

Proceed as for Apricot Pudding a la Ceres; serve with wine arrowroot sauce.

GREENGAGE PUDDING.

Stone enough greengages to fill a prepared pudding basin, and add 6 ozs sugar; boil 2 hours.

GREENGAGE JAM ROLL PUDDING.

Spread the paste with greengage jam, no additions being required with this pudding; finish as for Marmalade Roll Pudding.

HALF PAY PUDDING.

¼ ℔ chopped suet.	¼ ℔ bread crumbs.
¼ ℔ flour.	2 tablespoons molasses.
¼ ℔ currants.	½ pt milk.
¼ ℔ raisins.	

Mix all well together; boil in a cloth for 3 hours;

serve with melted butter sauce. The above is an excellent substitute for plum pudding, at a small expense.

HASTY PUDDING.

Boil one stick cinnamon with 1 qt milk; while boiling, shake into it three tablespoons of flour; stir until it thickens, then pour into a deep dish; stir in 1 oz of butter and some sugar, grate nutmeg on the top and serve.

HASTY ARROWROOT PUDDING.

Proceed as for Hasty Pudding, with the exception of shaking in; the arrowroot should be mixed in a little cold milk, and then added to the boiling milk.

HONEY PUDDING.

To ¼ ℔ clear honey add 6 ozs butter, beat to a cream, and 4 ozs bread crumbs; beat altogether for 10 minutes with 8 yolks of eggs; put into a mould and boil for 1½ hours, serve with Seville orange arrowroot sauce.

INDIAN MEAL MUSH PUDDING.

Boil some Indian meal as for porridge, using milk instead of water; drop the meal gradually into the boiling milk, stirring briskly between each handful as well as when dropping it in; boil well, sweeten and flavor to taste; pour it into a mould, and in a few minutes it will be ready to turn out, still hot; pour over it melted butter sauce.

LEMON PUDDING.

Chop ¼ ℔ suet very fine; mix with ½ ℔ bread crumbs, the zest and juice of two lemons, 6 ozs sugar, and 3 eggs; put into a mould or cloth, and boil for 2 hours; serve with lemon arrowroot sauce.

MACARONI PUDDING.

Break ¼ ℔ macaroni into inch lengths; put on in a stewpan with 1 qt milk; simmer until tender; then pour over it 2 tablespoons of bread crumbs; when cold, add 6 yolks and 2 whole eggs, a dariole of cream, and a glass of noyeau; sweeten to taste; put into a buttered basin; tie over and boil as usual; serve with macaroni sauce.

MAGNUM BONUM PLUM PUDDING.

Stone the plums, filling a prepared basin with them; add sugar ½ ℔ and sufficient butter; boil for 2 hours.

MARMALADE ROLL PUDDING.

Make a suet paste; roll it out rather thin than otherwise; cut it neatly into a convenient length; spread this with orange marmalade; slightly egg the edge of the paste; roll it up and tie in a cloth in the form of a bolster; boil for 1 ½ hours; cut off the ends before serving.

MARROW PUDDING A LA FORTESCUE.

¼ ℔ marrow.
½ ℔ beef suet, chopped fine.
6 ozs flour.
¼ ℔ sugar.
6 ozs citron.
6 ozs muscadine raisins, stoned.

4 apples, chopped fine.
½ ℔ apricot jam.
½ gill cream.
½ gill brandy.
5 eggs.
Nutmeg to taste.

Mix and tie in a buttered cloth and boil for 5 hours; serve with marrow pudding sauce.

MEDLAR PUDDING.

Proceed as for Pear Pudding.

MIRABELLA PLUM PUDDING.

Fill a prepared pudding basin with Mirabella plums 6 ozs of sugar and a pat of fresh butter; boil for 2 hours.

MIRABELLA PLUM PUDDING A LA CERES.

Stone sufficient Mirabella plums; roll them in sugar and finish as for apple and cream puddding a la Ceres.

MELON PUDDING.

Peel and cut a lemon into convenient pieces; put into a prepared pudding mould, with alternate layers of sliced apples; add 6 ozs sugar and 2 tablespoons of cream; boil 2 hours.

MICHAEL ANGELO'S PUDDING.

2½ lbs curd (as for cheese cake).

10 eggs (leaving out the whites of four).

1 lb stoned rasins.

¼ lb preserved gage and apricot.

¼ lb dried cherries, cut up and soaked in brandy.

6 ozs sugar.

6 ozs brown bread crumbs.

3 ozs chopped citron.

1 glass each of brandy and rum.

Beat the whites stiff and mix well; tie in a cloth and boil as plum pudding; serve with reduced wine sauce in a boat.

MINCEMEAT PUDDING.

1 lb mincemeat.

¼ lb bread crumbs.

Zest and juice of a lemon.

4 eggs, whisked.

1 glass brandy,

Mix and boil in a cloth for 3 hours; serve with German sauce, in a boat.

MINCEMEAT ROLL PUDDING.

Spread the paste with 1 lb of mincemeat, mixed with a couple glasses of brandy; finish as for marmalade roll pudding.

MINCEMEAT AND APRICOT ROLL PUDDING.

Spread the paste thinly with apricot jam, and strew with mincemeat; finish as for Marmalade Roll Pudding.

MULBERRY PUDDING.

Proceed as for blackberry pudding.

NACTARINE PUDDING.

Proceed as for apricot pudding.

NECTARINE PUDDING A LA CERES.

Proceed as for apricot pudding a la Ceres; serve with wine arrowroot sauce.

NAHANT PUDDING.

Proceed as for Princess pudding, using ½ lb pineapple jam (melted); add the juice of a lemon, and serve with greengage jam sauce.

NEWPORT PUDDING.

Proceed as for Princess pudding, using 1 lb greengage jam, pureed; add half a lemon and a glass of sherry; serve with greengage jam sauce.

OATMEAL PORRIDGE.

Put on a stewpan with 1 pt or more of water, according to the quantity to be obtained; when the water is boiling shake fine oatmeal in with the left hand, stirring it continuously with a wooden spoon in the right hand until it forms a sort of smooth paste; add salt and serve in soup plates. It is generally eaten with cold milk.

ONE, TWO, THREE PUDDING.

First, ½ lb flour.   Third, ½ lb chopped suet.
Second, ½ lb molasses.

Mix well, adding a teaspoon baking powder; boil in a cloth for 4 hours, and serve with brandy plum pudding sauce.

ORANGE PUDDING.

Proceed with a couple of oranges, the same as for lemon pudding, adding the juice of half a lemon: serve with orange arrowroot sauce.

PARISIAN PUDDING.

¼ lb chopped marrow.
6 ozs flour.
¼ lb apricot jam.
¼ lb chopped apples.
¼ lb dried cherries.
¼ lb orange, lemon and citron peel.

Teaspoon mixed spice. '
Zest of two oranges.
4 eggs.
Glass of brandy.
Pinch of salt.
½ pint cream.

Mix well, butter and flour a plain mould; fill up with the pudding; tie over lightly with a cloth; boil about 4½ hours; serve with cold sauce, in a boat.

PARISIAN MARROW PUDDING.

6 ozs rice flour.
½ lb veal suet.
¼ lb chopped marrow.
¼ lb vanilla sugar.
2 ozs blanched pistachios.
2 ozs dried cherries, cut up.
¼ lb bruised macaroons.

½ doz apples, chopped fine.
A little grated nutmeg.
1 glass each of cream, maraschino and noyeau.
One whole egg, and the yolks of ten.

Mix and boil in a buttered cloth for 4 hours; when ready to serve stick fillets of pistachios over the pudding; serve with marrow pudding sauce, round the base.

PEACH PUDDING.

Peel, stone and halve enough peaches to fill a prepared pudding basin; place over this ¼ lb sugar, the juice of half a lemon, and three drops of essence of almonds; boil about 1¾ hours.

PEACH PUDDING A LA CERES.

Proceed with peaches as for Apricot Pudding a la Ceres; flavor the pastry cream with a few drops of peach essence; serve with wine arrowroot sauce.

PEAR PUDDING.

* Proceed as for Apple Pudding, adding the juice of a lemon.

PEARL BARLEY PUDDING.

Wash ½ pt pearl barley; put it into a stewpan with 3 pts milk, ¼ lb sugar, and a little nutmeg; place over a slow fire and when properly swelled take it out, flavor to taste, add 4 eggs, and boil in a basin for one hour; serve with black cherry arrowroot sauce.

PINE APPLE PUDDING.

Cut off the outside of a small pine-apple; slice, core and cut it up into convenient pieces, which parboil in a little weak syrup; place the pine with slices of apple in alternate layers in a prepared pudding basin; add 6 ozs sugar; boil 2½ hours.

PISTACHIO AND APPLE PUDDING A LA CERES.

Make the pudding as for Apple and Cream Pudding a la Ceres, using 20 apples, and adding ½ lb apricot jam and 4 ozs blanched pistachios; when the pudding is turned out, mask as usual with apricot jam, adding chopped pistachios; serve with pistachio sauce round the base.

PLUM PUDDING (1.)

1 lb stoned raisins.	½ ℔ moist sugar.
1 ℔ currants.	Zest of two lemons.

6 ozs candied orange,	½ oz mixed spice.
lemon and citron peel,	Pinch salt.
cut up.	5 eggs.
1 lb beef suet, chopped.	Half a tumbler milk.
1 lb flour.	2 glasses of brandy.

Mix well together; pour into a mould; tie over with a cloth and boil from 5 to 6 hours; serve with brandy sauce, in a boat.

PLUM PUDDING (2.)

1 lb suet.	3 ozs blanched almonds.
1 lb currants.	Spice to taste.
1 lb raisins.	2 glasses brandy.
½ lb brown sugar.	1 glass rum.
½ lb mixed peel.	4 eggs.
¼ lb flour.	A little milk.
3 ozs bread crumbs, or	
Savoy cake.	

Boil 5 hours in a mould or cloth, and serve with brandy plum pudding sauce.

PLUM PUDDING (3)—CHEAP.

½ lb chopped beef suet.	1 teaspoon salt.
10 ozs flour.	1 teaspoon baking powder.
¼ lb currants.	Zest of a carrot, grated.
¼ lb raisins.	1 glass wine.
2 ozs sugar.	A little milk.

Tie up in a cloth and boil for 4 hours; serve with brandy plum pudding sauce.

PRESERVED CHERRY AND APPLE PUDDING A LA CERES.

Proceed as for Apple and Cream Pudding a la Ceres, adding preserved cherries; flavor the pastry cream with Kirschwasser, and serve with wine arrowroot sauce.

PRINCESS PUDDING.

Cream ½ lb butter in a basin with a wooden spoon; beat in ½ lb sugar and ½ doz eggs (one at a time) together with ½ lb raspberry jam pureed, the juice of a lemon and a few drops of cochineal; mix with ¾ lb flour; put into a mould, tie over with a cloth and boil 3 hours; serve with raspberry sauce.

This pudding is also made with strawberry jam in place of raspberry, in which case serve with strawberry sauce.

PUMPKIN PUDDING.

Peel and cut into convenient pieces a small pumpkin; parboil it, and mix with about the same quantity of apples, 2 tablespoons apricot jam, 6 ozs sugar, a few drops of lemon juice and some of the zest; put into a prepared pudding basin, and boil for two hours.

QUINCE JAM ROLL PUDDING.

Spread the paste with a thin layer of puree of apples, and a layer of quince jam over this; finish as for Marmalade Roll Pudding.

RAISIN AND APPLE PUDDING A LA CERES.

Proceed as for Apple and Cream Pudding a la Ceres, using 20 apples and adding ½ lb raisins; serve with orange arrowroot sauce.

RASPBERRY PUDDING.

Fill a prepared pudding basin with picked raspberries, adding about 6 ozs of sugar and 1 gill of cream; boil about 1½ hours.

RASPBERRY PUDDING A LA CERES.

Proceed with 2 lbs fresh raspberries as for Strawberry Pudding a la Ceres; serve with wine arrowroot sauce.

RASPBERRY AND CURRANT PUDDING.

Fill a prepared pudding basin with equal quantities of picked raspberries and currants; add about 10 ozs of sugar; boil 1¾ hours.

RASPBERRY JAM ROLL PUDDING.

Spread the paste with raspberry jam, adding the zest and a little of the juice of a lemon; finish as for Marmalade Roll Pudding.

RED GOOSEBERRY PUDDING.

Proceed as for Green Gooseberry Pudding, using ¾ lb sugar.

RED AND GREEN GOOSEBERRY PUDDING A LA CERES.

Roll ¾ lb each of picked green and red gooseberries in ½ lb sugar; finish as for Cherry Pudding a la Ceres; serve with wine arrowroot sauce.

RED GOOSEBERRY JAM ROLL PUDDING.

Heat about 1 lb red gooseberry jam in a stewpan, with a little lemon juice; rub it through a coarse wire sieve; spread the paste and finish as for Marmalade Roll Pudding.

RED CURRANT PUDDING.

Fill a prepared pudding basin with red currants, about ½ lb sugar, and the zest of two oranges; boil about 1¾ hours; serve with whipt cream in a boat.

RED CURRANT JAM ROLL PUDDING.

Spread the paste with red currant jam and raspberry mixed; finish as for Marmalade Roll Pudding.

RHUBARB PUDDING.

Skin and cut the rhubarb into small pieces; fill a prepared pudding basin with it; add about 10 ozs sugar; boil 2½ hours.

RHUBARB JAM ROLL PUDDING.

Make a stiff puree of rhubarb; sweeten to taste, and finish as for Marmalade Roll Pudding.

RICE PUDDING.

Boil a large cupful of rice in water for five minutes; drain off the water and put the rice on again in milk; let it boil until soft, stirring it occasionally to prevent it from burning; when done, put into a basin with a of pat butter, the zest of a lemon, a little nutmeg, and half a glass of brandy; sweeten to taste, and add 5 eggs; boil ¾ hour in a basin; serve with marrow pudding sauce.

RICE AND ORANGE MARROW PUDDING.

Boil 1 lb of rice well in milk with ¼ lb butter, and ¼ lb sugar, on which two oranges have been rubbed; when the rice is tender add 2 ozs chopped marrow, 2 ozs of butter, a glass of brandy and sufficient orange marmalade; mix the whole with 2 whole eggs and the yolks of 8; boil in a cloth for about 3 hours; serve without sauce.

SAGO PUDDING.

Boil 3 ozs of sago in 1 pt milk until tender; when cold add 5 eggs, a few bread crumbs, and sugar and brandy to taste; boil in a buttered basin (tied over with a cloth) for about 1½ hours; serve with black cherry arrowroot sauce.

ST. CATHERINE'S PLUM PUDDING.

Proceed as for Mirabella Plum Pudding.

SARATOGA PUDDING.

Proceed as for Princess Pudding, using 1 ℔ apricot jam pureed, the juice of a lemon and one glass of brandy; finish and serve with apricot jam sauce.

STRAWBERRY PUDDING.

Proceed as for Raspberry Pudding, adding the juice of half a lemon.

STRAWBERRY PUDDING A LA CERES.

Roll 2 ℔s of picked strawberries in 6 ozs of sugar; finish as for Apple and Cream Pudding a la Ceres; serve with wine arrowroot sauce.

STRAWBERRY JAM ROLL PUDDING.

Proceed as for Marmalade Roll Pudding, using strawberry jam and the juice of half a lemon.

SUET PUDDING.

Make a rather thick batter of 1 ℔ flour, ½ ℔ chopped suet, 3 eggs, a teaspoon of baking powder, some grated nutmeg, sugar, salt and water; boil in a cloth for 3 hours; serve with melted butter sauce.

SULTANA PUDDING.

Soak 3 ozs Sultana raisins in 1 glass of rum; add this to ½ ℔ flour, 6 ozs chopped suet, ¼ ℔ sugar, 3 eggs, and a little milk to form it into a paste; boil it in a buttered ba in for 2 hours; serve with almond and raisin sauce.

SULTANA MARROW PUDDING A LA FORTESCUE.

Proceed as for Currant Marrow Pudding, a la Fortescue, substituting Sultana raisins for currants; serve with marrow pudding sauce.

TAPIOCA PUDDING.

Proceed with 3 ozs of Tapioca as for Sago Pudding.

TAYMOUTH PUDDING.

1 ℔ beef suet, chopped fine.	Zest of 2 lemons.
¾ ℔ moist sugar.	A little salt·and milk.
¼ ℔ bread crumbs.	3 yolks of eggs, and three whites (whipped.)
2 teaspoons mixed spice.	

Mix the above ingredients to the consistency of plum pudding; tie in a cloth and boil 5 or 6 hours; serve with cold sauce, in a boat.

TURKISH PUDDING.

Moisten and pass ¾ ℔ figs through a sieve; add 6 ozs each of sugar, chopped suet and bread crumbs; 2 eggs and a cup of peel; mix well and put into a mould; boil 4 hours, and serve with Trafalgar sauce.

UNCLE TOM'S PUDDING.

½ ℔ flour.	6 ozs raisins.
6 ozs suet.	1 gill milk.
6 ozs molasses.	A little lemon zest.

Put into a mould and boil 2 hours; serve with Uncle Tom's Carolina sauce.

VEAL SUET PUDDING.

Pour 1 qt boiling milk over ½ ℔ chopped veal suet, ½ ℔ bread crumbs, ¼ ℔ dried cherries and 3 eggs; sweeten and flavor to taste; tie in a cloth, and boil 2½ hours; serve with brandy plum pudding sauce.

WHITE CURRANT PUDDING.

Make the pudding in the usual manner with 6 ozs of sugar, adding sufficient apricot jam; serve with whipped cream, in a boat; boil 1½ hours.

WHITE HEART CHERRY PUDDING.

Fill a prepared pudding basin with white heart cherries; add 10 ozs sugar and the juice of half a lemon; boil about 2 hours.

WHITE GRAPE PUDDING.

Proceed as for Black Grape Pudding, using apricot jam in place of red currant jelly.

CHAPTER V.

BAKED PUDDINGS.

ALMOND AND RAISIN PUDDING.

Mix ½ lb blanched and finely chopped almonds, and the same quantity of muscatel raisins, with a pastry cream; add a glass of noyeau, and bake in a buttered dish.

ALMOND PUDDINGS A LA BOLENO.

Blanch, cut and beat to a paste in a mortar, ½ lb sweet and ½ oz bitter almonds, with a spoonful of water; add to this paste 3 ozs of butter melted in a glass of hot cream, 4 eggs, sugar to taste, and a glass of curacoa; bake in buttered dariole moulds, and serve with walnut sauce.

ALMOND PUDDING A LA MONGLAS.

Blanch, cut and beat in a mortar 6 ozs of sweet almonds and 6 bitter ones, with a little plain water; mix the paste with the beat yolks of 6 eggs, 4 ozs butter, the zest and juice of one lemon, 1 glass of sherry, 1½ pts cream, and sugar to taste; pour into a buttered pudding dish, sprinkle the top with chopped almonds, and bake until properly set.

ALMOND CHEESE CURD PUDDING.

Blanch and pound ¼ lb sweet almonds and 8 bitter ones, with one glass of orange flower water; add ¼ lb sugar, ¼ pt cream, and the whites of two eggs beat stiff; bake as for cheese curd pudding.

APPLE PUDDING A LA DOUGLASS.

Pare and core ½ doz apples; fill the hearts with moist sugar, and a clove; place them in a buttered pie dish, and fill up with a light batter mixture, flavored with a glass of sherry; sweeten to taste and bake.

APPLE PUDDING A LA WASHINGTON.

Make a stiff apple jam with a little apricot mixed; let it cool in a jam pot, and then proceed as for apricot pudding a la Washington; serve with pear sauce.

APPLE OR PEAR PUDDING A LA CHICAGO.

Proceed as for cherry pudding a la Chicago, substituting a puree of apples or pears.

APRICOT OR PEACH PUDDING A LA CHICAGO.

Proceed as for cherry pudding a la Chicago, substituting a compote of apricots or peaches.

APRICOT OR PEACH PUDDING A LA DOUGLASS.

Peel the apricots or peaches; place them in the bottom of the dish, as for apple pudding a la Douglass; dust them with sugar and squeeze lemon juice over them; flavor the batter with two glasses of brandy.

APRICOT PUDDING A LA WASHINGTON.

Line a mould with puff paste trimmings, worked up with a little extra flour; turn sufficient apricot jam into the center of the lined mould, the same as for a mould of jelly; fill up with a firm, plain custard; bake until quite set; serve with apricot sauce.

ARROWROOT PUDDING.

Boil 1 pt milk; stir in a spoonful and half of arrowroot (mixed smooth with a little cold water); stir this over the fire until thick, and sweeten to taste; add the yolks of 4 eggs, 2 whole ones, and a half glass of brandy; rim a pudding dish with puff paste, fill it with the pudding, and bake for half an hour.

ARROWROOT CHERRY PUDDING.

Put in a buttered dish a compote of cherries; put ½ pt milk and ¼ pt cream on the fire, with 2 ozs sugar, some cherry syrup, and a few drops of cochineal and lemon juice; stiffen this when boiling with some arrowroot; pour over the compote and bake.

A great variety of arrowroot puddings, with various fruits, etc., can be made from this recipe.

BAKEWELL PUDDING.

Line a pie dish with puff paste cuttings; put in a layer of strawberry jam about an inch thick, and fill up with the following mixture: ½ ℔ butter and ½ ℔ sugar, well beat together, adding 8 yolks and the whites of 4 eggs beat; flavor with a glass of brandy, and bake in a moderate oven.

BATH PUDDING.

Decorate a mould with dried cherries; take 3 Bath buns, split and spread with some preserve, rejoin and place them up the center of the mould; fill up with a cold custard of 5 yolks and 1 whole egg, and 1 pt cream flavored with cloves; bake and serve with white cherry sauce.

BATTER PUDDING.

Pour 4 tablespoons of flour into a basin; add about 1

pt milk by degrees until quite smooth, a pinch of salt, and 5 eggs; flavor to taste, and bake in a buttered dish.

BEETROOT PUDDING.

Make a puree of ¾ ℔ cooked beetroot; add ½ pt cream, 4 yolks and 2 whole eggs, and a glass of brandy; bake in a buttered dish, and serve with a dust of sugar.

BLACK CURRANT PUDDING A LA CHICAGO.

Work the black currants as for raspberry and currant pudding a la Chicago; finish as for cherry pudding a la Chicago.   •

BLACK CURRANT PUDDING A LA WASHING-TON.

Reduce 1 lb of black currant jam over the stove, being careful not to burn it; put it back into the pot, and when it is cold proceed as for apricot pudding a la Washington;   serve with black currant sauce.   .

BLOOD ORANGE PUDDING A LA CHICAGO.

Proceed as for raspberry and currant pudding a la Chicago, with a compote of blood oranges.

BREAD AND BUTTER PUDDING.

Cut slices of French roll very thin; butter on one side; put a layer of bread and butter and a layer of currants and candied fruits alternately in a buttered dish; make a cold custard of 4 eggs and 1 pt milk, sweetened and flavored to taste; fill up with this; let it stand for ten minutes, and bake in a moderate oven.

BROWN BREAD PUDDING.

Proceed as for *steamed* brown bread pudding, adding half pint of cream; bake in a buttered dish.

CALIFORNIA PUDDING.

Chop and pound to a paste $\frac{1}{4}$ lb candied orange peel; put into a stewpan in which $\frac{3}{4}$ lb each of butter and sugar have been melted; stir altogether, and add the yolks of 12 eggs; put into a buttered dish and bake.

CANADA PUDDING.

When mush of Indian meal boiled pudding is nearly cooked, stir in about 1 lb of some sort of jam, 3 glasses of shrub, and sweeten to taste; bake in a buttered dish

CALVES' FEET PUDDING.

Bone three calves' feet; boil them with the bones in 3 qts water until tender; strain off, reserving the liquor for other purposes; press the best of the meat between two dishes; when cold mince up fine, and mix with $\frac{1}{2}$ lb sultanas, 2 glasses of sherry, the juice of half a lemon, and $\frac{1}{4}$ lb sugar; fill a buttered dish three parts full with this, and fill up with batter pudding mixture, flavored with two glasses of brandy; sweeten to taste and bake.

CHARLOTTE OF APPLES.

Cut, core and quarter about 20 apples; put them on the corner of the stove in a covered stewpan with $\frac{1}{4}$ lb butter until thoroughly done; then reduce the pulp over a quick fire with a wooden spoon, and add $\frac{1}{4}$ lb sugar with a little orange zest. Butter a plain mould; cut some small round pieces of bread with a French or cornet cutter, dip them in clarified butter, and place them in miroton round the bottom and sides of the mould; fill up with the puree of apples; cover the top with a round piece of bread dipped in clarified butter; place a cover on the top of the mould and bake for about $\frac{3}{4}$ hour; serve with a dust of sugar.

CHARLOTTE OF BLACK CURRANTS.

Reduce 2 qts of black currants with 2 ozs butter and
6 ozs sugar; finish as for charlotte of apples.

CHARLOTTE OF PEARS.

Proceed with pears, as for a charlotte of apples, with
the addition of 4 yolks of eggs, and the juice of half a
lemon to the puree.

CHERRY PUDDING A LA CHICAGO.

Prepare a compote of cherries; put them into a deep
buttered tart dish; cover an inch deep with a rich frangipan mixture (see- frangipan and apple souffle), flavored
with noyeau, which again cover with boiling cream
thickened with arrowroot; bake, and before serving, dust
with sugar, and salamander.

CHERRY PUDDING A LA DOUGLASS.

Proceed as for damson pudding a la Douglass, with a
compote of cherries; flavor the batter with a glass of
noyeau.

CHEESE CURD PUDDING OR CHEESECAKE.

Mix with the dry heat curd of 3 pts milk, 6 ozs of
well washed and picked currants, sugar to taste, a little
lemon zest, and the yolks of 4 eggs beat in ½ pt scalded
cream, add 1 glass of brandy; mix well and put into a
tourte tin lined with puff paste; bake, and serve with a
dust of sugar.

To make the curd, put new milk into a clean pan and
set it by the side of the fire so that it will keep blood
warm; put a spoonful of rennet into it, not too much, or
it will make the curd hard and the whey very salt; in a
a short time it will separate into curd and whey; cut the
former into small pieces with a knife.

A large variety of cheesecakes may be made from the above recipe by the addition of proper flavors and materials.

CITRON PUDDING.

Line a flat tourte tin with puff paste; lay at the bottom 3 ozs citron peel, cut very thin; beat 3 ozs of butter to a cream, work in the same of sugar and 3 eggs; pour this over and cover with another ounce of citron cut as before; bake and serve with a dust of sugar and whipped cream in a boat.

CLEREMONT PUDDING.

Cut some thin slices of bread; stamp out with a 2-inch circular cutter about 40 or 50 rounds, fry in butter and place them in alternate layers with 1 ℔ stoned cherries, in a buttered pudding dish; fill up with a cold custard of 4 eggs and 1 pt milk, flavored with one glass of each brandy and wine; sweeten to taste and bake of a rich color.

CORA LYNN DARIOLE PUDDINGS.

Line some dariole moulds with puff paste, put a small piece of butter in each, and fill with the following mixture: Take a large spoonful of flour, mix it with 1 egg, 5 yolks, 3 spoonfuls of sugar, 8 dariole moulds full of cream, 4 macaroons bruised fine, and a little orange flower water; bake, and serve with black currant jelly sauce.

CORN STARCH PUDDING.

Mix 3 tablespoons corn starch in a little cold milk; put 1 qt of milk on the fire with a little cinnamon and the rind of a lemon; sweeten to taste; when nearly boiling, stir in the mixed corn starch and boil (stirring it briskly) for four minutes; take out the cinnamon and rind, and when cool, stir up with it *thoroughly* 3 beat eggs; put into a buttered dish and bake.

COTTAGE PUDDING (CHEAP).

Put into a deep dish ½ ℔ rice, ¼ ℔ moist sugar or molasses, 2 qts milk, and 2 ozs of dripping; it will take some time baking.

CUSTARD PUDDING.

Put 1 pt milk into a stewpan with half a stick of cinnamon, the rind of a lemon, and three cloves; bring this to a boil, and strain it over 4 yolks and 4 whole eggs beat; mix well with the whisk, adding one glass each of brandy, rum and noyeau, and a little pineapple syrup; bake slowly in a buttered dish, and serve with whipped cream in a boat.

CRECI PUDDING.

Mix together 1 ℔ raw carrot grated, 1 ℔ bread crumbs, the yolks of 8 and the whites of 4 eggs beat in ½ pt cream, ½ ℔ melted butter, ½ pt sherry, 2 spoonfuls of orange flower water, and sugar to taste; pour into a dish lined with puff paste; bake about an hour.

DAMSON PUDDING A LA CHICAGO.

Stew ½ pt damsons in a sugar boiler as for raspberry and currant pudding a la Chicago; finish as for cherry pudding a la Chicago.

DAMSON PUDDING A LA DOUGLASS.

Put 1 pt damsons into the bottom of a dish with ¼ ℔ sugar; flavor the batter with two glasses of rum; proceed as for apple pudding a la Douglass.

4

DATE PUDDING.

Stone and pound to a paste ½ ℔ dates; add the juice of a lemon, 6 ozs butter, ¼ doz eggs, 2 glasses of brandy, ¼ ℔ sugar, and 2 ozs bread crumbs; mix well together and bake for 20 minutes in a buttered dish.

DUNDEE MARMALADE PUDDING A LA WASHINGTON.

Reduce sufficient orange marmalade over the fire; let it cool in the pot and proceed as for apple pudding a la Washington; serve with Seville orange arrowroot sauce.

EGERTON PUDDING.

Cream ¼ ℔ of butter with a wooden spoon in a stew-pan; add 6 ozs sugar and lastly 5 eggs beat as usual, and a glass of noyeau; pour into a dish lined with puff paste; bake about half an hour.

EGG PUDDING.

Mix together and put into a buttered dish ½ ℔ chopped beef suet, ¼ doz eggs boiled hard and minced, and 6 ozs Sultana raisins; fill up with a cold custard of 3 eggs and 1 pt milk, flavored with 2 glasses of brandy, and sweetened to taste; bake about half an hour.

EGG CHEESE CURD PUDDING.

Boil with lemon peel and cinnamon, 1 qt milk or cream; add 8 eggs well beat and a little salt; sweeten and flavor with two glasses of rum; stir and let this boil until it curdles, and the whey is completely separated; drain it well on a sieve, add ¼ ℔ butter, put into a dish lined with puff paste, and bake.

FRENCH BARLEY PUDDING.

Boil 6 ozs French barley until soft; stir in 6 ozs of butter, ¼ ℔ sugar, and the yolks of 2 eggs, and three whole ones; add a few orange flowers, and bake in a buttered pudding dish.

GERMAN PUDDINGS.

Mix ¼ ℔ butter and ¼ ℔ sugar; add ¼ ℔ flour, 4 eggs, the zest of a lemon, and ½ pt milk; stir all well together; bake in dariole moulds and serve with melted butter sauce.

GOOSEBERRY PUDDING A LA CHAUNTRY.

Stew some green gooseberries until they will puree through a sieve; when cold, add 6 ozs butter, ¼ ℔ Savoy biscuit, sugar to taste, 4 eggs, and one glass of brandy; mix well, put into a buttered dish, bake, and serve as usual with a dust of sugar.

GOOSEBERRY PUDDING A LA CHICAGO.

Make a gooseberry fool; finish as for Cherry Pudding a la Chicago.

GOOSEBERRY PUDDING A LA WASHINGTON.

Reduce some gooseberry jam, let it cool in a jam pot; proceed as for Apricot Pudding a la Washington; serve with red gooseberry sauce.

GREENGAGE PUDDING A LA DOUGLASS.

Proceed as for Apricot or Peach Pudding a la Douglass, with 2 doz greengages.

GREENGAGE PUDDING A LA WASHINGTON.

Proceed with greengage jam as for Apricot Pudding a la Washington; serve with greengage jam sauce.

GROAT PUDDING.

Soak ½ ℔ whole groats in 1 pt milk for 12 hours; add

¼ ℔ Sultana raisins, 6 ozs veal suet chopped fine, four eggs, and sweeten to taste; bake in a buttered dish 1½ hours.

GROUND RICE PUDDING.

Mix in a stewpan 3 ozs ground rice, half a stick of cinnamon, 1½ pts milk, and the zest of a lemon; sweeten to taste, put it on the fire, and stir with a wooden spoon until it boils; then pour it into a basin; when cool, add 4 eggs; bake for half an hour in a buttered dish; grate a little nutmeg on the top and serve. The cinnamon should not be left in the pudding.

HOGARTH PUDDING.

Add the yolks of 10 eggs to 1 pt milk; flavor with half a glass of rum and a few drops of essence of almonds; bake in a very moderate oven until quite set in the pudding dish. This forms a cheap substitute for almond pudding.

IONELLA PUDDING.

Have some macaroni boiled tender; cut it into pieces 1½ inches long; line a pie dish with puff paste cuttings; put in a layer of macaroni, and the following preserves in equal quantities: apricot and raspberry jam, orange marmalade, and apple jelly; half fill the dish in this manner; fill up with a cold custard of 4 eggs, ¾ pt milk and ¼ pt cream; flavor to taste and bake.

IPSWICH PUDDING.

Steep in 1¼ pts cream 3 ozs bread crumbs and a spoonful or two of water; beat the yolks of 8 eggs and the whites of 5 with ¼ ℔ sugar; mix all with ¼ ℔ melted butter; stir well over a slow fire until it thickens; line a dish with puff paste; pour in the mixture and bake for half an hour..

ITALIAN CITRON PUDDING.

Beat well together 1 pt cream and the yolks of ½ doz eggs; add ¼ ℔ sugar, ¼ ℔ citron, cut fine, 2 spoonfuls of flour, and a little nutmeg; put the mixture into a mould; decorate on the bottom with citron, cut fancifully; bake and serve with black currant sauce (1).

LEMON PUDDING.

1 pt cream.	4 whites of eggs, beat.
½ ℔ ratafias.	½ grated nutmeg.
Juice and zest of ½ doz	12 ozs powdered sugar.
lemons.	Cinnamon to taste.
12 yolks of eggs.	

Mix the above together with a whisk for five minutes; put a border of puff paste round a buttered tart dish; put the batter into this dish; strew chopped pistachios over the top, and bake for 1½ hours; serve with a dust of sugar.

LEMON CHEESE CURD PUDDING.

Cut into slices four sponge biscuits, and soak them in a gill of cream; add the zest and juice of three lemons, with ¼ ℔ each of butter and sugar, a little mixed spice and three eggs; bake as for Cheese Curd Pudding, decorating with candied lemon peel.

LEMON PUDDING A LA JOSEPHINE.

Proceed as for Orange Pudding a la Josephine, substituting lemons in place of oranges.

MACARONI PUDDING.

Boil ½ ℔ Naples macaroni in water until half done; cut it in lengths, and finish boiling in milk; when done, add 4 beat eggs and a glass of brandy; sweeten to taste, and bake in a buttered dish, with a few bits of

butter on the top; serve with grated nutmeg and a dust
of sugar.

MANFRED APPLE PUDDING.

Pare, core and slice 1 ℔ apples in a small stewpan
with a stick of cinnamon, 4 cloves, and a little water;
when the apples are soft, sweeten to taste, pass them
through a sieve, and add the yolks of 4 eggs, ¼ ℔ butter,
and the zest and juice of a lemon; mix well and bake
for half an hour in a dish lined with puff paste.

MARROW PUDDING.

Put a large cupful of bread crumbs into a basin; pour
over it 1½ pts of thin boiling cream, and let it swell;
chop fine ½ ℔ marrow, and add this to the crumbs, with
2 ozs of stoned raisins, 2 ozs currants, 5 eggs, and a little
grated nutmeg; sweeten to taste; pour into a baking
dish and bake.

MARROW CITRON PUDDING.

Pour over a French loaf, cut in slices, ½ pt boiling
milk; when soaked, put it on the fire in a stewpan, and
work it into a paste with a wooden spoon; then pound it
in a mortar with 2 whole eggs and the yolks of six; after
which put the whole in a stewpan, with the zest of a
lemon, ¼ ℔ citron, chopped fine, 2 ozs macaroons,
bruised, 3 ozs currants, 3 ozs muscadine raisins, 6 ozs
marrow chopped fine, and a glass of sherry; sweeten to
to taste and bake in a mould; serve with marrow pudding
sauce.

MONTEITH APRICOT PUDDING.

Pour 1 pt boiling cream over 6 ozs bread crumbs;
when cold, add the yolks of 4 eggs, a glass of sherry,
and sweeten to taste; stone, peel and pound 10 apricots;

mix them with the above ingredients adding the beat whites of 3 eggs stirred in lightly at the last; bake in a battered dish.

MONTEITH NECTARINE PUDDING.

Proceed with Nectarines as for Monteith Apricot Pudding.

MONTEITH PEACH PUDDING.

Proceed with peaches as for Monteith Apricot Pudding, adding a few drops of peach kernel essence.

MEHL BRIE PUDDING.

Take $\frac{1}{2}$ ℔ flour, $\frac{1}{2}$ ℔ sugar, $1\frac{1}{2}$ pts milk, $1\frac{1}{2}$ pts cream, and a pinch of salt; stir the whole with a wooden spoon in a stewpan over the fire, until it is reduced to half; place an untinned baking dish over the stove to get hot; spread the mixture over the baking sheet very thinly, brown it, remove from the fire, cut enough rounds from it with a circular cutter to fill a buttered dish; turn sufficient orange marmalade over this, fill up with a plain cold custard, and bake until set.

NORBERRY PUDDING.

Line a mould with trimmings of puff paste; fill it with flour; bake it and remove the flour; fill up with the following preparation: Mix in with 1 pt double cream, 3 whole eggs and 4 yolks, add a dariole mouldful of apricot syrup; sweeten to taste; bake carefully until set; serve with apple jelly sauce.

A great variety of puddings may be made by varying the above recipe.

ORANGE PUDDING.

Proceed as for Lemon Pudding, but double the quantity of oranges may be used, owing to their not containing as much acid as lemon; but the zest of three will be sufficient.

ORANGE PUDDING A LA JOSEPHINE.

Boil the peel of 8 or 10 oranges in a little boiling water until tender; pound it in a mortar; add ¼ ℔ clarified butter, two tablespoonsful of cream, 2 ozs sponge biscuit crumbs, the juice of one orange, 4 yolks and one whole egg; put into a tourte tin lined with puff paste; decorate the top with candied orange peel, and bake.

ORANGE PUDDING A LA CHICAGO.

Proceed with a compote of ½ doz oranges as for Raspberry and Currant Pudding a la Chicago.

ORANGE CHEESE CURD PUDDING.

Proceed with oranges as for Lemon Cheese Curd Pudding; decorate with candied orange peel.

PATRICIAN APPLE PUDDING.

Mix ½ ℔ apples (when grated or finely chopped) with ½ ℔ sugar, 6 ozs butter, the juice and zest of a lemon, and 5 eggs, leaving out the whites of two; line a dish with puff paste, and bake for ½ hour.

PATRICIAN APRICOT PUDDING.

Proceed with a puree of ½ doz apricots as for Patrician apple pudding.

PATRICIAN BLACK CURRANT OR PINE APPLE PUDDING.

Proceed as for Patrician apple pudding with a puree of black currants, or pine apple.

PATRICIAN DAMSON PUDDING.

Proceed as for Patrician apple pudding with a puree of ½ pt damsons.

PATRICIAN GOOSEBERRY OR RHUBARB PUDDING.

Proceed as for Patrician apple pudding with a gooseberry or rhubarb fool.

PATRICIAN GREENGAGE, STRAWBERRY OR RASPBERRY PUDDING.

Make these puddings as for Patrician apple pudding, with a puree of 10 greengages, ½ ℔ strawberries, or ½ ℔ raspberries.

PATRICIAN PEAR PUDDING.

Proceed with pears as for Patrician apple pudding.

PEAR PUDDING A LA DOUGLASS.

Proceed with pears as for apple pudding a la Douglass, squeezing the juice of a lemon over them, and omitting the cloves.

PINE APPLE PUDDING A LA WASHINGTON.

Make this pudding with some pine apple jam, reduced stiff; finish as for apricot pudding a la Washington.

PISTACHIO PUDDING.

Mix ½ ℔ blanched and very finely chopped pistachios with a frangipan and apple souffle mixture, and flavor with kirschwasser; put into a dish, and bake with a few bits of butter on the top for 15 or 20 minutes; serve with chopped pistachios strewed over the top.

POOR MAN'S PUDDING.

To 1 ℔ of hot mashed potatoes add ¼ ℔ suet, 2 ozs flour, a little sugar, and as much milk as will give it the consistency of a suet pudding; put it into a buttered dish and bake a fine brown.

POTATO CHEESE CURD PUDDING.

Boil or roast ½ ℔ good mealy potatoes; take off their skins and press them fine; then reduce ¼ ℔ good butter to a cream; mix this with the yolks of 3 eggs, 3 ozs powdered loaf sugar, a piece of stale Savoy or pound cake crumbled, and a little essence of lemon; mix as for pound cake, adding the potato pulp after the butter and sugar, using a few currants if desirable.

POTATO FLOUR PUDDING.

Stir four spoonsful of the flour mixed in a little cold milk into 1 qt boiling milk sweetened and flavored well; add five eggs beat, and a glass of rum; bake in a buttered dish for a quarter of an hour.

POTATO PUDDING.

Mix ½ ℔ potatoes boiled and rubbed through a sieve, 6 ozs sugar, and 6 ozs clarified butter, with 6 yolks of eggs and the zest of a lemon; beat up the whites stiff and add; bake in a buttered dish.

POULETTE APPLE PUDDING.

Boil as for Rice pudding ¼ ℔ ground rice; mix this with some candied orange, lemon and citron peel cut fine, to the puree of a dozen apples baked; add sugar to taste, a little cinnamon powder, and the yolks of ½ doz eggs; stir in the six whites beat firm, and put into a mould, lined with puff paste trimmings; bake for more than half an hour and serve with damson sauce.

QUINCE PUDDING A LA WASHINGTON.

Proceed with quince jam, sharpened with the juice of half a lemon, as for Black Currant pudding a la Washington.

RASPBERRY PUDDING A LA WASHINGTON.

Proceed as for Strawberry pudding a la Washington, substituting raspberry jam; omit the whipt cream, and serve with raspberry jam sauce.

RASPBERRY AND CURRANT PUDDING A LA CHICAGO.

Proceed as for Cherry Pudding a la Chicago, substituting the following preparation of raspberries and currants for the compote of cherries: Put ½ ℔ each of raspberries and red currants into a sugar-boiler, with 6 ozs sugar, for five minutes over the fire; add a little arrowroot, and half a glass of curacoa.

For strawberries, proceed in the same manner, omitting the currants.

RHUBARB PUDDING A LA CHICAGO.

Proceed as for Cherry pudding a la Chicago, with a stiff rhubarb fool.

RICE PUDDING.

Wash a large cupful of rice in cold water; boil it in water for six minutes; drain off the water and put the rice on in 1½ pts milk; let it boil until soft, stirring occasionally to prevent it burning; when done, put it into a basin, stir in a pat of butter, and when cold add 4 eggs, a little ground cinnamon, grated nutmeg and lemon zest; sweeten to taste, and bake in a buttered pudding dish, in a moderate oven, putting a few bits of butter over the pudding; when done serve with a dust of s .gar.

SAGO PUDDING.

Proceed with 6 ozs of sago as for Tapioca pudding.

SAXON PUDDING.

Put into a basin about 6 spoonfuls of flour, a teaspoon of salt, and a little grated nutmeg; mix this gradually with 1 qt milk, $\frac{1}{2}$ doz eggs, $\frac{1}{4}$ ℔ moist sugar, and a glass of brandy; line a dish with paste trimmings; put in the batter, and bake in a moderate oven.

SEMOLINA PUDDING.

$\frac{3}{4}$ ℔ semolina.	1 pt cream.
6 ozs sugar.	1 tablespoon orange flower
$\frac{1}{2}$ ℔ butter.	water.
8 eggs.	2 ozs ratafias.

Mix the semolina with the sugar, orange flower water, half the butter, two eggs, the cream and salt, in a stewpan; stir this over the fire until it boils, then continue stirring until it is smooth and detaches from the sides; withdraw it from the fire, and gradually mix in the remainder of the eggs, butter, and bruised ratafias; put this into a mould, put the mould into a deep saucepan half full of hot water, place in the oven and bake for $1\frac{1}{4}$ hours; serve with red currant jelly sauce.

SIMPLE PUDDINGS.

Beat four eggs; mix $\frac{1}{4}$ ℔ flour with 1 pt milk very smoothly; add it to the eggs, and sweeten and flavor to taste; bake for about 25 minutes in buttered teacups filled three parts full; serve with melted butter sauce.

STRAWBERRY PUDDING A LA WASHINGTON.

Proceed as for Apricot Pudding a la Washington, substituting strawberry jam for the apricot; serve with strawberry sauce, and whipt cream, in a boat.

STRUNG PUDDING.

Line a tourte tin with puff paste; put in this a thick and well flavored frangipan custard (see frangipan and apple souffle); string this across the top, which is done by means of a piece of puff paste rubbed down on the pastry slab with flour and water, until it can be pulled out into strings; bake in a moderate oven.

SWISS PUDDING.

Put a layer of bread crumbs, a layer of sliced apples, and a layer of apricots, in alternate layers, in a buttered pudding dish, the last layer being of bread crumbs; fill up with a mixture of half cream and half milk, sweetened to taste; bake and serve with a dust of sugar.

TAPIOCA PUDDING.

Put $\frac{1}{4}$ ℔ tapioca into a stewpan with $1\frac{1}{2}$ pts milk, $\frac{1}{4}$ ℔ sugar, 2 ozs butter, and the zest of a lemon; put on the fire, and when tender stir until it boils; remove it, add 4 eggs, and bake in a buttered dish for $1\frac{1}{2}$ hours.

VERMICELLI PUDDING.

Put $\frac{3}{4}$ pt milk and 1 gill cream, together with half a stick of cinnamon and four cloves, on the fire in a stewpan; when it comes to a boil, take out the cinnamon and

cloves, and stir in 3 ozs broken vermicelli; put this into
a basin and let it cool; add 4 eggs, 2 ozs butter, and
sweeten to taste; pour into a buttered dish, and bake
with a few pieces of butter on the top; serve with
grated nutmeg and a dust of sugar.

WAFER PUDDING.

Mix together 2 tablespoons of flour and half a spoonful of sugar; add 3 well beat eggs, and stir until as
smooth as butter; melt 1½ ozs butter in 1 gill hot cream;
when cold mix all well together, and flavor with lemon
zest; put into dariole moulds buttered, with a dried
cherry in the bottom of each; bake for about 10 minutes
in a quick oven and serve with reduced wine sauce.

CHAPTER VI.

Pastry Cream Puddings.

To make the pastry cream for puddings, boil $\frac{1}{2}$ pt each of milk and cream, with the peel of a lemon and some sugar; put this into a stewpan with the yolks of $\frac{1}{2}$ doz eggs and two spoonfuls of flour; mix this with a wooden spoon and dilute with the above; stir over the fire until it boils, and work it well for five or six minutes; then mix in $\frac{1}{4}$ lb clarified butter with the paste; put it into a basin and stir until cold; if it is too thick add a little cream.

To prepare and bake pastry cream puddings, line a flat tourte dish (previously buttered) with trimmings of puff paste; spread the bottom with the ingredients intended to be used, over which pour some of the pastry cream; bake for about an hour; when done slip the pudding from the tourte tin onto a dish, which has been previously spread with whipt cream, about $\frac{1}{4}$ inch thick; serve immediately. All pastry cream puddings are baked and served in the same manner, so that, in the following recipes, for brevity's sake, only the fillings are given.

Fresh fruit pastry-cream puddings.—Where puddings with pastry cream are made of fresh fruits, the following additional directions need to be observed; put the fruit pureed or otherwise prepared, in the bottom of a small earthenware pudding dish, previously lined and rimmed with puff paste; fill up with pastry cream; bake half an hour; mask with whipt cream on the top, and serve immediately. In the following recipes where fresh fruit is intended to be used it is so marked in brackets after the name of the pudding.

ALMOND PUDDING.

Beat to a paste in a mortar $\frac{1}{4}$ ℔ blanched sweet al-. monds and four bitter ones, with one glass of noyeau and one of plain water; mix with some pastry cream; bake in a lined tourte tin and serve as usual.

APPLE PUDDING (FRESH.)

Make a puree of $\frac{1}{2}$ doz apples and $\frac{1}{2}$ ℔ apricot jam; put this in the bottom of a small earthenware pudding dish, previously lined and rimmed with puff paste; fill up with pastry cream flavored with cloves; bake half an hour; mask with whipt cream on the top and serve immediately.

APRICOT PUDDING (FRESH.)

Proceed as for Fresh Peach pudding, substituting a little apricot syrup to taste, for the peach kernel essence in the pastry cream.

APRICOT JAM PUDDING.

Spread the bottom of a lined tourte tin with a small pot of apricot jam and the juice of half a lemon; fill up with pastry cream.

BLACK CURRANT PUDDING (FRESH.)

Proceed as for Fresh Red Currant pudding.

BRANDY PUDDING.

Flavor some pastry cream with 3 glasses of French

brandy; finish as usual with the addition of a few chopped cherry kernels sprinkled on the top.

CHERRY PUDDING (FRESH).

Proceed with a compote of $\frac{1}{2}$ ℔ cherries as for Fresh Damson pudding.

CHOCOLATE PUDDING.

Scrape three fillets chocolate; melt in two glasses of sherry over the fire; mix with pastry cream and finish as usual.

CITRON PUDDING.

Cut one cap of citron in very small dice; mix this with some pastry cream; pour into the tourte dish and cover with very thin strips of citron.

COCOANUT PUDDING.

Add a grated cocoanut and a glass of maraschino to some pastry cream.

COFFEE PUDDING. ·

Flavor some pastry cream with essence of coffee and two glasses of brandy; finish and serve as usual.

CURACOA PUDDING. ·

Flavor some pastry cream with three glasses of curacoa; add the juice of a small orange and a little lemon juice.

DAMSON PUDDING (FRESH).

Stone $\frac{1}{2}$ ℔ ripe damsons; pass them over the fire in a sugar boiler with $\frac{1}{4}$ ℔ sugar, for five minutes; place them in the prepared dish and finish as usual.

FILBERT PUDDING.

Shell and blanch $\frac{1}{2}$ ℔ filberts and proceed as for Almond pudding.

5

GINGER PUDDING.

Put a layer of preserved ginger at the bottom of the pudding; fill up with pastry cream, flavored with ginger syrup.

GOOSEBERRY PUDDING (FRESH).

Put a stiff gooseberry fool in the bottom of the prepared dish.

GREEN FIG PUDDING (FRESH).

Cut ½ doz ripe green figs into slices, and proceed as for Fresh Pear pudding.

GREENGAGE PUDDING (FRESH).

Stone 8 or 10 fresh greengages, and finish as for Pear pudding.

GREENGAGE JAM PUDDING.

Proceed as for Apricot Jam pudding, substituting greengage jam.

KIRSCHWASSER PUDDING.

Flavor some pastry cream with two glasses of kirschwasser; finish as usual, decorating the pudding with dried cherries.

LEMON PUDDING.

Proceed as for Orange pudding, substituting lemon zest and juice, and decorating with candied lemon peel.

MACAROON PUDDING.

Mix ¼ lb bruised macroons, and two glasses of madeira with some pastry cream; fill the lined tourte tin with this; cover the top with fillets of almond; finish and serve as usual.

MARASCHINO PUDDING.

Flavor some pastry cream with three glasses of

maraschino; finish and serve as usual, with the addition of half a glass of maraschino poured over the pudding.

MARMALADE PUDDING.

Spread the bottom of the lined tourte dish with orange marmalade; squeeze over this the juice of a small orange; pour over this pastry cream and finish as usual.

MINCEMEAT PUDDING.

Add a glass of brandy to $\frac{1}{2}$ ℔ mincemeat; put this at the bottom of the lined tourte tin; fill up with pastry cream; flavor with two glasses of brandy, and finish as usual.

NOYEAU PUDDING.

Proceed as for Maraschino pudding, with the addition of the juice of half a lemon.

ORANGE PUDDING.

Add the zest of three oranges and the juice of one, to pastry cream; finish as usual, decorating the top of the pudding with candied orange peel.

ORANGE FLOWER PUDDING.

Mix a dariole mould full of orange flowers with some pastry cream, and finish as usual.

PEACH PUDDING (FRESH).

Peel, halve, and stone $\frac{1}{2}$ doz ripe peaches, and proceed as for Fresh Pear pudding; add a few drops of peach kernel essence to the pastry cream.

PEAR PUDDING (FRESH).

Peel, core and slice thinly four or six mellow pears put them in the bottom of a prepared dish with 2 ozs sugar; fill up with pastry cream, and finish as usual.

PINE APPLE PUDDING (FRESH).

Peel and cut up a small pine apple in thin slices; take out the middle with a round cutter; place the pine rings in a copper sugar boiler with some weak syrup, and simmer until tender; place these in rather a larger sized prepared dish than the small one generally used; finish as usual, adding some of the syrup reduced, to flavor the pastry cream.

PINE APPLE JAM PUDDING.

Proceed as for Apricot Jam pudding, with pine apple jam, sharpened with the juice of half a lemon.

PINK NOYEAU PUDDING.

Proceed with pink noyeau as for noyeau pudding, adding a few drops of cochineal.

PUNCH PUDDING.

Flavor the pastry cream with three glasses of Jamaica rum, and one glass of very strong green tea; finish and serve as usual.

QUINCE JAM PUDDING.

Proceed with quince jam as for apricot jam pudding, adding the juice of half a lemon and a little apple jelly to the jam.

RASPBERRY PUDDING (FRESH).

Pick $\frac{3}{4}$ ℔ raspberries, and place them at the bottom of the prepared dish with $\frac{1}{4}$ ℔ sugar; finish as usual, adding the juice of a lemon to the pastry cream.

RASPBERRY AND CURRANT PUDDING (FRESH).

Take $\frac{1}{4}$ ℔ each raspberries and picked red currants; pass them over the fire together in a copper sugar boiler, with ¼ ℔ sugar, for five minutes; place them in the bottom of the prepared dish, and finish as usual.

RASPBERRY JAM PUDDING.

Proceed as for Strawberry Jam pudding, substituting raspberry jam.

RATAFIA PUDDING.

Soak 2 ozs ratifias in two or three glasses of sherry; place these at the bottom of the lined tourte tin, and cover with pastry cream; flavor with a little essence of ratafia; finish and serve as usual.

RED CURRANT PUDDING (FRESH).

Proceed with 1 pt red currants as for Fresh Damson pudding.

RED GOOSEBERRY JAM PUDDING.

Proceed with red gooseberry jam, as for Apricot Jam pudding.

RHUBARB PUDDING (FRESH).

Make a stiff rhubarb fool, and finish as usual.

RICE PUDDING.

Boil 2 ozs rice in milk; sweeten and pass it through a tammy; add a glass of double cream, and spread the bottom of a lined tourte tin with it; grate a little nutmeg over the top, and fill up with some pastry cream; flavor with cinnamon, and finish as usual.

STRAWBERRY PUDDING (FRESH).

Proceed as for raspberries, adding the juice of half a lemon only, to the pastry cream.

STRAWBERRY JAM PUDDING.

Put a small pot of strawberry jam, sharpened with the juice of a lemon, at the bottom of the lined tourte tin; fill up with pastry cream and finish as usual.

VANILLA PUDDING.

Flavor the cream with two tablespoonsful of vanilla sugar; finish as usual, serving with a dust of vanilla sugar.

WALNUT PUDDING.

Proceed as for Almond pudding, with 2 doz walnuts shelled and peeled, and substituting a glass of brandy for the noyeau.

CHAPTER VII.
SWEET SOUFFLES.

To prepare Souffle Cases, see Chapter I.

ALMOND SOUFFLE.

Pound ½ ℔ almonds with a little water; work this paste into lemon souffle mixture, with one glass of noyeau.

ANGELICA SOUFFLE.

Chop up three sticks of candied angelica; work in with lemon souffle mixture; finish with a few drops of essence of almonds.

APPLE SOUFFLE.

Peel, core, and slice up a dozen apples; put them in a stewpan with 3 ozs of butter, the zest of a lemon, and a little nutmeg; set over the fire until the apples are done, stirring occasionally to prevent them burning; add about 5 ozs bread crumbs, and sugar to taste; remove from the fire, stir in seven yolks of eggs, ¼ pt cream, and a glass of brandy, adding the whites beat; pour into souffle lining, and bake about ¾ hour; remove the paper, put it in the souffle case immediately, with a dust of sugar on top, and serve.

APRICOT SOUFFLE.

Melt 1 ℔ apricot jam over the fire; puree it and add to lemon souffle mixture, in which not quite so much milk has been used.

BEIGNETS SOUFFLES.

Put about a pint of water into a sauce pan with a few grains of salt, a piece of butter the size of an egg, and as much sugar, with plenty of grated lemon peel. When the water boils, throw gradually into it sufficient flour to form a thick paste; then take it off the fire, let it remain ten minutes, and work into it three or four eggs, reserving the whites of one or two, which whisk to a froth, and mix into the paste. Let it rest a couple of hours, then proceed to fry by dropping pieces of it, the size of a walnut, into hot lard. Serve piled up on a dish with powdered sugar over, and a lemon cut in quarters; or make an incision in each beignet, and insert a small piece of jam or jelly.

BLACK CURRANT SOUFFLE.

Proceed with 1 ℔ black currant jam, as for Apricot Souffle.

BREAD SOUFFLE.

Boil 1 pt milk, and pour it over the crumbs of three French rolls; when soaked, rub the bread through a sieve; sweeten and flavor to taste with spices; add the yolks of ½ doz eggs, and eight whites beat stiff; bake as usual.

BROWN BREAD SOUFFLE.

Boil 1 pt cream, and pour it over ¾ ℔ brown bread crumbs, two pats of butter, 6 ozs sugar, the zest of a lemon, and nearly a teaspoon cinnamon powder; stir the whole over the fire until it forms into a sort of smooth paste; remove and add 8 yolks of eggs; finish with the whites beat stiff as usual.

BYRON SOUFFLE.

Put a layer of frangipan and apple souffle mixture on the bottom of a souffle lining; a layer of sponge cake cut in slices and soaked in wine, and some apricot jam; proceed thus in alternate layers until the dish is full; bake about 20 minutes; take out of the oven and mask the top with meringue; dust with sugar, and when this is dried in the hot closet, remove the paper and serve in silver case.

CARAMEL SOUFFLE.

Flavor lemon souffle mixture with a tablespoonful of well made burnt sugar, and two glasses of brandy.

CHERRY PUREE SOUFFLE.

Pick the stalks from 2½ ℔s cherries; pound them in a mortar so as to break the stones; they must then be placed in a small preserving pan, with about ½ pt claret and 12 ozs sugar; let this boil; remove the scum as it rises, and after they have boiled about 10 minutes rub the whole through a sieve, and then pour it into a souffle case; cut 12 pieces of bread in the shape of eggs; fry in butter; drain and place them in close circular rows in the puree; fill up with pastry cream; bake for about 1½ hours, and send to the table in the silver souffle case.

CHERRY SOUFFLE.

Mix ¼ ℔ preserved cherries, and ½ glass each of brandy and noyeau, with lemon souffle mixture.

CHINESE SOUFFLE.

Make a strong decoction of tea, which mix with lemon souffle mixture, adding a glass of brandy.

CHOCOLATE SOUFFLE.

Scrape four fillets of chocolate; melt it in a little sherry, and work it with lemon souffle mixture.

CITRON SOUFFLE.

Add ¼ ℔ citron, chopped fine, and the zest of an orange, to lemon souffle mixture.

COFFEE SOUFFLE.

Put 6 ozs of whole coffee in a stewpan over the fire for a few minutes; then throw over it 1½ pts boiling milk and cream; let it stand at the corner of the stove for 20 minutes; strain and make lemon souffle mixture with this, instead of the plain milk, adding a glass of brandy. Essence of coffee is a very good substitute for the berry, and for quickness preferable.

CURACOA SOUFFLE.

Make a lemon souffle mixture, to which add two glasses of curacoa, and the juice of half a lemon.

DANTZIC SOUFFLE.

Add two glasses of Dantzic liquor, with a little orange zest, and the juice of half a lemon, to lemon souffle mixture.

DUNDEE SOUFFLE.

Proceed with 1 ℔ orange marmalade as for Apricot Souffle.

FILBERT SOUFFLE.

Blanch and pound ½ ℔ filberts, and proceed as for Almond Souffle.

FRANGIPAN AND APPLE SOUFFLE.

Boil 1 pt milk and ½ pt cream, with the peel of a lemon, half a stick of cinnamon, and 2 ozs sugar; thicken with a tablespoonful of the best Bermuda arrowroot; take out the peel and cinnamon and stir in 6 yolks of eggs; let this cool; butter a souffle case; slice some apples at the bottom; cover with apricot jam; cover this with the frangipan, and again with the apple and jam in alternate layers, which repeat until the dish is full; bake in a moderate oven for one hour.

A great variety may be made from this recipe.

GARIBALDI SOUFFLE.

Cut some macaroni up small; use it in alternate layers in the souffle lining with lemon souffle mixture.

GINGER SOUFFLE.

Prepare a lemon souffle mixture, adding 6 ozs preserved ginger, cut up into very small dice.

GOOSEBERRY SOUFFLE.

Proceed as for Apple Souffle with a stiff puree of 3 pts of green gooseberries; add extra sugar to taste.

GREEN FIG SOUFFLE.

Put on in a stewpan 8 green figs with 6 ozs of sugar, and the juice of half a lemon; when done puree them; reduce and mix with lemon souffle mixture.

GREENGAGE SOUFFLE.

Proceed with 1 ℔ greengage jam as for Apricot Souffle, adding the juice of half a lemon.

GROUND RICE SOUFFLE.

Dilute two tablespoons ground rice with half a pint of milk, and the same of cream; bring it to a boil, stirring all the time; remove from the fire; flavor and sweeten to taste; add 2 ozs fresh butter, and the yolks of seven eggs; stir in the beat whites; and bake as usual.

INDIAN SOUFFLE.

Grate two small cocoanuts, and add to lemon souffle mixture, with a glass of rum.

KIRSCHWASSER SOUFFLE.

Add three glasses of kirschwasser and the juice of half a lemon, to lemon souffle mixture.

LEMON SOUFFLE.

Stir $\frac{1}{4}$ ℔ butter with 6 ozs potato flour in a stewpan over the fire, 6 ozs sugar and the zest of three lemons; form this into a smooth paste, diluting it gradually with nearly 1 qt milk; when well mixed, remove from the fire and stir in 8 yolks of eggs (one at a time); beat the whites stiff and stir in; pour into souffle lining, and bake $\frac{3}{4}$ hour; remove the paper, put it in the souffle case immediately, with dust of sugar on top, and serve.

MACAROON SOUFFLE.

Mix 6 ozs bruised macaroons, and a glass of noyeau, with lemon souffle mixture.

MARASCHINO SOUFFLE.

Proceed as for lemon souffle, using three glasses of maraschino.

NECTARINE SOUFFLE.

Proceed with a dozen nectarines as for peach souffle, omitting the essence of almond.

NOYEAU SOUFFLE.

Proceed as for Lemon Souffle, using three glasses of noyeau

ORANGE FLOWER SOUFFLE.

Make a mixture as for lemon souffle, adding a small handful of orange flowers.

ORANGE SOUFFLE.

Proceed as for lemon souffle, using the zest of oranges.

PANCAKE SOUFFLE.

Make about 1 doz English pancakes; spread each one with apricot jam, and a layer of lemon souffle mixture; make a pile of these; bake for about half an hour, and serve with a dust of sugar.

PEACH SOUFFLE.

Stone and peel ten ripe peaches; stir them over the fire in a stewpan with $\frac{1}{2}$ lb sugar; add this to lemon souffle mixture, with two or three drops of essence of almonds.

PEAR SOUFFLE.

Peel, core and chop up ten pears; finish as for Apple Souffle.

PINE APPLE SOUFFLE.

Cut $\frac{3}{4}$ lb preserved pine apple into small dice; add this and a little of the syrup, to lemon souffle mixture.

PISTACHIO SOUFFLE.

Blanch and chop very finely 6 ozs pistachios; add them with half a glass of brandy to lemon souffle mixture.

PLUM SOUFFLE.

Stone 2 doz plums; put them on the fire with $\frac{3}{4}$ lb sugar for ten minutes or more; press them through a sieve, and mix the puree with lemon souffle mixture.

POTATO SOUFFLE.

Peel and boil in milk 6 or 8 potatoes; make a puree of them with the milk (not too soft); add 2 ozs each of butter and sugar, 6 yolks of eggs, and the whites beat.

PUNCH SOUFFLE.

Add two glasses of Jamaica rum, one of a decoction of tea, and the juice of half a lemon, to lemon souffle mixture.

QUEEN'S SOUFFLE.

Cut the crumb of two French rolls in slices; put them in a stewpan with eight macaroons, 1½ ozs sugar, the zest of a lemon, and sufficient butter; pour over this 1 pt boiling milk; cover and let it simmer at the corner of the stove until the bread has absorbed the milk, then work it with a wooden spoon; when well worked, remove it from the fire, and work in 6 yolks of eggs; rub it through a tammy with 1½ gills boiled cream, add 8 beat whites, and finish as usual.

QUINCE SOUFFLE.

Proceed as for Apple Souffle, with three quinces and four apples.

RASPBERRY SOUFFLE.

Proceed with 1 ℔ raspberry jam as for Strawberry Souffle, adding the juice of half a lemon only.

RHUBARB SOUFFLE.

Proceed as for Gooseberry Souffle, with about the same quantity of stiff rhubarb puree.

RICE SOUFFLE.

Put ¼ ℔ rice with 1 pt cream, ½ pt milk, a little lemon

zest, 2 ozs butter and 2 ozs sugar; simmer this over a
slow fire until tender; remove from the fire, and mix in
8 yolks of eggs; stir in the beat whites, and bake as
usual.

SAGO SOUFFLE.

Proceed as for Tapioca Souffle.

SEMOLINA SOUFFLE.

Put into a stewpan 10 ozs of semolina, 5 ozs sugar, 6
ozs butter, 1 pt cream, and a little orange flower water;
work the whole over the fire until it assumes a smooth
paste; stir in 8 yolks and the whites, beat as usual.

STRAWBERRY SOUFFLE.

Proceed with 1 ℔ strawberry jam as for Apricot
Souffle, adding the juice of a lemon.

SURPRISE NOUKLES.

Make a petit chou, sweetened with vanilla sugar; form
it into balls with a little flour, introducing a dried cherry
into each one; boil them in water for 5 or 6 minutes;
drain them on a sieve; place them in a souffle dish with
¾ pt sherry and a little syrup; bake for about 40 minutes;
serve with a dust of sugar.

TAPIOCA SOUFFLE.

Boil 1 qt cream and milk, and pour over it 10 ozs tapioca; simmer it very gently until soft and mellow; remove it from the fire and sweeten and flavor to taste;
add seven yolks of eggs, a pat of butter, the whites beat,
and bake as usual.

TURKISH SOUFFLE.

Boil 2 doz figs for five minutes in a weak syrup; pass

them through a sieve with the juice of a lemon, and add to lemon souffle mixture.

VANILLA SOUFFLE.

Make a lemon souffle with vanilla sugar, instead of common sugar, adding a glass of brandy.

WALNUT SOUFFLE.

Blanch and pound 2 dozen walnuts with two glasses of sherry; finish as for Almond Souffle.

CHAPTER VIII.
DUMPLINGS.

APPLE DUMPLINGS—BAKED.

The same as boiled apple dumplings, using butter paste; bake about forty minutes; serve with a dust of sugar. *A variety of fruit dumplings may be made from the above recipe.*

APPLE DUMPLINGS—BOILED.

Use russet apples if procurable; pare and cut them in half; take out the cores, and fill the cavities with sugar, apricot jam, and a clove; join the halves, and enclose them in suet paste; boil them in cloths for about ¾ hour; serve with melted butter sauce.

BREAD DUMPLINGS—BAKED.

Put ½ pt milk into a stewpan, with 2 ozs of each butter and sugar; while boiling stir in sufficient bread crumbs to form a stiff paste; stir until it detaches from the sides; remove it and stir in 2 whole eggs one at a time, and 3 ozs citron cut in small dice; bake on a buttered baking sheet in the form of buns; serve with a dust of sugar, and melted butter sauce in a boat.

COLLEGE DUMPLINGS.

Mix some bread crumbs with about half the quantity of beef suet, the same of currants, and some chopped

7

preserved peel, flavored with mixed spice and sugar; add 4 eggs and 4 glasses of port wine; mould this into the size and shape of duck's eggs; if they are not moist enough to bind well, add a little more wine; they require to lay a short time before moulding, as they bind much easier; they must also be baked on double sheets to prevent them burning; bake in a sharp oven, and serve with brandy plum pudding sauce.

EGG DUMPLINGS.

Make a batter of 1 pt milk, two well beaten eggs, a pinch of salt, one teaspoon baking powder, and flour enough to form it to the consistency of pound cake; drop it by the tablespoonful into fast-boiling water; four or five minutes will boil them; serve with syrup or lemon juice; they may be also served round, or with boiled beef, with butter and pepper on each.

HARD DUMPLINGS.

Make a paste of flour and water, a little butter and salt, and a teaspoon of baking powder; make it into balls about the size of billiards; boil about $\frac{3}{4}$ of an hour in a pot with a piece of beef.

NET OR CROCHET DUMPLINGS.

Dumplings boiled in crochet or net cases, which will give them the appearance at table of being carved.

NORFOLK DUMPLINGS.

Make a stiff batter of 1 ℔ flour, a little milk, 2 eggs, a teaspoon baking powder, and a pinch of salt; work this into balls the size of eggs; roll them in flour; drop them into boiling water; boil for 40 minutes; drain and serve with boiled meat.

OATMEAL DUMPLINGS.

Mix some oatmeal with half the quantity of chopped suet; season with pepper and salt, and a little shred onion; bind together with egg and boil in cloths.

POTATO DUMPLINGS WITH HALF GLAZE.

Add 3 yolks of eggs, 3 ozs melted glaze, a pat of butter, and pepper and salt to taste, to some mashed potatoes; let this cool; form it into balls; enclose in suet paste; boil in cloths, and serve on a vegetable dish with half glaze, in conjunction with boiled meats.

POOR MAN'S DUMPLINGS.

Make as for Poor Man's pudding, only a little stiffer; bake in the form of dumplings, and serve with a dust of sugar.

QUICK FLASH DUMPLINGS.

Mix a little chopped suet with an equal quantity of bread crumbs, a handful of currants, the zest of a lemon, two yolks, and two whole eggs; roll them into the form and size of eggs, and put them into fast boiling water; when done, they will rise to the top; serve with melted butter sauce, in a boat.

RICE APPLE DUMPLINGS.

Parboil some rice in milk and sugar until sufficiently stiff to enclose an apple prepared as for boiled apple dumplings; tie the rice dumplings up in cloths; boil for forty minutes, and serve with melted butter sauce.

SUET DUMPLINGS (1).

Proceed as for boiled suet pudding, omitting the eggs, and boiling in fast boiling water, in the form of dumplings without cloths; serve with melted butter sauce.

SUET DUMPLINGS (2).

Mix 1 teaspoon baking powder with every pound of flour in a dry state; mix and boil immediately, without letting it stand.

YEAST DUMPLINGS.

Make a light dough of 2 lbs of flour, $1\frac{1}{2}$ ozs German yeast, pinch of salt, and some milk; let it rise in a warm place; in about an hour the dough will be ready to use; mould them round as for buns, and boil fast for about 15 minutes in a good deal of water; serve with melted butter sauce.

CHAPTER IX.

COLD PUDDINGS.

APRICOT COMPOTE PUDDING.

Take about ½ lb rice, more or less, according to the size of the mould; put it on with milk in a stewpan, and cook it rather stiff; flavor with lemon zest, cinnamon and sugar; butter a plain mould slightly; spread it with rice an inch thick; put a compote of apricots in the cavity; cover it over with rice; let the pudding set; turn it in its dish; mask with whipt cream, and pour apricot sauce round the base.

A great variety of puddings may be made from this recipe by using the compotes or purees of different fruits, separately or mixed, and substituting appropriate sauces.

CHICAGO APPLE PUDDING.

Make a puree of about 2½ doz apples; add ½ lb apricot jam; put this into an oiled earthenware mould; when firm, turn it out on its dish; mask with whipt cream, and serve with cold sauce.

CHICAGO APRICOT PUDDING.

Proceed as for Chicago Apple pudding, with a puree of 2 doz apricots, adding ¼ oz isinglass.

CHICAGO BLACK CURRANT PUDDING

Proceed as for Chicago Apple pudding, with a puree of black currants, adding ½ oz isinglass.

CHICAGO PEAR PUDDING.

Proceed as for Chicago Apple pudding, using a puree of pears and adding ¼ oz clarified isinglass.

CORN STARCH PUDDING.

Four spoonfuls of corn starch to 1 qt milk; dissolve the corn in some of the milk, putting the rest on in a stewpan; add sugar; when this nearly boils, pour in the mixed corn, and boil (stirring it briskly) for four minutes; add some white noyeau or maraschino, to taste, and pour into an earthenware mould; when cold, turn on its dish, and pour round it any of the fruit sauces (cold).

DIPLOMATIC PUDDING.

Set a plain mould in ice; put a thin layer of clear jelly at the bottom, which decorate tastefully with dried cherries and pistachios; cover with another layer of jelly; decorate the sides in the same manner, dipping the cherries, etc., in jelly first to make them adhere; place a mould lining within, and fill the space between the two moulds with jelly, by degrees; when set, fill the lining with warm water, and quickly withdraw it; fill up with the following custard: Make a hot custard of one pint of cream and six yolks of eggs, sweetened and flavored to taste; add about 1 oz of clarified isinglass; serve with cold sauce, round the base; most of the following Diplomatic puddings being served in this manner.

DIPLOMATIC PUDDING A LA CHICAGO.

Cut some very thin rings of ripe raw apples; immerse a plain mould in ice; stick the rings dipped in clear jelly all round the sides and bottom of the mould; put a layer of pink jelly at the bottom; when set, introduce the mould lining, and by degrees fill up the space between the moulds with pink jelly; when this is also set, remove the mould lining with hot water as usual; fill up with the custard, mixed with a puree of apples; serve with cold sauce round the base.

DIPLOMATIC PUDDING—ALEXANDRA.

Put a thin layer of clear jelly at the bottom of a plain mould; make some blanc mange, and set it in a small dish; cut it into the form of a neat cross; put this at the bottom of the mould, and cover with a layer of pink jelly; when set, introduce the lining, and fill up the space with pink jelly in the usual manner; when this is also set, remove the lining and fill up with the custard; serve with cold sauce round the base.

DIPLOMATIC PUDDING—ALMOND.

Proceed with ¼ ℔ finely chopped blanched almonds as for Pistachio Diplomatic pudding, flavoring the custard to taste.

DIPLOMATIC PUDDING—ANGELICA.

Decorate the mould with angelica, cut fancifully, and proceed as for plain Diplomatic pudding; cold sauce.

DIPLOMATIC PUDDING—ARROWROOT.

Set a plain mould in ice; put a thin layer of clear jelly at the bottom; decorate this fancifully with a royal sweet garnish custard; ornament the sides in the same manner, dipping the custard in jelly; put a layer of jelly at the bottom; fix in the lining; fill round with jelly, and when set, remove the lining as usual; fill with some firm made arrowroot, flavored with cherry syrup, and ¾ oz isinglass added; serve as usual.

The above may be varied by using white royal custard and pink jelly.

DIPLOMATIC PUDDING—CARAMEL.

Proceed as usual with plain jelly; fill up with the custard, flavored with a tablespoonful of well made burnt sugar, and a glass of French brandy; when turned out, place over it a cover of caramel sugar, spun on an oiled mould one size larger than that used for the pudding; cold sauce.

DIPLOMATIC PUDDING—CHERRY.

Proceed as usual with clear cherry jelly, in an un-decorated mould; fill up with the custard, flavored with essence of cherry kernels; cold sauce.

DIPLOMATIC PUDDING—CHOCOLATE.

Proceed as usual with plain jelly (but the mould decorated), working in four fillets of scraped chocolate in making the custard.

DIPLOMATIC PUDDING—DANTZIC.

Proceed as usual in an undecorated mould, with Dantzic jelly, putting it round the space in layers to prevent the gold sinking to the bottom; fill up with the custard, flavored with Dantzic liqueur; cold sauce.

DIPLOMATIC PUDDING—FROZEN.

Proceed as usual with a rather weaker jelly, flavored with rum, the mould to be set in salt and ice; extract the lining; reset the mould in the pickle; when ready to serve, fill up the mould with vanilla cream ice, and very carefully turn the Diplomatic frozen pudding out, dipping the mould as usual into warm water; serve on a napkin or frozen stand.

DIPLOMATIC PUDDING—LEMON.

Proceed as usual with lemon jelly, filling the centre with the custard, flavored with the zest of two lemons; cold sauce.

DIPLOMATIC PUDDING—MARBLE.

Mask a plain mould with whipt sweet jelly; fill up with the custard.

DIPLOMATIC PUDDING—ORANGE.

Proceed as for Lemon Diplomatic Pudding, using orange jelly and zest; cold sauce.

DIPLOMATIC PUDDING—PINK NOYEAU.

Proceed as usual with pink noyeau jelly, flavoring the custard with white noyeau; cold sauce.

DIPLOMATIC PUDDING—PISTACHIO.

Chop very fine $\frac{1}{4}$ ℔ blanched pistachios; mix with $\frac{1}{2}$ pt clear jelly; mask a plain mould with all this, and fill up with the custard, mixed with $\frac{1}{4}$ ℔ finely chopped almonds, and flavored with a glass of noyeau; cold sauce.

DIPLOMATIC PUDDING—SILVER.

Break six leaves of silver into a maraschino jelly; proceed as for Dantzic Diplomatic pudding, using the same precaution regarding the silver; fill up with the custard flavored to taste; cold sauce.

DIPLOMATIC PUDDING—THOUSAND-LEAF.

Fill a plain mould with alternate and very thin layers of the Diplomatic custard and pink jelly; cold sauce.

DIPLOMATIC PUDDING—VANILLA.

Proceed as usual with jelly flavored with vanilla liqueur; fill up with the custard, flavored with 2 ozs of vanilla sugar; cold sauce.

DIPLOMATIC PUDDING—VICTORIA.

Proceed as usual with some clear maraschino jelly in which six leaves of gold have been broken, and 1 oz pistachios, blanched and filleted, have been added; use this jelly in layers to prevent the gold leaf and pistachios from sinking to the bottom; fill with the custard, with ½ lb of apricot jam pureed, added to it; serve with cold sauce; the mould must not be decorated.

DOROTHY'S CURD PUDDING.

Boil with lemon peel and cinnamon, 1 qt of milk or cream; add to it 8 eggs; sweeten and flavor with rum; stir and let it boil until it curdles, and until the whey is completely separated; then drain it on a seive, and put into a mould with holes in it, to let the whey drain wholly off; when firm, turn it out, and serve with cold sauce.

GARIBALDI PUDDING.

Half fill a souffle lining with frangipan and apple souffle mixture, flavored with some liqueur; fill up with a compote of some fruit; mask the top half an inch thick with whipt cream; put in the souffle case and serve with chopped pistachios on the top.

A great variety can be thus made.

MELE PUDDING.

Beat up with a whisk six yolks of eggs over hot water, as for Savoy cake, with 6 ozs of sugar, ¾ oz clarified isinglass, a glass of sherry, half a glass of maraschino, the juice of three lemons, and ½ oz pistachio kernels; when up, remove the beat until cold; then stir in lightly the whites of six eggs, beat; put sufficient of the mixture into a plain mould; set and serve with cold sauce round the base.

MINUTE PUDDING.

Place on the bottom of a dish ½ doz finger Savoy biscuit and 1 doz macaroons; soak them with sherry; cover with a frangipan and apple souffle mixture, filling up the dish with whipt cream; strew the top with bruised ratafias and serve.

QUEEN'S PUDDING.

Add 1 ℔ bread crumbs to 1 qt milk, ¼ ℔ sugar, the zest of a lemon, 2 ozs butter and four eggs; bake in a buttered pie dish; when done, spread the top of the pudding with apricot jam, and mask with meringue; set in the hot closet, and serve cold with whipt cream in a boat.

SURPRISE SOUFFLE.

Half fill a prepared souffle lining with a compote of fruits; fill the lining up with a frangipan and apple souffle mixture, flavored to taste; fill up with about three inches of sweet whipt jelly; when set, strew the top with bruised ratafias; remove the paper, put into the silver souffle case and serve.

A great variety may be made from this recipe.

TIPSY PUDDING A LA GENOISE.

Make a Genoise in a plain mould and proceed as for Tipsy Pudding a la Savoy, soaking the exterior with brandy and noyeau syrup.

TIPSY PUDDING A LA SAVARIN.

Make a Savarin cake in a plain mould and proceed as for Tipsy Pudding a la Savoy, soaking the exterior with syrup; flavor with rum and lemon.

TIPSY PUDDING A LA SAVOY.

Bake a Savoy cake in a plain mould; when cold, cut out the centre, leaving an inch of cake all round; fill the centre with a Diplomatic custard flavored with chocolate, but not until half set; when firm, turn it on a dish and soak the outside with sherry.

VENICE PUDDING.

Cut up ½ ℔ greengage, apricot, and dried cherries; soak these in wine and brandy; make a custard as for Diplomatic pudding; place a plain mould in ice; put a layer of jelly at the bottom, ornamenting with dried cherries and pistachios; fill up with alternate layers of the fruits and custard with some Savoy biscuit soaked in brandy between; when set, turn out on its dish and serve with whipt cream garnish.

CHAPTER X.
FRIED PUDDINGS.

CABINET CUTLETS.

Cut a cold cabinet pudding (see steamed puddings) up in slices; cut these into the form of cutlets with a tin cutter of that shape; egg and bread-crumb them; fry in lard, drain on paper and stick a piece of almond into the narrow end to form the bone; dish *en miroton* on a silver dish and pour round them melted red currant jelly.

CASSEROLES OF RICE A LA SURPRISE.

Put on in a stewpan 1 ℔ rice; boil with milk and a little sugar until stiff; tighten it with a wooden spoon, and set at the corner of the stove for a few minutes; turn this out on a buttered dish, and flatten it to the thichness of 2 inches; when cold stamp out carefully with a patty cutter; trim top and bottom; egg and bread crumb them; cut a circle on the top with a smaller cutter; fry in lard; cut the top piece off, scoop out the interior and fill as follows; half fill the casseroles with a hot compote of any fruit desired, and fill them up with a hot custard of ½ pt cream, thickened with arrowroot; add three yolks of eggs and a glass of rum; sweeten to taste; cover the casseroles, and serve them on a napkin.

CHICAGO PUDDINGS.

Take ¼ ℔ stale Savoy cake crumbs; ¼ ℔ currants; ¼ ℔ fine chopped suet, a tablespoon of sugar, and some mixed spice; make the puddings into balls with the yolk of four eggs; fry of a light color in butter; serve with a dust of sugar, and melted butter sauce.

CROQUETTES OF NOUILLES.

Make some nouilles (see Nouilles paste); mix them with a custard (as for Casseroles of Rice), extra stiffened; when cool, form them into balls; egg and bread-crumb them twice; fry in lard; drain and serve on a napkin.

CUSTARD PUDDING.

Egg and bread-crumb an ordinary custard pudding (see steamed puddings); fry it in lard; when done drain on paper, and dish on a napkin, with a large spoonful of orange marmalade on top; serve with Seville Orange Arrowroot sauce in a boat. A small pudding should be used, as it is quicker warmed through.

DARIOLE CUSTARD PUDDINGS.

Take eight cold dariole puddings (see steamed puddings); cut each one across into three with a sharp knife, and join them together with apricot jam; very carefully egg, bread-crumb, and fry them in lard; drain on paper, dish on a napkin, and serve with a teaspoon of orange marmalade on top of each; Seville orange arrowroot sauce in a boat

GAUFFRES.

Beat ¼ ℔ butter to a cream in a basin, with a wooden spoon; mix with this six yolks of eggs (one by one), three spoonsful of flour, the zest of a lemon, ½ pt double cream (whipt), and six whites of eggs (beat); make the gauffre irons hot on both sides, pour in a little clarified butter for the first baking; bake the gauffres in the irons over the charcoal fire, quickly; serving with a dust of sugar and cinnamon powder.

INDIAN MEAL DOUGHNUT PUDDINGS.

Pour ½ pint boiling milk over ¼ ℔ Indian meal; when cool, add ½ ℔ flour, ¼ ℔ butter, 2 ozs sugar, ¾ oz German yeast, 2 eggs, and a little ground cinnamon; if not stiff enough, add a little more flour; let it rise; roll out about ½ inch thick; stamp with a round cutter, and fry in lard.

LEMON BEIGNETS.

Make a petit chou, flavored with lemon zest and sweetened to taste; form this into small balls, and fry in hot lard; drain, dish on a napkin, and serve with a dust of sugar.

By altering the flavors, a great variety may be made from this recipe.

MUSH PUDDING.

Cut a cold Indian meal boiled pudding, out of the basin, in slices an inch thick; fry in lard and serve with with sugar, or with butter, pepper, salt, and meat.

PLUM PUDDING.

Cut slices of cold boiled plum pudding, stamp out with a round cutter; fry in fresh butter; drain on paper; dust with sugar; bar across with a red hot skewer, and serve on a napkin.

PLUM PUDDING BEIGNETS.

Cut some cold boiled plum pudding into slices ¼ inch thick; stamp this out with a round cutter; mask the rounds with pastry cream made very thick with arrowroot; bread-crumb, and then egg and bread-crumb them;

fry in hot lard; drain on paper; dish *en miroton* on a napkin; serve with a dust of sugar, with cold sauce, in a boat.

RICE CROQUETTES.

Put in a stewpan ¼ lb rice; cover with cream and a little sugar; simmer this at the corner of stove with the cover on; stir it occasionally, and when to the consistency of a not too stiff paste, flavor with noyeau; let it cool; form it into balls; egg and bread-crumb them; fry in lard; drain and serve hot on a napkin.

A great many varieties in both form and flavors may be made from this recipe.

SANDWICH CUSTARD BEIGNETS.

Cut a cold steamed custard pudding into rounds ½ inch thick, with a round cutter 2 inches in diameter; split with a sharp knife, spread with apricot jam, and rejoin them, forming a sandwich; egg, bread-crumb, and fry them in lard; drain on paper, and serve on a napkin; use raspberry jam sauce.

YEAST GAUFFRES.

Melt ½ lb butter; add this to ¾ pt cream, 6 ozs flour, a few currants, 6 eggs, and ¾ oz German yeast; let this rise about two hours before it is wanted; proceed as for Gauffres.

CHAPTER XI.
FRITTERS.

APPLE FRITTERS.

Cut six or eight apples into not too thick slices, cutting the core cut of each slice with a round cutter, and with a larger cutter form it into a ring; lay them in a dish with a little powdered sugar, lemon juice and brandy; let them stand in this for an hour; dip them in prepared batter, fry in hot lard, drain on paper, and serve with a dust of sugar.

To prepare the batter for frying fritters, put ½ ℔ of flour in a basin, making a well in the middle; add one whole egg and a pinch of salt; form a rather thick batter with old or pale ale, stirred with a wooden spoon, and adding by degrees about ½ pt salad oil.

APPLE FRITTERS—PLAIN.

Stir minced apples rolled in sugar, with a little finely chopped suet, into a stiff batter; drop this from a large spoon into hot lard, and fry.

APPLE FRITTERS—A LA CHICAGO.

Beat up the yolks of two eggs with a little warm milk; add ½ ℔ of flour, ½ oz dissolved butter, a pinch of salt, and sufficient warm milk to make the batter of such consistency that it will drop from the spoon; stir it well, make it quite smooth, and, lastly, beat into the mixture

8

the whites of two eggs previously well whisked. Peel some apples, cut them into thick slices, stamping out the core from the middle of each slice; dip them in the batter, covering them well over, and fry on both sides in boiling lard, or clarified dripping; lay the fritters on sheets of blotting paper before the fire; serve very hot, with pounded sugar strewed over. It is a great improvement if the slices of apple be steeped in a marinade of wine or brandy, lemon peel or cinnamon, for two or three hours before frying.

APRICOT FRITTERS.

Proceed with apricots, as for Peach fritters.

BANANA FRITTERS.

Strip the bananas of their skins, and slice them in half lengthwise; proceed as for Apple fritters.

CHERRY FRITTERS.

Proceed with unstoned cherries, as for Damson fritters.

CINTRA FRITTERS.

These are prepared from the remains of brioche, baba, or any other cake; which ever is used for the purpose should be first cut in slices $\frac{1}{4}$ inch thick, and stamped out with a round tin about 1 inch in diameter, placed in a dish, and soaked with the following mixture, viz.: 1 gill cream, 1 oz sugar, and a tablespoon orange flower water. Previously to frying these fritters, let them be dredged over with flour; fry of a light color; dish them up without a napkin, and pour some diluted preserve of any kind most convenient round the base.

CORN FRITTERS.

A teacup of milk, 3 eggs, 1 pt green corn (grated), a little sugar, and as much flour as will form a batter; beat the eggs, yolks and whites separately; to the yolks add the corn, sugar, milk, and flour enough to form the batter; beat the whole well; stir in the whites, and drop the batter, a spoonful at a time, into hot lard.

CREAM FRITTERS.

Cut stiff cold corn starch pudding into slices; dip the slices in cracker dust and egg, and fry, laying them on brown paper to free them from grease; serve with powdered sugar.

CURRANT FRITTERS.

Proceed with currants, as for Plain Apple fritters.

CUSTARD FRITTERS.

Boil 1 pt milk with cinnamon and lemon, adding 4 ozs sugar, 1 oz flour, a pinch of salt, and $\frac{1}{2}$ doz eggs, beat all together, and steam this custard in a plain mould previously spread inside with butter; when done firm and quite cold, let it be carefully cut into square pieces, dipped in frying batter in which there has been mixed a little cream, and dropped separately in hot frying fat; when they have obtained a light color all over, drain and dish them up with some kind of preserve round the base.

DAMSON FRITTERS.

Take some large fine damsons; roll them in sugar and a little brandy; dip them in fritter batter, and pick them out one at a time; fry them in lard; drain and dish on a napkin in pyramid form; serve with a dust of sugar.

DATE FRITTERS.

Stew 2 doz dates in weak syrup flavored with brandy; lay them in a dish with powdered sugar and a little lemon juice; finish as for Damson fritters.

GERMAN FRITTERS.

Roll out about 12 ozs of brioche paste about $\frac{1}{8}$ inch thick; moisten slightly with a paste brush dipped in water; place small balls of preserve upon this, at distance of two inches from each other; cover over with some of the same paste rolled out thin, similarly to the first piece; with the edge of the thumb press down all round each lump of preserve; stamp these out with a round tin cutter, and place them in rows on sheets of buttered paper upon a baking sheet; fry them in hot frying fat of a light color; when done, dish them on a napkin; dredge them over with cinnamon powdered with sugar, and serve.

GREENGAGE FRITTERS.

Halve and stone 1 doz greengages; finish as for Damson fritters.

MEDLAR FRITTERS.

Peel and cut up $\frac{1}{2}$ doz medlars into the shape of half moons; fry and finish as for Apple fritters.

MELON FRITTERS.

Peel and cut a ripe melon; slice, cut and finish as for Apple fritters.

NECTARINE FRITTERS.

Proceed with nectarines, as for Peach fritters.

ORANGE FRITTERS.

Cut $\frac{1}{2}$ doz oranges as for compote; toss them up in a basin with some sugar and brandy, and finish as for Apple fritters.

PEACH FRITTERS.

Peel and quarter $\frac{1}{2}$ doz peaches, and finish as for Apple fritters.

PEAR FRITTERS.

Proceed as for Apple fritters, coring with the small cutter, and stamping out with a pear-shaped cutter.

PINE APPLE FRITTERS.

Peel, slice and core a small ripe pine; cut each slice into four; stew them for five minutes or more in a weak syrup flavored with brandy; dip the pieces in fritter batter, and finish as for apple fritters.

POTATO FRITTERS, (1).

Boil 2 large potatoes, scraping them fine; beat 4 yolks and 3 whites of eggs, adding to the above one large spoonful of cream, one of sweet wine, a little lemon juice and nutmeg. Beat this batter until extremely light; fry in hot lard; serve with wine or other appropriate sauce.

POTATO FRITTERS, (2).

Slice potatoes thin; dip them in batter and fry; serve with white sugar, sifted over them. Lemon peel and a spoonful of orange-flower water should be added to the batter.

PORTUGUESE FRITTERS.

Put 6 ozs. of rice into 1 pt milk, 4 ozs. sugar, 2 ozs.
butter, and a little cinnamon and lemon peel; boil very
gently over a slow fire about ¾ hour, by which time the
rice will have entirely absorbed all moisture. Mix in
3 yolks of eggs, and then make up this preparation of
rice into balls the size of large walnuts, introducing into
the center of each a teaspoonful of orange marmalade;
egg and crumb them over carefully, placing them in a
wire frying basket, and immerse them in hot frying fat.
As soon as they have obtained a light color, drain, and
dish them up on a napkin; sugar them over and serve.

PUDDING FRITTERS.

These are prepared with the remains of any kind of
custard puddings—such as cabinet, ground rice, arrowroot, etc., or even plum pudding. The pudding intended
to be used for the purpose should be cut in neat squares,
egged over and bread-crumbed, and being fried of a
light color, may be dished either with or without preserve.

For further instructions see Chapter X on Fried
Puddings.

RASPBERRY FRITTERS.

Make a batter of a pint of milk, 1 egg, a little salt,
and enough flour to make a mixture that will drop from
a spoon. Add a cup of fine raspberries, with a tablespoonful of granulated sugar mixed with them. Fry in
hot lard and dust with powdered sugar.

RHUBARB FRITTERS.

Skin and cut some fine rhubarb into inch lengths;
stew them in syrup flavored with brandy, till tender;

drain them, put them into fritter batter, and pick them out quickly; fry in hot lard and serve with a dust of sugar.

RICE FRITTERS.

Boil 1 cup of rice in 1 pt milk until soft and all the milk is absorbed; remove and add the yolks of 3 eggs, 3 ozs. butter and 1 oz. sugar; when cold add the whites of the eggs, whipped to a dry froth; drop in spoonfuls in plenty of lard, made hot for the purpose; fry a deep buff color; serve with cream, wine and lemon sauce.

SPANISH FRITTERS.

Cut the crumb of a French roll into lengths as thick as the finger, in any shape to please the fancy. Soak in some cream or milk, nutmeg, sugar, pounded cinnamon and egg. When well soaked, fry of a nice brown; and serve with butter, wine and sugar-sauce.

CHAPTER XII.

PANCAKES.

BUCKWHEAT PANCAKES.

Mix a large cupful of lukewarm milk with about ¼ ℔ buckwheat flour; add 3 eggs, and sufficient milk to form it into a smooth batter; let it stand in a warm place for an hour; add a teaspoonful of baking powder; fry as usual; serve rolled up, with sugar and lemon juice.

ENGLISH PANCAKES.

Put into a basin four spoonsful of flour, one of sugar, and the zest of a lemon; mix smoothly with two eggs; add milk and cream to the consistency of double cream; fry the pancakes thin and on both sides, giving them the well known toss to accomplish this feat; dust them with sugar; sprinkle lemon juice over them, and roll them up; cut off the ends, and serve very hot on a napkin.

FRENCH PANCAKES.

Mix in a basin 3 ozs flour, 3 ozs sugar, ¼ ℔ bruised macaroons, 1 teaspoon orange-flower water, 1 pt cream, a little milk, and the yolks of ½ doz eggs; to fry, put a little clarified butter into the omelet pan, make it hot, fry a very little of the batter at a time, on one side only; drain on paper; spread with apricot jam; form a pile on a silver dish; salamander the top, and serve very hot.

GERADEAU PANCAKES,

Often called French Pancakes; 4 eggs; 4 ozs butter; 4 ozs sifted sugar; 4 ozs flour; ¼ grated nutmeg; 1 good pint of milk. Beat the eggs well and butter to cream, add the sugar, flour, and nutmeg, then the milk, and beat well. Put on buttered plates or tins, and bake in quick oven. Serve with lemon juice and sifted sugar, or preserved fruit.

GERMAN PANCAKES.

Proceed as for Swiss Pancakes, spreading pastry cream between each, and serve with currant jelly sauce

INDIAN MEAL PANCAKES.

Beat four eggs; add a little milk, and form into a paste with sufficient Indian meal; add nearly 1 pt milk, and about a teaspoon of baking powder; work smooth; fry as for English pancakes, rolling them up with butter, sugar, nutmeg, and lemon juice.

IRISH PANCAKES.

Beat 8 yolks and 4 whites of eggs; strain into 1 pt. cream, adding sugar and nutmeg to taste; set 3 ozs butter on the fire; stir it, and as it warms pour it to the cream, which should be warm when the eggs are put to it; mix smooth with about ½ pt flour; fry very thin; serve one on the other.

JENNY LIND PANCAKES.

5 eggs; 6 ozs flour; enough milk to make a thin batter; ¼ grated nutmeg; salt to season. Beat the eggs well and add the flour, salt and a little of the milk; beat all to a smooth batter; then add slowly the rest of the milk, beating all the time to a thin batter or thick

cream. Let the frying pan be *hot;* oil it, and pour in thin; when brown lift over; when done, sprinkle with nutmeg. Spread on the jelly, roll up, and sprinkle with sugar. They should be sent to the table as soon as possible, and are never good unless eaten at once; but if this is not possible, put them in the oven and let glaze. To have the cakes very light it is necessary to beat the whites and yolks separately, as for fritter batter.

NEW ENGLAND PANCAKES.

Mix 1 pt cream, five spoonsfuls flour, 7 yolks and 4 whites of eggs, and a pinch of salt; fry in fresh butter, and strew between each, sugar and cinnamon.

ORANGE PANCAKES.

Peel a few nice oranges, cutting them in slices crossways; cover the first pancake with them; sugar over according to taste; lay another over this, which sprinkle with sugar; bake and serve.

PANCAKES—PLAIN, (1).

Take six eggs, break them separately into a cup to ascertain that they are fresh; put them into a basin, whisk them well, then add half a pound of flour, and half a teaspoonful of salt; beat to perfectly smooth batter, add sufficient milk to make it the consistency of thick cream. Place a small frying-pan on the fire, and when quite hot put in a piece of butter or lard; when it is nearly boiling, pour in about half a teacupful of batter, or rather more, according to the size of the pan; fry until it is of a delicate brown, then turn it carefully with a slice, and when brown on the other side, sprinkle some pounded sugar over it; take it out with the slice, and place it on a dish before the fire. Proceed in like manner until sufficient are cooked for a dish; serve immediately. Never place one plain pancake upon another. Lemon-juice and sugar or jam are served with pancakes.

PANCAKES—PLAIN, (2).

Mix in a basin with a spoon 4 oz flour, 4 eggs, a little salt, a few ratafias, some grated lemon peel, and 1 pt milk or cream; fry spoonfuls of this batter with a little butter in small frying pans over a clear fire; the pancakes must be fried on both sides, and when done, folded up with sugar inside, and dished upon a pancake drainer on its dish, to allow all grease to run off from them.

French pancakes may be made by introducing some preserves in the ordinary pancakes.

PANCAKES A LA CELESTINE.

Proceed as for Scotch Pancakes; when all are made, spread one with pastry cream, cover with a pancake; spread the latter with red currant jelly, cover again; spread the third with apple sauce; cover and spread the fourth with cranberry sauce or jelly; cover and sift over sugar; repeat with the rest. Serve at table like cake.

A great variety may be made by simply varying this recipe.

PANCAKES WITH APRICOT JAM.

Take six ounces of flour, four ounces of butter, four eggs, half an ounce of sugar, five gills of cream, a small pinch of salt; cut a piece of crumb of bread to a dome shape, fry it in clarified butter, fix it in the center of a dish with a little sticking paste, and put the dish in the oven; mix in a basin the flour, sugar, salt, and eggs; melt the butter in the cream and add it, by degrees, to

the flour and eggs in the basin, so as to make a smooth
batter; should this be too thick, add a little cream;
warm a pancake pan, brush it over with clarified butter;
pour in two tablespoonfuls of the batter and spread it
so as to cover the bottom of the pan entirely; fry the
pancake until it is colored on one side, and turn it over
on to the dome shaped block of bread, the uncolored
side outwards. Spread a layer of warm apricot jam,
previously rubbed through a hair sieve, on the top of
the pancake and keep the batter hot; fry the remainder
of the batter in the same way, coloring only one side of
the pancake, putting them one above the other on the
block of bread, and spreading each one over with the
jam; when all the pancakes are fried, stand one above
the other, dredge some *fine sugar* over the top, glaze
with a red hot salamander, and serve at once. The pancakes may be spread with any kind of jam or jelly,
warmed, instead of the apricot jam.

RICE PANCAKES.

Boil ¼ ℔ rice flour in 1 qt thin cream, stirring it all
the while until thick; when cold, stir in ¼ ℔ sugar, four
spoonfuls of flour, and ½ doz beat eggs; if not stiff
enough add more flour; fry and serve as for English
pancakes, with ground rice sauce, in a boat.

SCOTCH PANCAKES.

1 pt milk; 2 ozs butter; 4 eggs; 1 teaspoon baking
powder, a pinch of salt, and about ¼ ℔ flour. Sift flour,
salt and powder together; add the milk, eggs and butter (melted); mix into a thin batter; have a small round
frying-pan, with a little butter melted in it; pour in ½
cupful of batter; turn the pan round to cover it with

the batter; place it on a sharp fire to brown; then hold
it up in front of the fire, and the pancake will rise right
up; spread each with marmalade or jelly; roll it up,
and serve with sliced lemon and sugar.

SWISS PANCAKES.

2 ozs butter; 2 ozs sugar; 6 ozs flour; 1 large apple,
peeled, cored and minced fine; ½ pt milk; ½ pt cream; 4
eggs; 1 teaspoon baking powder; nutmeg and cinnamon
to flavor.

Sift the flour with the powder; add to it the butter
(melted), the sugar and eggs, beaten together and diluted with the cream and milk; add the flavorings; fry
on one side only. Serve them piled one on the other,
with sugar strewed between each cake.

VANILLA PANCAKES.

Make a pancake batter of 6 yolks of eggs, ½ pt cream,
3 spoonfuls of flour, and a glass of brandy; beat the
whites, and whip into the mixture: fry as for English
pancakes; dust vanilla sugar over each one, and serve
in a pile on a silver dish.

CHAPTER XIII.

Miscellaneous Articles of Sweet Pastry.

ALMOND PASTRY.

Pound three ounces of almonds, one-quarter pound of butter, and two ounces of loaf sugar, with a little rosewater till it becomes a thick paste; spread it on a buttered tin, bake in a slow oven. When cold divide into eight pieces, put a spoonful of preserve on each piece, and cover with whipped cream.

APPLE CHARLOTTE.

Cut from a loaf of bread a number of slices of uniform thickness (one-quarter to three-eighths of an inch); butter a plain mould and all the slices of bread; shape one of them round to fit the botton of the mould, and another one for the top; cut the rest in pieces an inch wide, and the height of the mould in length; lay one of the round pieces at the bottom of the mould, and line the sides with the small pieces, carefully smearing the edges with the white of egg, so as to make them hold together well. Stew a quantity of apples with plenty of brown sugar, a little water, the juice and the thin rind of a lemon, and a piece of cinnamon; when thoroughly done, pass them through a hair sieve; fill the mould with this puree, put on the round slice of bread for the cover, and set in a quick oven for about an hour and a half.

APPLE TRIFLE.

½ pt good apple sauce, well sweetened and flavored with grated lemon peel, 4 eggs, ½ pt milk, 2 ozs sugar; heat the milk, and pour over the beaten yolks and sugar; put back in a farina-kettle, and stir until it begins to thicken, say about eight minutes; set by in a shallow vessel to cool; beat the whites very stiff, then whip gradually into the apple. When all is in, and well beaten, pile up in a glass dish, and pour the cold custard about the base.

BALLONS D'OR.

Take 1 oz. of sweet almonds, blanched and pounded smooth, 3 tablespoonfuls peach marmalade, or any other kind of jam, 2 ozs. fine bread-crumbs and 2 well beaten eggs. Beat well together, then add 1 oz of butter, melted to the consistency of cream. Half fill some buttered cups with the mixture and bake twenty minutes in a slow oven.

CHARTREUSE OF ORANGES.

Make a very clear orange jelly with a pint and a half of water, six oranges, sugar to taste, a wineglassful of sherry, and an ounce and a half of isinglass. Divide two or three oranges into quarters, and with a sharp knife carefully remove from each quarter every particle of skin of any sort. Have two plain moulds, one about an inch and a quarter more in diameter than the other. Pour a very little jelly at the bottom of the larger

mould, and place it in a layer of orange quarters prepared as above (if too thick, they should be split in two
lengthways); cover them with more jelly, but only put
enough to get a smooth surface. Lay this on ice to set.
When it is quite firm, put the small mould inside the
large one, taking care to place it exactly in the middle,
so that the vacant space between the two moulds is of
the same width. In this vacant space dispose prepared
orange quarters, filling up the interstices with jelly until
the whole of the space is filled up. Place the mould
upon ice, and proceed to whip a pint of cream with half
an ounce of isinglass and some sweetened orange juice,
which must be added to it a very little at a time, else
the cream will not rise into a froth. When the cream is
ready and the jelly set, remove the inner mould by pouring warm water into it, and fill up the inner space of
the chartreuse with the cream. Set it on ice for an
hour, turn out, and serve.

ICEING PASTRY.

When nearly baked enough, take the pastry out of the
oven, and sift over it fine powdered sugar. Replace in
the oven, and hold over it, till the sugar is melted, a hot
iron salamander. The above method is preferred for pastry
to be eaten hot. For cold, beat up the whites of two
eggs well; wash over the top of the pies with the brush,
and sift over this a good coating of sugar; cause it to
adhere to the crust; trundle over it a clean brush
dipped in water till the sugar is moistened. Bake again
for about 10 minutes.

SNOWBALLS.

¼ ℔ raw rice, 1 qt fresh milk, 5 tablespoonfuls of su-

gar, a little nutmeg. Wash the rice in several waters
and boil in the milk (always in a farina-kettle), adding a
little salt and 5 tablespoonfuls of sugar, with a pinch of
nutmeg. Stew gently until the rice is soft and has
soaked up the milk. Fill small cups with the rice,
pressing it down firmly, and let it get cold. At dinner-
time, turn it out upon a large flat dish, or pile within a
glass bowl. Eat with sweetened cream.

TROPICAL SNOW.

10 sweet oranges, 1 cocoanut, pared and grated, 2
glasses sherry, ¼ ℔ powdered sugar, 6 bananas. Peel
and cut the oranges small, taking out the seeds. Put a
layer in a glass bowl and wet with wine, then strew with
sugar. Next, put a layer of grated cocoanut; slice the
bananas thin, and cover the cocoanut with them. When
the dish has been filled in this order, heap with cocoanut. Eat soon, or the oranges will toughen.

CHAPTER XIV.

MISCELLANEOUS PUDDINGS.

BAKEWELL PUDDING.

This pudding, so-called, is famous throughout England. It is made of a puff-paste, a layer of any kind of
jam, and then on top of the jam some chopped almonds,
and filled up with a rich custard.

BIRD'S NEST PUDDING.

Pare 1 doz apples and take out the cores withou;
breaking them; fill the holes where the cores came out,
with sugar, after placing the apples in an earthen pudding dish. Make a batter of 1 qt milk, ½ doz eggs and
sufficient flour; pour this over the apples, and bake until
the fruit is soft. Serve with cream sauce.

BUBBLE PUDDING.

One quart of fresh milk, 5 eggs, well beaten, 3 tablespoonfuls of corn starch, 1 tablespoonful of sugar, nutmeg to taste, pinch of soda in the milk. Scald the milk,
stir in the corn starch, cook one minute, and pour upon
the beaten eggs and sugar. Season, whip up well; pour

into a round-bottomed mould, well-buttered, fit on the top, set in a pot of boiling water, boil three-quarters of an hour, turn out upon a dish, and eat with wine sauce. It will almost certainly break in two on the way to the table, hence the name.

CABINET PUDDING.

Save cake crumbs till sufficient to make the size pudding needed; assort all the best parts, those parts that are not burned, or to which paper is not attached, leaving them in good sized chunks; place them in a mould or pan; take one quart of sweet milk, $\frac{1}{4}$ ℔ sugar, 3 eggs; beat well together and pour upon the cake, adding a few currants or raisins. This pudding is always baked or steamed. The pudding can be made any size, but as the cake crumbs always contain sugar and eggs, $\frac{1}{4}$ ℔ sugar and 3 eggs are sufficient to 1 quart milk.

CHICAGO PUDDINGS.

Crumble a pound of sponge cakes and some cocoanut grated in a basin; pour over a pint and a half of rich cream previously sweetened with a quarter of a pound of loaf sugar, and brought to a boiling point. Cover the basin, and when the cream is soaked up stir in it eight well beaten eggs. Butter a mould, arrange four or five ounces of preserved ginger round it; pour in the pudding carefully and tie it down with a cloth; steam or boil slowly for an hour and a half; serve with the syrup from the ginger, which should be warmed and poured over the pudding. In the way of *ambrosia*, so-called: Peel and slice twelve sweet oranges, a grated cocoanut added, and a cup of powdered sugar. Arrange this in layers in a cut-glass compote, having the cocoa-

nut and sugar for the crowning point; it must be served
directly after it is prepared. Opposed to this are
orange snow-balls: Boil some rice for ten minutes, drain
and allow it to cool; pare some oranges closely; spread
the rice, as many portions as there are oranges, on some
pudding cloths; tie the fruit, surrounded by the rice,
separately in these, and boil the balls for one hour; turn
them out carefully on a flat dish of green majolica,
sprinkle them with a quantity of sifted pounded suga
candy; serve with sauce or sweetened cream.

COLD CORN-STARCH PUDDING.

Take 1 qt of boiling milk, 6 ozs sugar, and 6 ozs corn-
starch; sift the sugar and corn-starch together; stir
into the boiling milk until it thickens; flavor according
to taste, and set in moulds previously wet with water, or
the white of an egg; set to cool; serve with sweetened
cold cream.

CORN-STARCH PUDDING.

A simple but sure way to make corn-starch pudding
is, first to boil 1 qt of milk. Take 4 ozs corn-starch, 6
ozs white sugar and 4 eggs; beat together the sugar and
eggs and corn-starch; put them into the boiling milk
stir briskly until the mass thickens; flavor with vanilla;
use cream sauce.

CRACKER PUDDING,

Is made by taking six milk crackers and rolling them
very fine. Let them soak in two teacupfuls of water;
add the grated rind and the juice of two large lemons,
and one-half pound of sugar. Make some puff paste
with which to line the pudding dish. Bake for half an

hour. This may be eaten with or without sauce. If with sauce, make that in this way: beat one egg, add a little water, thicken it with corn-starch, sweeten to taste. Reserve a little of the rind for flavoring. Let it just come to a boil.

INDIAN PUDDING—BAKED.

Soak 1 ℔ of corn meal in 2 qts of milk or water; pour into 3 qts of boiling milk, and cook the same as mush. When thoroughly boiled, add 1 ℔ of brown sugar, ½ pt molasses, a little ginger and 1 doz eggs; bake the same as for rice pudding. This pudding can also be steamed in moulds. Serve with brandy sauce.

NEW ENGLAND, OR BREAD PUDDING.

Take any quantity of bread; soak it in cold water in order to extract the yeast (as the latter would make the custard sour); squeeze the water out as dry as possible. Make a custard as follows: 1 qt milk; ½ ℔ sugar; 4 eggs; a little molasses; some ginger and nutmeg; pour upon the bread; bake or steam until done. This makes New England Pudding, Washington Pudding, etc.

NOTTINGHAM PUDDING.

One pint sifted flour, 3 gills of milk, 1 gill rich cream, 6 apples, 4 eggs, a saltspoon of salt. Pare the apples and take out the cores without cutting them. Mix the batter very smooth and pour over the apples. Bake one hour. Serve with wine or cream sauce.

POUND PUDDING, ETC.

One ℔ of sugar and 1 ℔ of butter; rub the same as

for pound cake; add 1 doz eggs, rubbing them into it; then add 1 pt milk, 2½ ℔s of flour and 3 ozs baking powder (or ½ oz soda and 1½ ozs cream tartar). Put the mixture into moulds and steam. With this mixture a great variety of puddings may be made. Add to it 2 ℔s of raisins, for Raisin or Malaga Pudding; add 2 ℔s currants, for Currant Pudding; add 2 ℔s citron, for Citron or Peel Pudding; grate and add the rinds of six lemons, for Lemon Pudding. By further adding 2 qts of blackberries, raspberries, or any other fruit, with the addition of about 1 ℔ flour, a variety of fruit puddings are produced. *Sponge Pudding* is made by taking ten eggs to 1 ℔ sugar; beat the same as for common sponge cake; when beaten light, mix into it 1 pt milk and 2 ℔s flour, with a little baking powder (or soda and cream tartar), the same as pound pudding. All the foregoing puddings are generally boiled or steamed.

QUEEN MAB'S PUDDING—(Cold).

Take one pint of cream, one ounce of isinglass, one ounce of mixed citron and lemon-peel, two ounces of preserved cherries, and sugar to taste; add half a wine-glassful of brandy; mix well, pour it into a mould, and ice.

RICE PUDDING.

Wash the rice well; soak it in sweet milk for a half hour; boil some milk; about 3 qts to ½ ℔ rice, and 1 qt to soak it in, making four quarts in all. When the milk boils, put the rice into it and stir very often, unless steam is used when it does not need stirring. When boiled, take ¾ ℔ white sugar and 8 eggs; beat together and pour into the rice; flavor with lemon or vanilla; pour into a pan or earthen dish and bake until it rises in the center; if left to bake any longer it is very apt to curdle: For this pudding, some use sweetened milk with a little thickening in it; some use hard sauce; while others again prefer brandy sauce. The above is called rice custard. A very nice rice pudding is made without eggs. After the rice is cooked, put with the above ½ pt of brandy and bake as usual; or it does very well without the brandy.

SNOW PUDDING.

Soak about 2 ozs gelatine in a very little cold water for an hour to two, add 2 gills of boiling water and the juice of two lemons. When cold and commencing to thicken, stir in the whites of three eggs beaten to a stiff froth. Beat rapidly for fifteen minutes, pour into a glass bowl and set away to grow firm. Make a boiled custard with the yolks of the three eggs, two gills of milk and 2 ozs of sugar. Pour this over the pudding (after it has hardened) if there is room in the bowl, or mould the gelatine in a form, turn it onto a platter, and serve with the custard poured around it.

SWISS PUDDING.

For a quart pie-dish, cut up 2 ℔s of apples, put them into a saucepan, add a ¼ pint of cold water and brown sugar to taste, also any flavoring liked. Lemon rind is very good with it. Simmer until the fruit is quite soft. Butter a pie dish very well, line it with bread crumbs, about 1 in. thick at the bottom and as many as will adhere to the sides. Beat the apple mixture until thoroughly light, adding one egg, beaten separately.

Put this into the dish, cover with a layer of bread crumbs. Put a few small pieces of butter on the top and bake 20 minutes or until the crumbs are nicely browned. Turn out on to a dish, and sift with white sugar.

TAPIOCA, SAGO AND FARINA PUDDINGS.

Wash, cook and prepare in the same manner as for rice pudding; observing, however, that the above ingredients need 4 eggs to each quart of milk.

THE COMPLETE

Practical Pastry Cook,

— IN —

THREE PARTS.

PART III.

Savory Pies and Puddings; Patties, Vol-au-Vents, Etc.

CHICAGO:

J. Thompson Gill, Manager Confectioner and Baker Publishing Co.,

1889.

CONTENTS.

CHAPTER I.

Miscellaneous Articles for Savory Pies, Puddings, etc., etc.

Anchovies, Essence of—Aromatic Herbaceous Seasoning
Aspic Jelly—Custard for Garnish—Custard for Garnish
(white)—Forcemeat of Liver and Ham for Raised Pies—
Farce or Forcemeat (2)--Forcemeat, Oysters—Financiere
Ragout—Fine Herbs for Puddings--Glaze -Glaze for
Pastry—Gravy for Fish Pies, etc.—Half Glaze—Jelly for
Game Pies—Jelly for Meat Pies—Mushrooms for Pud-
dings—Panada for Puddings—Potato Paste—Quenelles
for Boudins—Rice Pastry for Savory Dishes—Roux—
Roux, brown—Roux, white—Stock—Stock, brown—Preser-
vation of Pastry.

ANCHOVIES, ESSENCE OF.

Remove the bones from a few Anchovies; beat into
paste with green chilies, or cayenne pepper and shallots;
mix with about 1 pt walnut catsup and ½ pt mushroom
catsup; preserve in well closed bottles.

AROMATIC HERBACEOUS SEASONING.

1 oz nutmeg.	3 ozs majoram.
1 oz mace.	2 ozs winter savory.
2 ozs cloves.	3 ozs thyme.
2 ozs peppercorns.	¼ oz cayenne pepper.
1 oz dried bay leaves.	½ oz grated lemon peel.
3 ozs basil.	2 cloves of garlic.

Pulverize in a mortar; sift through a fine sieve, and
put away for use, in a dry, well corked bottle.

ASPIC JELLY.

1 qt good stock broth.	1 sprig of thyme.
6 shallots.	6 cloves.
2 bay leaves.	4 ozs gelatine.
mace, q. s.	

Place in a stew-pan upon the fire and stir until the gelatine becomes thoroughly dissolved, when remove from the fire to cool. Whip three whites of eggs with ½ pt cold water and a tablespoon tarragon vinegar, and having well mixed this in with the aspic, stir over the fire until it boils; after allowing it to boil ten minutes, pass through a jelly-bag or napkin; it will then be fit for use.

CUSTARD FOR GARNISH.

Make a cold custard of ten yolks of eggs and ½ pt good clear stock; steam this in a prepared pudding mould; when cold, cut into fancy shapes, and serve in consomme, etc.

For *sweet custard for garnish*, use cream in place of stock, adding half a glass of rum and a very little sugar.

CUSTARD FOR GARNISH—WHITE.

Make a cold custard of 6 whites of eggs, just broken with the whisk, and not quite ½ pt melted (but not hot) clear stock; season, steam and serve as above.

For *sweet custard for garnish* (white), use cream in place of stock, adding half a glass of white noyeau, and a little sugar.

FORCEMEAT OF LIVER AND HAM, FOR RAISED PIES.

Take equal quantities of calf's liver and fat bacon; cut into square pieces the size of a walnut; fry the pieces of bacon in a large stew-pan, and when about half done add the liver; season with aromatic herbaceous seasoning, a clove of garlic and a little salt. As soon as the liver is about half done, first chop fine, and then pound the whole in a mortar until reduced to a smooth substance, and force this through a wire sieve; put in a basin for use.

FARCE, OR FORCEMEAT (2).

To $\frac{1}{2}$ ℔ veal cutlet, from which cut off all the sinews, add $\frac{1}{2}$ ℔ bacon or ham, cutting off all the rind and outside. To this add $\frac{1}{4}$ ℔ dressed ox-tongue. Chop all very fine, after which, pound in a mortar till quite smooth. Add a little parsley, mixed herbs and shallot, and a small portion of truffles, if they are to be had. These herbs must also be chopped fine. Mix and season with pepper and salt, powdered mace, ground allspice and one egg. For game, chicken, pigeon, etc., add the liver of the several birds.

FORCEMEAT, OYSTERS.

Open and beard 2 doz fresh oysters, and preserve the liquor; mince them finely, pound to a smooth paste, and mix with 5 ozs finely grated bread crumbs, 1 oz butter, the rind of half a lemon chopped fine, cayenne, salt, pepper and minced parsley; when well mixed, bind together with the unbeaten yolk of an egg, and a small quantity of the oyster liquor, added very gradually.

FINANCIERE RAGOUT.

Place in a stew-pan, ready cooked, a few cockscombs, button mushrooms, truffles, quenelles, and scollops of sweetbreads; add $\frac{1}{2}$ pt brown sauce (flavored if possible with game), a glass of sherry or madeira, and a small pinch of cayenne; boil together for three minutes, and serve for garnishes of vol-au-vents, patties, etc.

FINE HERBS FOR PUDDINGS.

Chop some parsley, some prepared mushrooms, and about four shallots; fry with 3 ozs butter; season with pepper and salt, and put by for use.

GLAZE

is made from clear stock, boiled down until it forms a sort of meat varnish or strong jelly. The knuckles of veal, the legs and shins of beef, and the shanks of mutton are particularly glutinous, and therefore the best for making glaze; it may be kept for some time in small jars, if kept dry.

GLAZE FOR PASTRY.

A rich yellow glaze is given to meat pies by brushing them over with the beaten yolk of an egg. A lighter glaze is given by using the white as well as the yolk, and a lighter still by the addition of a little milk; or, for sweet dishes, by brushing the pastry with sugar and water.

GRAVY FOR FISH PIES, ETC.

Take any common fish, such as eels, flounders or pike, or a mixture of one or two kinds; cut into small pieces and put in a stew-pan; to 2 lbs fish put 1½ pts water, pepper, salt, two bunches of parsley, a sprig each of majoram and thyme, a blade of mace, and a crust of bread toasted brown and hard; simmer gently for an hour or more, then strain; thicken with flour and butter, and a teaspoon of anchovy essence, or 2 or 3 pounded anchovies. If *brown* gravy is wanted, the fish must be fried before it is stewed.

HALF GLAZE

is the best stock reduced over the fire to a half glaze; it must be used sparingly.

JELLY FOR GAME PIES.

Take the bones of birds and the various cuttings from veal, tongue and other meats; add a little parsley, sweet-herbs and shallot; cover with broth or water; reduce the quantity by simmering to one-half; dissolve and add gelatine; season with pepper, salt and mace; strain through a seive, and put into pies, as directed.

JELLY FOR MEAT PIES.

Take 1½ lbs of the knuckle or neck of veal, and ½ ℔ of the shin of beef; cut them into small pieces, and put into a sauce-pan with ¼ pt good beef stock; simmer gently for a half hour, then add 2 pts more stock, a shallot, 3 ozs undressed lean ham, ¼ teaspoon bruised celery seed tied in muslin, a clove, a small bunch of savory herbs, and ½ doz peppercorns. Simmer slowly for 3 or 4 hours or until the liquid will jelly. If quickly boiled the jelly will not be so clear. Strain the gravy, add salt if required, and put aside until quite cold, so that the fat may be entirely removed.

MUSHROOMS FOR PUDDINGS.

Put into a stewpan 3 ozs. of butter, with a little water, a pinch of salt, and a few drops of lemon-juice; cut the end, or dirty parts, off 1 doz mushrooms, wash them quickly in three or four waters, and turn or peel them neatly with a sharp vegetable knife, throwing them into the prepared liquor as they are done; place them on the fire, boil with a cover on for about four minutes; put by in the liquor.

PANADA FOR PUDDINGS, QUENELLES, ETC.

Put on in a stewpan ½ pt best white broth, flavored with shallot and a little parsley, and sufficient bread crumbs to form it into a sort of paste; set at the corner of the stove to swell, then stir in a pat of butter; stir until it detaches from the sides of the stew-pan and is quite firm to the touch; put it on a buttered plate, flatten, let it cool, and use as directed.

POTATO PASTE.

Bake 1 doz large white potatoes, and when done and just out of the oven, rub their pulp through a clean wire sieve; put this into a stew-pan with 2 ozs butter, 4 yolks of eggs, nutmeg, pepper and salt; stir the paste over the fire until it ceases to adhere to the sides of the stew-pan; roll it out on the slab with flour, remembering that as this paste possesses little elasticity it must be handled with care, and when rolled out to the size and in the form of the dish which has to be covered with it, the cover should be divided into two or four parts (according to the size of the pie); by this contrivance it will be more easily adjusted on the top by gently pressing the joints together with the flat part of the thumb; parts of the paste can be used to decorate the surface of a pie in the usual way.

QUENELLES FOR BOUDINS.

Scrape with a knife all the best part from 2 ℔s of leg

of veal; cut in slices, leaving the fibre or skin part only, which put into the stock pot to avoid waste; pass the pulp of meat thus obtained through a wire sieve; pound this with half the quantity of finished panada; add ½ pt double cream, 2 whole eggs, and seasonings to taste; use as directed. Quenelles may be made of other meats, fish, game, poultry, etc., in a similar manner.

RICE PASTE FOR SAVORY DISHES.

Put seasoned cutlets of veal, lamb, chicken, or game, already dressed, into a pie-dish; cover the meat with a layer of rice which has been boiled to a stiff paste in a little milk, with pepper, salt and onion for seasoning; brush over with egg, and put into the oven for a minute or two to color the paste lightly. A little egg mixed with the rice will make it adhere better.

ROUX

is simply a mixture of flour and butter, which, when baked, is used for thickening soups and gravies; it should be kept in a covered jar, and will remain good for months. A teaspoonful is generally sufficient to thicken a pint of gravy, etc.

ROUX—BROWN.

Dissolve ¼ ℔ fresh butter; skim well, let stand for a minute, and pour it away from the impurities, which will settle at the bottom. Put the clear, oily part into a sauce-pan over a slow fire, and shake into it about ¼ ℔ fine flour, or as much as will make a thick paste. Stir constantly, heating slowly and equally until it is very thick and of a bright brown color; put into a jar till needed.

ROUX—WHITE.

Proceed as above, but be careful to remove the paste from the fire before it has acquired any color. White roux is used for white sauces.

STOCK.

Cut 1 ℔ of shin of beef into small pieces; put into a clean stewpan with a few bones (broken up small), and about five pints of water. Trimmings of meat or poultry, if convenient, may also be thrown into the pot, as well as a little bacon rind which has been first scalded or scraped. Bring the contents of the pan slowly to the boil; carefully remove the scum as it rises, and throw in a spoonful of cold water now and then to assist it in doing so. An onion with a clove stuck into it, a turnip, a carrot, two leeks, a few outer sticks of celery, with a little salt and pepper may be added, if liked. Draw the sauce-pan to the side of the fire, and let its contents simmer very gently, keeping it covered, excepting when it is necessary to take off the lid for the purpose of skimming. Strain into an earthenware pan, and remove the fat when it forms on the surface. It should simmer about four hours.

STOCK, BROWN.

There are various ways of browning stock; the best is to let it boil to a glaze when making it, letting it color itself over the fire. Stock made from bones cannot, however, be thus colored, and in this case Liebig's extract may be used. Brown thickening may be employed when the stock is to be thickened as well as browned, though it must be remembered that after it is added the stock must simmer by the side of the fire, that it may throw up the fat, which should be removed. Liquid browning, which can be bottled and used as required, may be made as follows: Put ¼ pt moist sugar in a stew-pan and let it remain over a gentle fire till it is melted; keep stirring with a wooden spoon till it is almost black; pour upon it 1 pt water, and let it remain until dissolved. Three or four drops will color 1 pt stock.

PRESERVATION OF PASTRY.

Pastry should never be put into a cold pantry directly it comes out of the oven, as the sudden change of temperature is likely to make it heavy. It may be kept good for several days if put into a tin box, when perfectly cold.

CHAPTER II.

SAVORY SAUCES.

Bechemel Sauce--Bohemian Sauce—Brown Sauce (Espagnol) —Cardinal's Sauce—Chestnut Sauce—Dutch Sauce— D'Uxelles Sauce — Grouse Sauce -- Poivrade Sauce — Steward's Sauce (maitre d'hotel)—Supreme Sauce—Tata Cold Sauce (Mayonaise)—Truffle Sauce—Venison Sauce— White Sauce.

BECHEMEL SAUCE.

Put 4 ozs flour into a sauce-pan with 2 ozs butter; knead these together smoothly by working them with a wooden spoon; add an onion, a carrot, some celery, parsley, a bay leaf and thyme (the vegetables cut thin), a little nutmeg, pepper and salt; moisten with 1½ pts milk; stir the sauce over the fire while it boils sharply for 20 minutes; then strain it through a tammy into a basin—afterwards to be immediately removed into a convenient-sized covered stew-pan or bain-marie, for use.

It is important when stirring a sauce upon the fire, to bear with some strength and a little tact on the edge of the bowl of the wooden spoon, so as to prevent the sauce from burning at the bottom of the stew-pan while it is being reduced, especially with such sauces as contain milk or cream.

BOHEMIAN SAUCE.

Sweat 3 ozs of chopped truffles over the fire, with a glass of sherry; add ½ pt brown sauce.

•

BROWN SAUCE.
(ESPAGNOL).

Put some well-finished brown roux into a stew-pan over the fire; stir in best brown stock until the consistency of single cream; clarify (as for white sauce), and when the butter is all off, pour it into a stew-pan, in which has been sweated, with a pat of butter, some lean ham (cut in small dice), some trimmings of mushrooms, one sliced shallot, and two glasses of sherry; reduce (as for white sauce) until the consistency of cream; squeeze through a tammy and put by for use.

CARDINAL'S SAUCE.

Put on in a stew-pan over the fire, some trimmings of fish, with a little white stock; make an essence of this; strain and boil it down to half; add a glass of sherry and ½ pt of uncreamed white sauce, reduced, and some live lobster spawn, rubbed through a sieve with a pat of butter; clarify at the corner of the stove, and squeeze through a tammy.

CHESTNUT SAUCE.

Peel and skin twenty-four chestnuts; simmer them over the stove in stock until tender; rub them through a tammy; add more stock if required, and a spoonful of brown sauce; season to taste.

DUTCH SAUCE.

Scrape a little horse-radish, and boil it in four spoonsful of elder vinegar; add ½ pt white sauce, and 5 yolks of eggs; pass through a metal search, and keep hot in the bain-marie until required.

D'UXELLES SAUCE.

Chop separately a sufficient quantity of prepared

mushrooms, three shallots, a handful of parsley, and 3 ozs truffles; pass the whole over the fire with 3 ozs butter, pepper, salt and a little nutmeg; add 1½ glasses sherry; reduce this to half; mix in 1½ gills white sauce, and thicken with 4 yolks of eggs. This is used for masking, etc.

GROUSE SAUCE.

Put some stock to trimmings of grouse and boil until an essence is obtained; strain and reduce it to half; add a glass of sherry and some brown sauce; let it simmer; squeeze through a tammy.

Most essences may be made in this manner.

POIVRADE SAUCE.

Put 2 ozs of butter into a stew-pan, with two onions, a shallot, a carrot, a turnip, cut into dice, two cloves, a bay leaf, and a sprig of thyme; stir constantly over a gentle fire until lightly browned; dredge over them a spoonful of flour, add pepper, salt, a glass of claret, half a glass of vinegar, and one of water; boil gently for a half hour; skim, strain and serve.

STEWARD'S SAUCE.
(MAITRE D'HOTEL.)

Chop a little parsley very fine, and squeeze it in a cloth; reduce some white sauce; and if for fish, add some of the essence made from the bones, and reduced in half a glass of sherry; pass through a metal search, and add the chopped parsley, with a little lemon juice.

SUPREME SAUCE.

Put some white sauce into a stew-pan, add some trimmings of chicken, and a little essence of truffles; reduce the whole over the fire; pass through a tammy for use.

TATA COLD SAUCE.

(MAYONAISE.)

Place two raw yolks of eggs in a round-bottomed basin, set in pounded ice; stir in briskly with a wooden spoon, some salad oil dropped in very sparingly at first; add a little salt and proceed stirring in the oil carefully, and using a little tarragon and French vinegar when required. When a sufficient quantity is thus made, and has the appearance of a light petit choux, season to taste; this is MAYONAISE. For tata sauce, reduce some of this with a little vinegar and cream, and stir in a little chopped tarragon.

TRUFFLE SAUCE.

Chop 2 ozs truffles very fine; sweat them over the fire with half a glass of sherry; add ½ pt Supreme sauce to this.

VENISON SAUCE.

Boil 2 glasses of port wine to half; add some red currant jelly and 1½ gills brown sauce; boil up and pass through a tammy.

WHITE SAUCE.

Put some well finished white roux into a stew-pan over the charcoal stove or hot plate; stir into this some best white stock to the consistency of single cream; when well mixed, set it at the corner of the stove to simmer, with the cover three parts over to allow the butter to rise; when taken off, place over a quick fire with some prepared mushrooms, stirring all the time until reduced to the consistency of double cream; pour in some boiled cream, pass through a tammy and put by for use.

2

CHAPTER III.

Raised Pies; Meat, Game, Etc.

Raised Pies—Raised Pies in Moulds—Paste for Raised Pies—
French Raised Pie—French Paste (Pate Brisee)—Hot
Water Paste—Three Quarter Paste—Cold Water Paste—
Additional Pastes—How to Ornament Game Pies—Game
Pie Shells.

RAISED PIES.

Raised pies may be made of any size and with almost
all kinds of meat, poultry or game, the only indispen-
sable requisite being that there shall be no bone in
them. They are usually served cold, and should be
rather highly flavored. The pastry of small pies is
generally eaten, but with large pies it is merely used as
a case in which to serve the savory preparation inside.
There is no difficulty in making the paste for raised
pies, but inexperienced cooks often find it difficult to
raise the walls of the pie; this latter is easier of accomp-
lishment if a tin mould is used.

For the manner of forming raised pies, both with and
without moulds, as well as for a variety of pastes suitable therefor, see Part I. Chapter 3.

Raised pies should be baked in a well heated but by
no means brisk oven, and if there is any danger of the
pastry being too highly colored, a buttered paper should
be laid over it. To ascertain when the pie is done
enough, run a skewer into the middle of it, and if it is

tender throughout, it is done. When the appearance of the pie is a consideration, it is a good plan to cut the top carefully out, and cover the meat with bright stiff aspic jelly, cut into dice. If this is not done, however, a little good bright gravy, which will form a jelly when cold, should always be poured into the pie through the hole at the top, whenever it is taken out of the oven. In summer time it is safer to stiffen this with a little dissolved isinglass. When a mould is used, richer pastry can be employed than without its use.

RAISED PIES IN MOULDS.

(*Use hot water paste or three quarter paste, as described below*):

The mould must be well buttered with a butter brush dipped in melted butter, taking care that every part is covered, or the crust will stick. To line the mould, the easiest way is to take a small portion of the paste, roll it out to the size of the bottom of the mould, where, press carefully down so as to lay quite level. Then, with the remainder of the paste (or sufficient of it to form a long strip the exact circumference of the mould, and about 2 inches wider than its depth) proceed to line the sides, pressing into the flutes or ornamental depressions with a small portion of the paste. Wet with a brush the extreme edge, so that where it falls on the bottom it may stick to the bottom piece only. Press this down close so as to make the crust water-tight, or the gravy will be lost. Trim off the top edges, and it is ready for the filling. This paste being dry and tough, is not generally eaten. (For additional instructions see Part I. Chapter 3).

PASTE FOR RAISED PIES.

In making raised pies the first consideration is, whether the pastry is intended to be eaten or not; if merely to form a mould in which to hold the meat, etc., it may be made firm and compact without much difficulty, and may be beaten with a rolling-pin, or kneaded with the knuckles, to make it stiff and hard. If the paste is intended to be eaten, greater care will be necessary.

When the pastry is not to be eaten; dissolve 3 or 4 ozs of lard in ½ pt of boiling water, and stir in as much flour as will make a stiff smooth paste; a little more than a pound being required. Knead it thoroughly with the fingers, and when it is sufficiently firm to keep its form when moulded, put it into a bowl, and cover with a cloth until it is nearly cold. Dredge a little flour on the pastry board, put the pastry upon it, and roll it with the hands into the shape of a sugar-loaf or cone, with the diameter of the lower part rather less than the size required for the pie. Place the cone upright, and flaten the top until it is half the height. Press it down with the knuckles of the right hand, at the same time forming the walls of the pie with the left. When the sides are smooth, and of equal thickness, fill the pie, roll out the cover, lay it on, and make a hole in the centre. Fasten the edges securely with a little egg, ornament the pie according to fancy, glaze it by brushing it over with the beaten yolk of an egg, and bake in a quick oven.

An easier way of shaping a raised pie, is to roll out the pastry to the required thickness, and then cut out a piece for the top and bottom, and a long strip for the sides. These pieces must be fastened with egg, and the edges pressed over one another, so as to be securely fastened. The pie is then finished as above.

When the pastry is to eaten; rub ¼ ℔ butter into 1 ℔ flour; sprinkle over it a pinch of salt. Pour another ¼ ℔ butter into a sauce-pan with ½ pt milk; stir over a gentle fire until the butter is dissolved; pour the liquid over the flour, and stir it to a smooth paste; dredge some flour over it; give it two or three turns, and mould it into the proper shape before it has had time to cool.

FRENCH RAISED PIE.

According to Ude this should be moulded as follows: Take a lump of paste the size of the pie to be made; mould it in the shape of a sugar-loaf; put it upright on the table, and with the palms of the hands flatten the sides of it; when these are equalized all round, and it is quite smooth, squeeze the point of the cone down to half the height of the paste; then hollow the inside by pressing it with the fingers, being careful to keep it in every part of equal thickness; fill it, roll out the cover, egg the edges, press them securely together, make a hole in the centre, lay a roll of paste round it, and encircle this with a wreath of leaves, or ornament the pie according to taste; glaze with the beaten yolk of egg, and bake from 2 to 3 hours in a well heated oven, if the pie is small; or if large, from 4 to 5 hours, the time being regulated by the nature of the contents and the size of the pie.

FRENCH PASTE (PATE BRISEE).

6 ozs butter,	pinch of salt,
1 ℔ flour,	cup of water.

Make rather stiff; lard or suet may be used in place of the butter.

HOT WATER PASTE.

Put 1 ℔ of flour on the table; spread it out with the back of the hand so as to form a hollow in the centre; put in 1 oz salt, and ½ pt of hot water with 4 ozs of dissolved butter; mix all together with the hand into a firm paste; work it compactly with both hands; roll it up in a cloth, and put it in a *warm* stew-pan for use.

THREE-QUARTER PASTE.

Mix 2 ℔s flour with 1½ ℔s butter, and rub well together. Add sufficient water to make the mass into a stiff dough; work it well.

COLD WATER PASTE.

Prepare 1 ℔ flour with a hollow in the centre; add ½ oz salt, 4 ozs butter, and ½ pt water; mix the whole into a firm compact paste.

(*For additional pastes, etc., for raised pies, etc., see Part I. Chapter* 3).

HOW TO ORNAMENT GAME PIES.

This may be done in three ways, some being applicable to all raised pies; (1) by using the plumage of the bird; (2) with aspic jelly; (3) by paste decorations (see Part I. Chapter 3). To proceed according to the first method,—before boning the bird, cut through the skin right down the breast from neck to rump in a straight line, very carefully removing the skin at the wings; cut these latter from the body, as also the head with the neck and the rump, leaving all these parts attached to the skin. Having done this, put the skin or skins on one side. Now take out the inside of the bird, cut out all the bones, and fill as usual This being done and the pie baked and cold, go on with the decoration. Taking the plumage if it be a pheasant (with the head, neck and wings attached) in the hand, pass a small skewer up the neck, right into the head, leaving about two inches of the skewer to put into the pie, to act as a prop. Cover the pie with a sheet of writing paper cut to its size, and arrange the plumage nicely and gracefully over it, pressing the skewer into the pie exactly where a proper posture of the bird will force it. A sprig of parsley put into the beak, and the whole thing is complete. If partridge or grouse, the tails of the birds are usually put together, the heads being over the edge of the pie.

GAME PIE SHELLS.

Take 2 lbs flour, into which rub 4 ozs butter; place in a sauce-pan on the fire $\frac{3}{4}$ pt water, with 4 ozs mutton suet and $\frac{1}{2}$ oz salt; when boiling, make a bay in the flour and mix. The paste should be stiff, and be either passed through a biscuit break or be well worked with the hands till it is firm and pliable; roll out the paste 1 inch thick, and with a piece of cardboard, the size and shape required (oval or round) placed upon it, cut out the bottom with a sharp knife, then cut out the middle in one piece, about 3 inches deep, and the length required. It is necessary to have a paste-brush and an egg to gloss the paste over, and also to make it stick together. Gloss the edge of the bottom over and place the middle on, bevel the two ends a little to make them fit, also to be of one thickness, then fill with bran, put a lid on, and if for show in a window, etc., cut some small leaves out of the paste, and decorate the lid; put a border round the bottom part of the shell, which ornament with the paste pincers. Cut some thin pieces of paste two inches long, and form chain work round the top, or vary the pattern at will; when ornamented, gloss over with egg, and let it stand till the next day, if possible; bake in a moderate oven.

These shells are used in the places of dishes, and are considered to look more noble. They are used for game, veal and ham, pate-de-foie-gras, etc. This paste is not generally eaten, but is only to make the table look artistic.

CHAPTER IV.

Meat and Game Pie Fillings, Pasties, Etc.

GENERAL NOTES.

In this and the following chapters a variety of recipes are presented—so great a variety, in fact, that the pastry-cook, can with a few variations, be able to produce every species of raised pies, patties, etc., that human ingenuity can invent. Although specific directions accompany most of the recipes, still the cook can often exercise his discretion as to the kind of paste to be employed, which should be carefully adjusted to the material used, so that it should not be too *moist* when done. In regard to seasoning, discretion must be used.

Raised pies and patties may also be made of canned meats, etc, which, however, need no special directions.

It is scarcely worth while to more than mention that patty cases, game pie cases,etc., can be filled with jellies, fruit purees, preserves, etc., for desert.

BEEF PIE (RAISED).

See rump-steak pie (2).

BEEF STEAK PIE.

Cut a piece of steak in very thin slices, put a small piece of suet or fat bacon on each slice, with a very small quantity of finely mixed parsley, pepper and salt, and powdered sweet herbs; roll up each slice, which

should be so cut that when rolled up each will form a
mouthful; make a layer of them in a pie-dish, rubbed
with shallot; on that put a layer of kidneys, par-boiled
for a minute or two, and cut in thin slices; then another layer of steak and so on until the dish is full; add
a dash of pepper and salt and pour in as much calf's foot
or aspic jelly as the dish will hold; cover with a short
crust; ornament, glaze, etc.; bake one and a half or two
hours.

BEEF STEAK AND OYSTER PIE.

Cut up about two pounds rump steak in collops the
size of a teacup; trim away unnecessary fat and sinew
without waste; season with pepper and salt; fry them
brown on both sides with about one ounce butter; shake
in two tablespoons flour; add two dozen oysters and
their liquor, a little catsup and chopped onion; shake
round gently over the fire, allowing all to simmer together for five minutes; arrange the collops of beef, etc.,
neatly in the pie-dish; add the sauce and a few cooked
potatoes; cover with paste; bake one hour.

BRIDE PIE.

Par-boil some veal sweet-breads and pieces of lamb;
cut them into slices; mix with them some slices of blanched
ox-palate, streaky bacon, one pint oysters, some roast
chestnuts, seasoning with salt, mace and nutmeg. When
the pie-dish is full, lay slices of butter on the top, cover
with paste and bake. When done lift up the lid and put
into the pie four raw eggs, beaten up with a little butter,
the juice of a lemon, and a glass of sherry.

CALF'S HEAD PIE.

(*A Scotch Cold Dish.*)

Scald and soak a moderate sized calf's head; put in a stew pan with a knuckle of veal, two onions, the rind of a lemon, cut thin, a small bunch of winter savory and parsley, two blades of mace, and a few white peppercorns, with as much water as will cover all, and let them simmer for a half hour. Remove the head and when it becomes cold, cut the meat into small, neat pieces, and after taking the skin from the tongue, do the same with the latter. Boil the broth by itself, with a small addition of gelatine till it is reduced to a strong jellified gravy. Cover the bottom of a pie-dish with thin slices of lean ham, then add a layer of the head and tongue, a little forcemeat made from the knuckle of veal, and hard yolks of eggs cut in two. Repeat the layers in the same order till the dish is full; season with nutmeg, pepper, salt and a little lemon peel. Pour over all as much jelly as the dish will hold, cover with good paste, and bake one hour. Eaten cold, this pie is most delicious.

CAPON RAISED PIE.

Line a mould or shape a pie large enough to hold the capon and forcemeat. Spread at the bottom a layer of forcemeat and some slices of truffles. Split a capon down the back, and take out the bones without injuring the skin; lay it breast downward upon a board, season with pepper, salt and spices; spread on it a layer of forcemeat one-half inch thick; put some slices of truffles on this and then another layer of forcemeat. Roll the capon over, make the skin meet at the back and shape it to fit the mould; lay it breast uppermost, on the forcemeat on the pie; sprinkle pepper and salt over it, lay on it some slices of truffles and cover with forcemeat; lay on top thin slices of fat bacon; put on the lid and finish as usual. When baked, let it cool one-half hour and pour into it through a hole in the top, a quarter pint savory gravy, reduced to jelly.

When quite cold this pie is served in a napkin, garnished with parsley. Slices of veal or ham may be used in place of truffles.

CHICKEN PIE. (1).

Take two young chickens, freed from bone; open one of the birds by the back and spread it upon a board; season with prepared seasoning and salt; fill in with forcemeat, (2) and close the bird so as to restore it to its original shape. Do the same with the other bird, taking care that both are equally fitted. Place in the mould, filling up the cavities with fillets of tongue and a few slices of bacon or ham, Should the mould not be quite full, put in some slices of veal, well seasoned. Bake, and when nearly cold, fill up with jelly.

In making the jelly for this pie, the bones and giblets of the chicken may be put in.

CHICKEN PIE. (2).

To a large tender chicken add about a half pound salt pork, chopped fine; lay on one layer of pork; pepper, and cover with pieces of chicken; another layer of pork and chicken, etc. Have three hard boiled eggs chopped up, and added with the chicken. Before laying on the top crust, place a few lumps of butter about the top, and add water to make as much gravy as desired.

CHICKEN POT-PIE.

An old chicken will do for this purpose—in fact, it is preferable to a very young one. Singe and draw the fowl, cutting it up in joints. Cover with cold water, and let it simmer, closely covered, for an hour or more, according to its age. Add three medium sized onions, sliced, some sprigs of parsley, salt and pepper, and continue cooking until the meat is tender and the onions done. Dish the bulky pieces such as the back, under part of the breast, and first joints. Make a batter with one egg, a cup of milk and a teaspoonful of baking powder sifted through enough flour to make it of proper consistency. Drop this into the boiling broth in small spoonsful. While the dumplings are cooking, which will take about eight minutes, heat to boiling half a pint of milk; pour this into the gravy after the rest of the meat and dumplings have been removed, and stir in a lump of butter and a large tablespoonful of flour wet with a little cold mi'k; boil for a minute and pour over the chicken. The dumplings should be served on a separate dish. Bake a piece of rich pie-crust the size of a dinner plate; break it into as many pieces as there are people to be served, and place as a broder around the dish containing this meat. This is chicken pie *par excellence*. If the fowl is old and fat, it would be advisable to remove as much as possible of the fat and skin, before cooking.

CHICKEN PIE, A LA SUPREME.

Cut small pieces as for fricassee; cover the bottom of a pie-dish with scallops of veal and ham, placed alternately; season with mushroom and parsley, pepper and salt: add a little white sauce; then add the pieces of chicken, arranged in neat order and on these place plover's or bird's eggs in each cavity; repeat the seasoning and the sauce; lay a few thin slices of trimmed, dressed ham on the top; cover with puff paste, ornament, egg, and bake one and a half hours.

CHICKEN AND HAM PIE.

Proceed as for chicken pie (2), using veal and ham in place of salt pork.

CHICKEN AND SWEETBREAD PIE.

Line a deep pie-dish with a good crust and spread a layer of forcemeat on it; put over this alternate layers of chicken cut into neat joints and sweetbread cut into small pieces, both seasoned with salt and cayenne; sprinkle over each layer a few mushrooms or truffles, chopped small; when the dish is nearly full, put some slices of hard-boiled eggs over the top, pour a little gravy over the meat, cover the dish with the same crust as it was lined with, brush over with beaten egg, and bake one to one and a half hours in a good oven. Just before serving, make a hole in the top and pour in some good gravy.

CHICAGO PIE.

Cut up sufficient pork in square pieces—fat and lean in equal proportions; season with pepper, salt and a small quantity of chopped sage-leaves. Finish as usual.

CHRISTMAS PIE.

Bone a fowl, a wild duck, pheasant, woodcock, etc.; having spread them open on the table, season with aromatic herbs, pepper and salt; garnish each with forcemeat; sew them up with small twine; place them on a sauce-pan with clarified butter, and set them to bake in a moderate heat, until they are done through, when withdraw from the oven and set to cool. Meanwhile place the carcasses in a stew-pan, with two calf's feet, carrot, celery, onion, a clove of garlic, two bay leaves, thyme, cloves, mace and salt; fill up with 4 qts water; boil, skim, and set aside to boil gently for 3 hours; strain, free from grease, and boil down to a thin glaze, and keep for use.

Line a raised pie mould with hot water paste; line the inside of the pie with forcemeat; arrange the baked fowl, etc. in the centre, placing at the same time layers of forcemeat and seasoning, until all the preparation is used up; put a cover of paste on top, egg and ornament; finish as for Game Pie.

DARTMOUTH PIE.

Mince 2 lbs mutton, from which all the fat has been cut away; add 1 lb finely shred beef suet, 1 lb well washed currants, 4 ozs sugar, salt and nutmeg to taste. Make a paste by boiling 2 ozs butter with 4 ozs beef suet, and working it into 8 ozs flour. Cover the mixture with this paste; bake 1½ hours.

DUCK PIE.

Previous to putting the duck in the pie-dish, boil it about ¼ hour, having first cut off the neck and wings, which should be stewed for a few minutes with the giblets in a stew-pan containing 2 ozs butter, a bunch of herbs, an onion sliced, an anchovy, a blade of mace, pepper, salt and cayenne; when the butter has dissolved pour in ½ pt boiling water, and stew gently one hour; strain and add the mixture to the gravy from the duck.

Cut up the duck neatly, and arrange it in the pie-dish, adding more seasoning if required; skim off all fat from the gravy, which should be cold, and pour it into the dish.   Cover with puff paste or any crust desired. Bake one hour.

FAVORITE MEAT PIE.

Take cold roast meat of any kind, slice it thin, cut it rather small, lay it with gravy, sufficiently peppered and salted, in a pie-dish.   If liked, a small onion may be chopped fine and sprinkled over it.   Over the meat pour a couple of stewed tomatoes, a little more pepper, and a thick layer of mashed potatoes.   Bake slowly in a moderate oven till the top is a light brown.

FIELDFARE PASTIES.

Take ½ doz birds—fieldfares, snipe, woodcocks, quails and young plovers—draw them and put the insides into a stew-pan with a little butter, first taking out any grit from the gizzards; when steamed enough, take them out, and put the birds into the butter to brown lightly; remove them, add a little more butter and stir in 3 or 4 eggs well beaten, with a cup of milk.   Spread a layer of forcemeat over the bottom of a dish, with a boiled sweetbread cut in dice, if obtainable; lay on the birds with their trails, seasoning with salt, pepper and lemon juice; the rest should be laid upon them, and a cover of paste over all.   Bake, and pour in a little rich gravy, when done.

FIFE PIE.

Skin a young rabbit and cut into pieces about the size of a small egg.   Prepare a forcemeat of the liver, parboiled and minced, some bread crumbs, a little fat bacon, and a seasoning of lemon-thyme, minced parsley, nutmeg, pepper and salt; moisten with an egg and make into balls. Cut 1 lb bacon into thin slices; free from rind, sprinkle with pepper, salt and nutmeg, and pack it with the balls, closely into a dish; pour in sufficient good gravy and a small glass of white wine; cover with puff-paste; bake 1½ hours.

FRENCH PIE (1).

Take 1 lb or 2 lbs veal (knuckle or breast); boil tender in as little water as possible; when cold, cut into squares, season highly with pepper, salt and lemon; let it boil slightly. Have two or three hard boiled eggs, which cut into slices, some small pieces of bacon and dressed sausage. Place part of the eggs, sausage and ham at the bottom of a pie-dish, and round the edges; fill up with veal and gravy, which when turned out will be a jelly. This makes a suitable dish for breakfast, lunch or supper.

FRENCH PIE (2).

Pass any remains of cold meat, free from fat or gristle, through a mincing machine, till finely minced; season according to taste and moisten with plenty of gravy; have ready some mashed potatoes, and after warming the mince in a sauce-pan, turn it out into a pie-dish; heap the mashed potatoes well up, spread bits of butter on the top, and place in a hot oven till brown. Any scraps may be used, the chief point being to mince everything well.

FOWL PIES.

See Game Pies, etc.

GAME PIE.

Take pheasants, partridges, woodcocks or snipes, or a mixture of some of them, etc.; bone and cut them up in convenient pieces, larding the breast pieces. Line a prepared mould with slices of bacon cut as thin as possible, and proceed to fill it with the pieces of game, truffles, previously cooked in white wine, and mushrooms cooked in lemon juice, filling up the interstices with forcemeat (2), being careful to pack the whole closely. When taken out of the oven pour in through the hole in the crust some hot aspic jelly. The next day take off the cover and lay on the top a layer of bright aspic chopped up, not too finely.

To serve; remove the pie from the mould; lay it on a clean white napkin; garnish according to fancy with parsley, etc.

GAME AND MACARONI PIE

Put ¼ ℔ pipe macaroni into a sauce-pan of boiling stock, and let it simmer till it is tender, but unbroken. Drain, and lay it at the bottom of a deep dish; place on it a layer of game (partridges, pheasants or grouse, etc.,) cut into neat joints, and stewed until they are three parts cooked; a few slices of raw, lean ham should be put amongst the game, together with a few chopped mushrooms. Season with salt and pepper. Place a layer of macaroni on the top, grate over it a little Parmesan cheese, and put little lumps of butter here and there. Pour some good gravy, mixed with cream or new milk, over the whole; cover with a good crust; bake about an hour in a moderate oven. Before serving add a little more boiling gravy and milk, if required.

GAME PIE—ENGLISH.

Trim the best end of the neck of venison, and rub it with mace, nutmeg, cayenne and salt; boil down the trimmings of venison and the inferior joints of a hare, to make gravy. Take the back and thighs of the hare, and after boning them, fill with forcemeat, using shallot and the raw liver minced. Line a dish with short crust; put in the venison and hare, filling up every space with forcemeat; add a little of the gravy, put on the cover, ornament the top and bake about 2½ hours in a hot oven. When venison is not liked, substitute the prime joints of another hare.

GAME PIE—HUNTING.

Make a stiff short crust for raised pies; bake in a moderate oven; cut into neat and rather small joints, one turkey, two pheasants, two partridges, two woodcocks, half a small hare, one grouse, one snipe, and one large ox-tongue. Stew them gently till tender; season rather highly, put them into the crust, pour over them a little of the gravy in which they were stewed, and strew on the top some finely chopped stewed mushrooms. Put on the lid, and warm the pie in a moderate oven, when wanted.

GAME PIE—PERIGORD (1).

This celebrated pie, composed of partridges and truffles, derives its name from Perigord, where truffles are abundant: to make, first line the crust of a raised pie with fat bacon; spread on it a forcemeat made by mincing and pounding liver and seasoning in the following proportions: ½ ℔ liver (the partridges' liver and a little calf's liver may be used), ¼ ℔ fat bacon, ¼ ℔ lean ham, 2 shallots, 4 ozs seasoning spices, one or two truffles, and pepper and salt. Stuff the partridges with this forcemeat and some truffles; place them on the crust, back downwards; fill up the vacant places with forcement and bacon; put a slice of bacon on the top; cover with paste, and bake 4 hours in a moderate oven. When the pie is baked nearly enough, fill up with some gravy, made by stewing the trimmings and a little isinglass.

GAME PIE—PERIGORD (2).

Soak sufficient truffles for two or three hours in fresh water, to loosen the earth about them; rinse well and scrub them with a hard brush; peel, mince the small and broken ones, and put aside. Truss, as if for boiling, as many partridges as required; bone, lard and season with salt, pepper and powdered spice. Make some highly seasoned forcemeat; mix with it the minced truffles; stuff the birds with the whole truffles and a portion of the forcemeat. Line a raised crust with slices of bacon, and forcemeat; place the birds in it backs downwards; fill the vacant places with forcemeat; lay a slice of bacon on top; put on lid, ornament and bake.

GAME PIES.

Very good pies may be made of game, either cut into joints, or, if the birds are small, put in whole. The seasoning should be rather high, and it is usual to put a beefsteak at the bottom of the dish. Game pies are often too much cooked, and thus the flavor is spoilt. A little good melted butter, mixed with claret, and a *soupcon* of lemon juice may be poured over the game, when it is to be eaten hot. Stewed macaroni is sometimes substituted for the beefsteak in pies.

GAME PIES (SMALL).

Bake some small raised pies with good eatable crust, in tin hoops about 3 in. across by 1 in high; paste sides and bottom, but not the tops. Fill with flour before baking; when baked, empty the flour out clean. Bone, stuff with forcemeat, and braize in a cloth, any kind of game; when done, put on a dish, tighten up the cloth by retying one end, place another dish on top, and some weights on it to press it down. When cold, cut up into small dice; fill the pie-cases with a mixture of this game and liver *foie gras;* level the surface, and cover over the top with chopped aspic jelly.

GAME PIE—SMALL BIRDS.

Season the birds highly with cayenne pepper and salt; they may be divided or not. Boil down any trimmings for gravy; put this with some good beef gravy, into a pie-dish, and lay in the birds with bits of butter over them; or a rumpsteak, well seasoned, may be laid in the bottom of the pie-dish, with the gravy from the trimmings; cover with puff paste and bake, but do not overdo it; if eaten hot, melted butter with claret and lemon juice may be poured into it through a funnel; but for a cold pie this is not necessary.

GIBLET PIE.

Thoroughly clean a set of goose giblets, and put them into a pan with 1 pt water, an onion, some black pepper, and a bunch of savory herbs; simmer 1½ hours; remove the giblets, allow them to cool and cut them into small pieces. Cut up 1 lb rump steak into thin slices, and line the bottom of a pie-dish with a few of them; place a layer of giblets on top of them, then cover the giblets again with the remaining slices of beef; strain the gravy in which the giblets were boiled, and pour it over the pie, seasoning with pepper and salt; cover with plain crust, and bake in a brisk oven 1½ hours.

If beefsteak is used, it must be stewed in a separate sauce-pan until nearly tender before being put into the pie; with rump steak this is not necessary. Chicken, cut into neat joints and seasoned with pepper, salt and pounded mace, may be used in place of beef.

A giblet pie should never be eaten cold.

GODIVEAU RAISED PIE.

Fill a raised pie with balls of Godiveau forcemeat, mixed with any savory ragout; pour over the whole a rich sauce. To make the *forcemeat* proceed as follows: Take 1 lb of the fillet of veal and 1½ lbs of good beef suet; remove the skin and gristle, chop the meat small and pound it in a mortar; add salt and pepper, half a nutmeg, grated, a spoonful of scalded and minced parsley, and one of chopped onions or chives; add, while pounding, two well-beaten eggs and a little water. Take the forcemeat up and put it in a cool place for an hour. It should have been so thoroughly pounded that no pieces are distinguishable; it should be made in a cool place and quickly.

GOOSE PIE.

This is made either with one goose, or what is better still, two green geese. Braize or stew them, and cut each goose into eight pieces; season and put them into a good raised pie crust. Or they may be put into a pie-dish with a short crust, in the usual way. A good-sized piece of butter should be put into the dish.

GOOSE PIE—ENGLISH,

Is made by boning a goose, turkey, fowl and· pigeon, and putting the turkey inside the goose, the fowl inside the turkey, and the pigeon inside the fowl. A strong raised crust is then fixed properly in form and all are put inside it, any vacancies being filled up with pieces of ham, tongue, or forcemeat. Clarified butter is poured over the whole, the lid put on, the crust brushed over with beaten egg, and ornamented. It should be well bound with three or four folds of buttered paper before being put into the oven.

GOOSE LIVER PASTY.

Take the livers of two fat geese and cut away the gall bag entirely; soak the livers in milk to whiten them. Mince very finely 1¼ ℔s veal and ¼ ℔ fat bacon; mix with them 2 ozs. of sardines cleared of skin and bone, lemon juice and rind, and chopped capers, all minced finely. Melt some butter in a stew-pan, put in the above articles, cover closely and steam gently until the meat is cooked, but not browned; then stir in 1 gill thick, sour cream, vinegar, white wine, pepper, salt, grated nutmeg and two well-beaten eggs. Line a pie mould with pastry, spread half the mince at the bottom and cut the livers in slices and lay them upon it; season with pepper, salt and cloves; spread the rest of the mince on top; cover, make a hole in the top, ornament and bake, but do not brown. The next day it may be put into hot water to

make it turn out more easily.   A few truffles are a great
improvement.

GROUSE PIE.   (1).

Line the edges of a pie-dish with good paste; put 1 ℔
rump steak, cut into convenient sized pieces, at the bottom; lay a couple of grouse on these.   If the birds are
large they should be cut into joints; if small, they may
be put in whole or in halves.   Season rather highly, with
salt, cayenne and pepper; pour ¼ pt. nicely flavored broth
over the grouse; cover with a good crust and bake about
one hour in a moderate oven.   If the pie is to be eaten
hot, a little more boiling gravy, to which has been added
a little lemon juice and some claret, may be poured
in before serving.

The *Scotch* fashion is to fry the grouse and steak in
cutlets, preparing the pie as above, and sometimes adding
stewed mushrooms and hard boiled eggs.

GROUSE PIE.   (2).

Proceed with grouse as for partridge pie.

GROUSE PIE.   (Scotch).

Pick and draw two or three young grouse; cut off the
wings and legs; tuck the drumsticks in through a slit
made under the thighs; singe the birds over a charcoal
flame; split them in halves; season and fry with butter
until half done; prepare also some collops of beef, season, fry and place them at the bottom of a pie-dish; add
chopped mushrooms, parsley and shallots, and a tablespoonful of Worcester sauce; place the fried halves of
grouse in neat order on this; add a little more seasoning,
and some hard boiled yolks of eggs; moisten with sufficient sauce, gravy or water, and a little salt, to reach up

to the sides of the pie-dish; cover with puff paste, and bake about 1¼ hours.

HARE PASTY.

Cut the hare into convenient sized pieces, and cook partially in a little gravy; spread a layer of forcemeat at the bottom of a buttered pie-dish; put the pieces of hare upon it and the rest of the forcemeat between them; sprinkle with finely minced shallots, chopped parsley, thyme, salt and pepper; lay over the whole a few thin slices of bacon; pour in ¼ pt. blood and ½ pt. of the gravy in which the hare was stewed; cover and bake. It may be eaten either hot or cold.

HARE PIE.

Skin the hare, cut into convenient sized joints; season these with pepper and two pounded cloves; fry them in hot butter ten or fifteen minutes and put them aside to cool. Line the edges of a pie-dish with good crust; arrange the hare and some forcemeat in alternate layers; cover the whole with thin slices of bacon, and pour over it ½ pt gravy, to which has been added a teaspoonful of red currant jelly and a glass of port wine; bake 1½ hours in a good oven, and serve hot.

HARE PIE—RAISED.

Cut a hare, which has hung for a week or two, into neat joints and bone it, if practical. When emptying it be careful to preserve the blood. Mince finely ½ ℔ each lean veal and fat bacon, pound them in a mortar, adding the blood in small quantities while pounding. Roll the paste in the proper shape, ½ inch thick; butter the mould, press the pastry into it, fill with alternate

layers of forcemeat and hare; fill the cavities with forcemeat and jellied gravy; lay two or three slices of bacon
on the top; put on the pastry cover; brush it over with
beaten egg; ornament the sides and top; make a hole in
the centre, and bake for three hours.

No gravy should be put into this pie until after it is
baked. It is to be eaten cold.

HUNTER'S PIE.

Take 2 ℔s of the best end of a leg of mutton; cut it
into chops, trim these neatly, remove all superfluous fat,
add pepper and salt; put into a stew-pan with a little
water and let them stew gently for ½ hour. Boil and
mash 3 or 4 ℔s good potatoes. Line a buttered pie-dish
with them, put in the meat and gravy, and shape a crust
over the top, of the remainder of the potatoes. Bake in
a good oven for ½ hour. If the pie is not nicely browned,
hold a red-hot salamander over it for a minute or two.
Just before serving, make an incision in the middle of
the crust and pour in a little boiling gravy.

ITALIAN PIE.

Cut thin slices of veal from the fillet, and prepare a
careful seasoning of thyme, parsley, a couple of sage
leaves, white pepper, cayenne and salt. Cover the
bottom of the pie-dish with the meat; strew the seasoning
over and lay thin slices of ham (previously dressed) upon
the top. Distribute forcemeat balls throughout, and fill
up the dish with veal, ham and forcemeat balls, and the
yolks of hard boiled eggs. Before baking, pour in ½ pt.
rich white stock, and a large cup of cream when the pie
is ready for the table. Cover the dish with puff paste,
put an ornament in the centre, which can be removed

to put in the cream; bake about 1½ hours in a quick oven.

KIDNEY PIE.

Take four veal kidneys and half its bulk in fat with each. Cut them into slices ¼ inch thick, season rather highly with salt and cayenne, and add half a teaspoonful of powdered mace for the whole. Cut the meat from a calf's foot and season it in the same way. Place a layer of kidney at the bottom of a pie-dish, strew over it two ozs. finely minced ham, and lay on this the slices of calf's foot. Repeat until the dish is nearly full. Put the hard boiled yolks of six eggs and half dozen forcemeat balls at the top. and pour over them ¼ pt. veal stock, flavored with lemon juice. Line the edges of the dish with a good crust, cover it with the same, and bake in a moderate oven. Though forcemeat balls are an improvement, they may be dispensed with.

Kidney pies are usually eaten cold.

LAMB PIE.

Take about 2 ℔s of the neck, breast or loin of lamb; cut it up into neat pieces and sprinkle over these sufficient salt, white pepper and minced parsley; put them into a pie-dish; take out some of the bones to stew for gravy and pour over them half ¼ pt. of cold water. Line the edges of the dish with good crust, cover it with the same and bake in a moderate oven. When the pie is sufficiently cooked, pour in a little good stock or meat jelly; bake 1½ hours. Lamb pie is usually eaten cold.

LANCASHIRE RAISED PIE.

Take 2 ℔s meat, (pork is most generally used), cut the lean into thin slices, seasoning each with pepper and salt. Stew the bones with half pint water, salt and pepper, for two hours, strain the gravy and set aside for use; when cold, it should be a stiff jelly. Melt over the fire in half pint water, about 4 ozs finely shred beef suet, with a pinch of salt. Put 1½ ℔s flour in a bowl, pour the boiling fat and water into the middle of it, and mix thoroughly, first with a spoon, and afterwards with the hands; knead to a stiff paste; cut off a piece large enough to form the lid of the pie; put the rest on the table and mould it into the form of a cone; flatten the sides with the palm of the hands, or when quite smooth press down the top of the cone with one hand, and with the other make the sides equally round. Great expedition is necessary, as the excellence of the pie depends upon its being placed in the oven while still warm.

Put in the lean meat, strew a little minced fat over each layer, and press it closely until the mould is full; egg the edges; roll out the cover and place it over the pie; make a small hole in the centre, through which the gravy can afterwards be put in; ornament with leaves of pastry, or according to fancy; brush over with the yolk of egg, and bake about 3 hours in a good oven. When the pie is done enough, pour a little of the jelly gravy (melted) through the hole in the top.

Lancashire raised pies are much more easily made in moulds. Beef suet is better than either butter or lard for this pastry, but if either of these latter is used, an extra ounce will be required for the same quantity of flour or water.

LARK PASTY.

Take 1 dozen larks, empty them, cut off their heads, legs and necks, and put into a saucepan with a few trimmings of veal, a sprig of parsley, one of thyme, a sliced carrot, and one pint water; let simmer gently till the liquid is considerably reduced and will jelly. Mince the livers of the larks finely and mix with half pound lean veal, half pound sausage meat, four ozs. unsmoked bacon, chopped parsley, powdered thyme, white pepper and salt; work up half of this forcemeat with a little light wine and fill the larks with it. Line a mould or pie-dish throughout with a good stiff crust; put a layer of loose mince meat at the bottom, lay the larks upon it and fill up with mince meat; place a few slices of bacon on top, cover, fasten the edges securely, and cut a slit in the middle through which the gravy may afterwards be poured; bake, and when sufficiently done strain the liquor into it through the hole in the top; ornament and let get quite cold before cutting. This dish is better to be kept a day or two before being eaten.

LARK PIE.

Take a dozen larks, empty them, cut off their heads, necks and legs; roll them in flour, and fill them with forcemeat. Place three or four slices each of bacon and lean ham at the bottom of a pie-dish; put the larks upon them and strew over them a little pepper, salt, parsley, and if required a shallot, cut into small pieces. Pour ½ pt weak stock over the whole, line the edges with good crust, cover and bake.

LARK PIE, A LA MELTON MOWBRAY.

Cut about 1 ℔ veal into small collops and fry them with an equal proportion of collops of ham or bacon, placing them at the bottom of a prepared pie-dish; fry 2 doz larks from which the gizzard only has been removed, by picking it out from under the thigh with the point of a knife; season with chopped parsley, truffle and shallot, pepper and salt, some mushroom catsup, button mushrooms, and a tablespoon of flour; moisten with ½ pt gravy or water, stir over the fire until it boils, and add the whole to the collops of veal, etc., contained in the pie-dish; cover with puff paste, aud bake 1½ hours.

LEICESTER PIE.

Cut 3 lbs pork (fat and lean) into pieces 2 in. long and ⅓ in. wide; season with pepper, salt and powdered sage, and put them aside. Mix a teaspoon of salt with 1 lb flour; stir into it with a knife, 4 ozs lard dissolved in ½ pt hot water; roll it out; line a greased tin mould with part of it; put in the pieces of pork; place the lid on top, and fasten the edges securely; bake in a moderate oven about 1¾ hours. The pie must be put into the oven when the paste is still warm.

LEICESTERSHIRE PIE.

Take 1 lb each cold fat bacon, cold roast beef or pork, and cored apples; line the edges of a pie-dish with crust made of drippings; fill with the meat and apples in alternate layers, seasoning each layer with salt, pepper and powdered ginger; pour ½ pt ale over all; place the lid on top, and bake 1½ hours in a good oven.

MELTON MOWBRAY PIES.

See Veal and Ham Pie.
See Yorkshire Veal Pie.
See Yorkshire Hare Pie.

MICHIGAN PIE.

Take 2 lbs chops from a neck of mutton; cut them

short and pare away some of the fat. Peel, core and slice about 2 lbs well flavored sour apples. Put a layer of them in the bottom of a pie-dish with a little sugar and ground allspice; place the chops next, and season with salt, pepper and finely chopped onion. Continue with alternate layers of apples and meat till all are used up. Make an ordinary crust, line the edges of the dish and cover over the top, adding $\frac{1}{4}$ pt gravy or water. Bake $1\frac{1}{2}$ hours in a moderate oven.

MUTTON PIE (1).

Trim a neck of mutton as for cutlets, removing the superfluous fat; separate the neck into thick cutlets; divide the short ribs and scrag end into equal sized pieces about 2 inches square; season highly with pepper and salt, and place in a stew-pan with enough water to cover the meat; set to stew for $\frac{1}{2}$ hour over a slow fire; the gravy must now be strained from the meat, freed from grease, and poured again into the meat; add six onions and eight potatoes; put the lid on the stew-pan, and set the whole to stew gently for another $\frac{1}{2}$ hour; arrange the cutlets, etc., neatly round the pie-dish; lift the potatoes and onions into the centre without smashing them; boil down the gravy to the quantity required to fill up the pie; sprinkle 2 doz oysters over the surface; cover the pie with potato-paste, bake for an hour and serve a sauce of gravy separately.

MUTTON PIE (2).

Make a seasoning of chopped parsley, powdered savory herbs, an onion, pepper and salt. Cut from 2 to 3 lbs neat chops from the loin or neck of mutton, free from bone and most of the fat; put them well covered

with the above seasoning, into a pie-dish. Cut three
kidneys into halves and each half into two parts; distribute them equally amongst the meat; pour in ½ pt
veal broth or water; bake with a puff or good suet
paste. A tablespoon of catsup and two of port wine
may be added to the gravy, with less water.

MUTTON PIES—SMALL.

See Mutton Patties.

OLIVE PIE—BEEF.

Make a good forcemeat of equal parts of suet, and
finely grated bread crumbs, with plenty of finely mixed
parsley, pepper, salt, grated nutmeg and the well beaten
yolk of an egg. Cut thin slices four inches long and
two wide from the inside of a fillet of beef; spread a
layer of forcemeat upon each slice, and roll it up
securely; place the rolls side by side in a deep pie-dish
piling them high in the centre; pour ½ pt gravy over
them; line the edges of the dish with good crust; place
a cover of the same on the top, and bake about 1¼ hours
in a moderate oven. A little wine and catsup will improve the gravy.

OLIVE PIE—VEAL.

Line the edges of a pie-dish with good puff paste.
Cut 2 ℔s fillet of veal into slices ¼ in. thick, 4 in. long
and 2 in. wide. Make a forcemeat with 4 ozs minced
veal, 4 ozs finely shred suet, 4 ozs grated bread crumbs,
3 tablespoons chopped parsley, a teaspoon mixed sweet
herbs, salt, pepper, powdered mace, grated lemon-rind,
and the yolks of eggs, well beaten. Season the slices of
veal with pepper and salt; place a slice of fat bacon on
each, and a little of the forcemeat, and roll them up

neatly and securely. Make the forcemeat which remains into balls; place them amongst the veal olives in a pie-dish, pour over them $\frac{1}{2}$ pt nicely seasoned gravy; line the edges of the dish with a good crust; place a cover of the same over the top, egg over and bake in a good oven. Lemon juice and sherry greatly improve the gravy. This pie is good eaten either hot or cold.

PARTRIDGE PIE. (1).

The mould being prepared, take 1 lb veal cutlets, cut into very thin slices, and with them cover the bottom of the pie; add a layer of forcemeat (2), then the partridges, which should be boned, filled with the forcemeat, then cut in half and placed on the layer below. Follow with a few more slices of veal and forcemeat, and between each layer place (if convenient) a truffle or two, chopped rather fine. Season the veal and partridges before putting them in the crust. Having proceeded thus far, put in a little water or broth. If truffles are used, and any are left, cut some into pieces about one inch long and half inch thick, and place them between each layer. *The mould must be filled.* This being so, put on a top crust (hot water paste); make a hole in the centre to let out the steam, and bake $1\frac{1}{2}$ to 2 hours in a moderate oven. When the pie is slightly cool, remove the false top and fill the pie up with jelly.

PARTRIDGE PIE. (2).

Pluck, draw and singe a brace of young partridges; season them inside and out, with salt, cayenne and pow-dered mace; cover with this rashers of bacon, and put into a stewpan with $\frac{1}{4}$ pt veal stock or water; put on the lid and let them simmer $\frac{1}{2}$ hour as gently as possible. Spread some forcemeat at the bottom of a pie-dish, take

4

out the birds and cut them into quarters; lay half the
bacon which was tied round them upon the forcemeat;
pack in the partridges and cover with forcemeat and
bacon; pour in three tablespoons of gravy in which the
partridges were simmered; line the edges of the dish
with good pastry and cover with the same; make a hole
in the centre and bake in a quick oven; before sending
to the table pour in $\frac{1}{4}$ pt good gravy slightly flavored
with lemon juice.

PATE DE GIBIER.

Bone four partridges, or two partridges and two
grouse; cut up a hare; season all with salt and cayenne;
put inside each partridge a good sized truffle and a portion of forcemeat; mould the pastry according to the
proper shape; cover the bottom of the pie with slices of
fat bacon; place upon this, half the hare with forcemeat,
then put in the partridges, etc., two with their breasts
upwards and two with their breasts downwards; place
the remainder of the hare and forcemeat upon these,
with a good slice of fat bacon and a bay leaf on top;
cover with pastry, ornament and bake; when done and
almost cold, pour into it through a hole in the centre $\frac{1}{4}$
pt dissolved gravy-jelly, made by stewing the bones in
water and mixing the stock with a little gelatine.

PATE DE FOIS GRAS—IMITATION.

Take the livers from three fine fat geese, *remove the
gall bladders carefully,* and lay the livers in milk for six
or eight hours to whiten them; cut them in halves and
put these halves aside for forcemeat.   Sort, wash, scrub
and peel $\frac{3}{4}$ ℔ truffles, carefully preserving the cuttings;
slice a third of them into narrow strips like lardoons

and stick them into the remainder of the livers $\frac{3}{4}$ inch apart; sprinkle over them pepper, salt and spice, and put in a cool place until the forcemeat is prepared. Cover the bottom of the pie with thin rashers of ham, fat and lean together; spread evenly on these, part of the forcemeat, then put in the three livers with the slices of truffles stuck in them, and afterwards forcemeat; intersperse amongst the contents of the pie the remainder of the truffles and cover the whole with two or three more slices of ham or bacon; cover with pastry, ornament, egg and bake.

PERIGORD PIE.

See Game Pie—Perigord.

PHEASANT PIE.

After boning a large bird, partly fill with fillets of veal and ham, cut in about $\frac{1}{4}$ in squares, and forcemeat, in equal proportions. The bird may now be put into the mould whole, or it may be cut into halves or quarters, afterwards filling up with jelly.

PICNIC PIE. (1).

Butter a deep pie-dish; quarter three hard boiled eggs and lay round the bottom to form a wreath, ornamenting the same with chopped parsley and strips of boiled tongue, to form a star. Have ready a par-boiled chicken, finely minced and highly flavored with mace, mushrooms, pepper, salt and chopped herbs. Put in layers of this, then strips of bacon, then chicken, till the dish is nearly full, and a good quantity of strong, clear, well-flavored jelly (made from chicken bones); put crust of butter and flour over whole. Bake $1\frac{1}{2}$ hours and turn out.

PICNIC PIE. (2)

Boned lereret, etc., and three boned pigeons. Force-meat balls of pounded chicken, flavored with herbs, salt, butter, three hard boiled eggs and truffles. All the above to be put in layers in a standing crust, and covered with aspic jelly.

PIE OF SMALL BIRDS.

The birds intended for this pie should be stuffed with the following preparation: Soak the crumbs of a French roll in a little milk; put it into a stewpan with 2 ozs butter, a little grated lemon peel, shallot, chopped parsley, nutmeg, pepper, salt, a pinch of aromatic herbs, and three yolks of eggs; stir over the fire until it becomes a compact paste, and use it to fill the insides of the birds. Line the bottom of the pie-dish with fried collops of beef and place thereon the birds in neat order; pour some fine herb sauce over these; add hard boiled yolks of eggs; cover with puff-paste; bake 1¼ hours.

PIGEON PIE. (1).

Having lined the mould, cover the bottom with about 1 ℔ rump steak, cut in thin slices and well beaten. Bone and stuff with forcemeat as many pigeons as may be required; fill with jelly. It is usual to add two or three hard boiled eggs, cut in quarters.

PIGEON PIE. (2).

After the bird has been thoroughly washed inside and out, and dried, fill it with a highly-seasoned and very savory forcemeat. Rub the inside with a compound of pepper, ground allspice, one pounded clove, and about the same weight of cinnamon, nutmeg and grated lemon peel. Put into a stew-pan one teacupful of lemon juice, one of orange juice, and one of port; four or five sprigs of parsley, and the same of sweet marjoram and thyme. Let this commence to boil, then put in the bird, and allow it to stew very slowly for nearly an hour. Keep the pan closed the whole time, and send to table as hot as possible, garnished with slices of lemon and red currant jelly, or pieces of cold aspic.

PLOVER PIE.

Pluck, draw and skin three plovers, and truss them as for roasting. Lay ½ ℔ rump steak, cut into convenient sized pieces, at the bottom of a moderate sized pie-dish, seasoning highly with pepper and salt; lay the birds upon them, and beside each bird place the yolk of a hard boiled egg. Clean one dozen mushrooms, cut the stalks off, and lay them at the top of the pie; pour in ½ pt good brown gravy. Line the edges of the dish with puff-paste, and finish as usual.

PORK AND APPLE PIE.

Cut a sufficient quantity of pork chops (free from fat) into three or four pieces each, leaving the bone attached to the meat; roll in flour and season with salt, pepper and allspice; peel, quarter, core and slice apples, in quantity and bulk about half that of the pork; invert a cup of cider or stock at the bottom of the pie-dish. At the bottom put a layer of pork, then apples, so on, finishing with sliced apples at the top. Pour in a small cupful of stock or cider; cover with a good solid crust.

PORK PIE.

Take the knuckle end of a leg of young pork, say 4 ℔s

or 5 lbs; take the meat off the bone; cut into thin slices, and season.   Be careful not to put in too much fat.

Make the jelly by boiling the bones, skin and trimmings, without fat; season with pepper, allspice, salt, two small onions, and two or three leaves of sage.   Both pie and jelly should be slightly warmed on filling in the jelly.

PORK PIES (1).

Pork pies are generally made of the trimmings taken from a hog when it is cut up; make and shape the pies according to directions below; the pies must be moulded while the paste is warm, and are more easily made with a mould.   (If a mould is not at hand, the pies may be moulded in a warmed jelly pot).   Cut the meat into small pieces, keeping the fat and lean separate; season with salt, pepper, finely shred sage leaves, (or powdered sage), and cayenne.   Pack the fat and lean closely into the pie in alternate layers until it is filled; put on the cover, press and pinch the edges and ornament; brush over with a well-beaten egg, and bake in a slow oven, as the meat is solid and requires to be cooked through. Neither water nor bone should be put into pork pies, and the outside pieces will be hard unless they are cut small and pressed closely together.   The bones and trimmings of the pork may be stewed to make gravy, which should be boiled until it will jelly when cold, and when this has been nicely flavored, a little may be poured into the pie after it is baked, through an opening made in the top.   When pies are made small they require a quicker oven than large ones.

Special Pastry for Pork Pies.—Put ¼ ℔ finely shred beef suet, (or 5 ozs lard, or ¼ ℔ mutton suet), and 1 oz fresh butter into a sauce pan with ½ pt boiling water and a pinch of salt; stir the mixture until the fat is dissolved, and pour it boiling hot into 1½ lbs flour; knead to a stiff paste, adding more water if required; shape the dough and get it into the oven while it is warm. If the pie is to be baked in a mould, lay a piece of the proper shape in the bottom; press long pieces in the sides, and fasten them to the top and bottom with white of egg. If a mould is not to be used, cut off as much pastry as will make the cover, and wrap it up in a cloth to keep warm; mould the rest with both hands into the shape of a cone, making the sides firm and smooth; press the top down with the knuckles of the right hand, and with the left press the outside closely to keep it firm and smooth, keeping the walls equally thick in every part; fill the pie, put on the cover, pinch the edges, fasten securely with the white of egg, ornament, egg over and bake in a slow oven if the pie is large, in a quicker oven if it be small.

PORK PIES. (2).

14 lbs flour.	4½ lbs lard.
2 ozs salt.	16 lbs pork, (free from bone
Seasoning, 3 ozs pepper and	and gristle.)
4 ozs salt.	

Sift the flour with 2 ounces of salt, four and a half pounds of lard; rub half of it in the flour, making a bay; the other half, put in a pan with three and a half pints of water; place it on the stove; when it boils pour into the bay, and mix at once with spatula, till the flour is well in, then finish with the hand; spread it out on the stone to cool a short time, then put it all together; weigh off pieces for the pies, and mould them round.

Suppose for a four-pound pie, one and three-quarters of a pound; or two-pound pie, one pound of paste; one-pound pie, half pound, and so on for all sizes. When moulded round knock them out, so that they are similar in shape to a cocked hat, flattened thicker in the middle than at the edge. Allow them to lie on the stone till they are comparatively stiff, but not too much so; then raising them, some by means of blocks, some by hoops: For a four-pound pie, an oval or elliptic hoop, its transverse or longest diameter eight inches, its conjugate or shortest diameter six inches wide and five inches high: A two-pound pie, a round hoop five inches in diameter, four high; push the thickest part of the piece of paste, that has been knocked out and laid by to stiffen, down the centre of the hoop to form a bottom, drawing it up the sides gradually, so as to be thinnest at the top. The size of the hoops can, of course, be regulated according to the pie required.

The meat required for the above would be sixteen pounds free from bone, also taking out what skin and gristle may be in it, and cutting it up fine in a meat machine; when cut mix it with six ounces of seasoning, with a quart of water, putting two pounds of meat in the four-pound pie, one in the two-pound, etc. When filled, the lid can be cut from the paste that is over, with the hoops in which they were raised, and placed on the pies, wetting the edges; afterwards trimming them, washing them down with egg, and decorating with fancy leaves and roses cut from the paste. The four-pound pie would require about two hours' baking in a nice oven, and the two pound, about an hour and a quarter, with either the hoops or paper round them.

PORK PIES. (Small).

4 lbs flour.   1 lb butter.
1 lb mutton suet.   Salt and pepper to taste.
8 lbs neck of pork.   A little powdered sage.

Dry the flour well, mince the suet, and put them with
the butter into a sauce-pan, to be made hot, adding a
little salt. When melted, mix it up into a stiff paste
and put it before the fire with a cloth over it until ready
to make up. Chop the pork into small pieces, season
with white pepper, salt and powdered sage; divide the
paste into rather small pieces, raise it in a round or oval
form, fill with the meat, and bake in a brisk oven.

POULARDE PIE.

See Capon Raised Pie.

PRAIRIE HEN PIE.

Choose two plump birds, pluck, draw and wipe them;
cut off the legs at the first joint, and remove the heads;
season them inside with pepper, salt, butter and minced
parsley, mixed together. Line a pie-dish with slices of
ham, and proceed as for game pie, using good beef
stock.

RABBIT PIE.

Cut a young rabbit into neat joints, lay them in luke-
warm water for ½ hour, then drain and dry. Cut ½ lb
streaky bacon into strips, and ¾ lb lean veal into inch
squares. Line the edges of a pie-dish with good puff
paste; put the veal into the pie, then the rabbit, and
lastly the bacon; intersperse the contents with forcemeat balls and hard boiled eggs, cut into quarters
lengthwise; season each layer with savory herbs;

moisten the whole with stock or water, but do not entirely cover the meat; finish as usual.

Truffles or mushrooms and port wine mixed with some good gravy, may be poured into the pie through a hole in the top, when it is taken from the oven.

RABBIT PIE—RAISED.

Take the meat from a fine young rabbit, cut it into small pieces, and season with salt, pepper and grated nutmeg. Cut ½ ℔ fat bacon into dice. Pack tightly in the mould the pieces of meat and bacon, interspersing amongst them the yolks of 3 or 4 hard boiled eggs, cut into quarters lengthwise; pour over all a little tomato sauce, or a spoonful or two of good gravy, which will jelly when cold.

ROOK PIE.

Skin and draw ½ doz young rooks; cut out the back-bones; season with salt and pepper; put them in a deep dish with ½ pt water; lay some bits of butter over them; cover the dish with a tolerably thick crust. Let the pie be well baked. Rooks require long stewing, or they will not be tender. The breasts are the only part of the birds which are really worth using, and when the other portions are put into the dish, care should be taken to cut out the spine and the flesh near it, to the width of ¾ in., or the pie will have a bitter taste.

RUMP-STEAK PIE (1).

Take about 3 ℔s rump-steak, the under cut being the best; cut in thin slices and beat; season and fill mould with alternate layers of meat, forcemeat, a few button mushrooms, and three hard boiled eggs, cut in slices. Fill the pie before it gets cold, with a jelly made with

½ ℔ beef gravy and 2 ozs gelatine, seasoned with pepper, mace, catsup and salt.

RUMP-STEAK PIE (2).

Take 2 ℔s rump-steak and cut them into small collops; season with minced parsley, pepper and salt; dust with flour and lay them around the prepared mould; fill with alternate layer of potatoes, thinly sliced, and meat.   Finish and bake.

SAVORY PIE.

Butter a pie dish very thickly, and cover the bottom with a layer of chopped mushrooms; place upon them 2 ozs tapioca soaked for 10 minutes in ¼ pt water; sprinkle over an onion and three sage leaves chopped fine; add 3 hard boiled eggs, chopped small, and season with salt and pepper; lay bits of butter on the surface; cover and bake.

SEA PIE.

This is made of any scraps of meat, properly seasoned.

SHEEP'S HEAD PIE.

Scald, clean and boil a sheap's head, also some feet; cut off the meat in neat pieces, packing them closely in a pie-dish;   season with salt, pepper and finely minced onion; lay bits of butter upon them and pour over a little of the liquor in which the head and feet were boiled.   Cover the dish with pastry and bake till done. When cold, take off the crust, and serve it cut into thin slices, garnished with parsley.

This makes a nice breakfast or luncheon dish.

SNIPE PIE.

Parboil the birds in bouillon and a little white wine,

seasoned with a grated onion, pepper, salt and nutmeg. Line a dish with forcemeat; put in the birds with a little of the soup, and small pieces of butter; cover with a thick layer of forcemeat; finish and serve with supreme or other sauce.

SQUAB PIE.

This is generally made of mutton. Take a deep dish and fill it with layers of mutton chops, apples cut as for other pies, and finely shred onions; season the layers with pepper and salt, and sweeten the apples with sugar; cover with a thick crust and bake 2 to 3 hours.

SWEETBREADS PIE.

Take two or more fresh sweetbreads; soak, blanch and cool then; cut each one into three pieces, and simmer $\frac{1}{4}$ hour in white stock with about 2 doz mushrooms. Lay them in a dish, put the mushrooms among them and also 6 or 8 forcemeat balls, the green tips of asparagus, and the hard boiled yolks of eggs. Thicken the gravy with white thickening, add pepper and salt, and pour over the meat. Lay slices of fat bacon on the top of the meat, cover with good pastry, and bake in a moderate oven.

Ox palates are often used in connection with sweetbreads, in making the above pie.

SWISS PIE.

Cut 3 lbs rump steak in moderate pieces, and split $\frac{1}{2}$ doz mutton kidneys; put both on the fire with enough water to cover them, with an onion cut in small rings, and seasoned with pepper and salt. Have some potatoes ready boiled, but not too much, cut them in quarters, brown them and put round the dish in rows on the top of the meat.

A pretty way of dishing this, is to put it in a game pie-dish.

TONGUE PIE.

Use equal parts of cold tongue and cold poultry or roast pork; season and place them in layers; add sufficient cold gravy to moisten the meat.

TRIPE PIE.

Tripe which is to be used for a pie should be stewed and allowed to jelly in the liquor in which it was boiled. Line the inside of a pie-dish with good pastry; put a slice of tender steak or a little undressed ham at the bottom of the dish; place upon this the tripe with the jellied gravy adhering to it; season with pepper and salt; place pieces of butter on the meat, and pour in two or three spoonsful of good brown gravy. Cover with a good crust and bake.

UNION LEAGUE PIE.

Take thin slices from a calf's head when cold, and some of the brains, pieces of cold lamb, pickled tongue, a few slices of bacon, and some hard-boiled eggs cut neatly into rings; with these fill a pie-dish. Season with pepper, salt and cayenne; arrange the meat in layers; see that all is well seasoned; fill up the dish with a rich gravy. Bake about an hour in a slow oven, with a cover of flour and water paste, and remove when cold. The pie must then be turned out on a dish. Garnish with parsley and pickled eggs, sliced.

VEAL PIES.

Any part of lean veal free from fat and bone may be used for a pie; the loin and the best end of the neck are

excellent for the purpose, when the bone and the greater
part of the fat are removed; slices from the fillet are
also very good. The knuckle, part of the leg, the breast,
and the shoulder may also be used, but they should be
partially stewed before being put into the pie, to render
them tender.

Veal pies may be made plain or rich, according to
choice. Ham or bacon, forcemeat balls, hard-boiled
eggs, sweetbreads, sausage, oysters, potatoes, mushrooms, truffles, etc., may all be introduced. If ham or
bacon has been cured with saltpetre, there is danger it
will make the veal red, and so spoil the appearance of
the pie; on this account dressed ham or bacon is to be
preferred. The following recipes for veal pies may be
varied to suit convenience and taste.

VEAL AND HAM PIE.

Cut 1½ ℔s veal-cutlets into small collops; also ½ ℔ ham
or streaky bacon; chop a few mushrooms, some parsley
and shallot, and fry these with 1 oz butter, in a small
stewpan; season with pepper and salt; add a little catsup, a tablespoon of flour and ½ pt gravy or water: Stir
this sauce over the fire till it boils, then add the juice of
half a lemon, and use it to mix with the veal and ham,
as they are placed in alternate layers in the pie-dish;
place hard-boiled yolks of eggs on the surface, cover
with puff-paste; when the pie is done, pour in a little
gravy.

VEAL PIE.

Put a piece of the knuckle of veal into a stewpan,
cover with water, let it boil up, and simmer till tender;
when cold, divide into small pieces. Butter a plain
round or oval shape, and cover the bottom with the

yolks and whites of hard-boiled eggs, neatly arranged;
place over these pieces of the meat and gristle, seasoning
with salt, pepper, pounded mace and grated lemon-peel;
pour in a little of the gravy in which the meat was
boiled, (which ought to form a strong jelly) and fill the
dish with the meat, hard-boiled eggs, and sliced beet-
root, so arranged that the color will contrast prettily:
pour in as much gravy as will cover the ingredients,
and bake in a good oven. When quite cold, turn it out;
it will have a glazed appearance.

VEAL PIE—RAISED.

Take 1½ lbs lean veal and 1 lb ham; cut three parts of
the veal into neat pieces and season with pepper and
chopped mushrooms; mince the remainder of the veal
with an equal quantity of fat bacon; pound the mixture
in a mortar, and season with salt and cayenne, a small
piece of onion; herbs and spices may be added to the
forcemeat if liked. Line a mould with pastry; cover
the bottom with forcemeat, and fill the pie with alternate
layers of thinly sliced ham, veal and forcemeat. Lay thin
slices of fat bacon on the top of the meat, put a bay-leaf
on that, finish and bake. Half an hour after the pie is
taken from the oven, pour into it through a pointed
strainer placed in the hole in the top, a little highly seasoned gravy, which will jelly when cold.

The jelly may be made by stewing a couple of hours, a
calf's foot and the bones and trimmings of the veal,
with an onion stuck with two cloves, a small bunch of
herbs, pepper, salt, grated nutmeg, in stock or water.
If liked, the pieces of veal in the pie may be larded.

VEAL PIES—RAISED, (Small).

Take the lean part of the best end of a neck of veal,

with half its weight of thinly sliced bacon; divide the
meat into inch squares.   Put the bones and trimmings
of the meat into a sacepan, cover with water, add flavoring ingredients, and stew the liquor until it is strong
enough to jelly when cold.   Put the veal into a stewpan,
cover with the strained stock, and add about 1 gill
cream, and a few mushrooms if desired; simmer gently
for an hour, then let it get cold.   Line some small pate
moulds; fill with the preparation, cover and bake till
done.   Serve cold.

VEAL PIE—Windsor.

Fill a dish with alternate layers of lean veal, cut in
slices ½ in. thick, and thin slices of lean ham; season
each layer with powdered mace and white pepper. Place
a dish with a weight over the meat and press it for ½
hour; pour upon it strong veal gravy, as much as will
jelly and cover it, when cold; add a slice of fresh butter;
cover with good pastry and bake.

VENISON AND HARE PIE.

Take the flesh in one piece from a neck of venison and
cut it to the length of the pie-dish; season with salt,
cayenne and pounded mace.   Divide the hare into pieces
not larger than an egg; take out the bones and fill the
cavities with good forcement.   Line the edges of a pie-
dish with good pastry; lay the venison in the centre and
arrange the pieces of hare closely around it; fill up the
empty space with forcemeat and lay 2 or 3 spoonsful of
jellied gravy on top. Cover, ornament and bake. When
done enough pour in, through a pointed strainer, a little
additional gravy, made of the trimmings of the hare and
venison, properly seasoned.

VEAL LIVER PATE.

Mix separately, and afterwards together, 1 ℔ calf's liver and 10 ozs. fat bacon; season with pepper, salt and pounded mace; add chopped parsley, 2 ozs. finely-minced lean ham, and an onion, sliced and browned in fat; mix thoroughly, and mix with them first the beaten yolks, and afterwards the well-whisked whites, of two eggs; line a mould with thin slices of fat bacon and put in the mince; place slices of bacon on the top and bake gradually; let get cold and turn it upon a dish; garnish with parsley.

VENISON PASTY.

This is generally made of the portions of the venison which do not roast very well, such as the neck, breast and shoulders. The pasty should properly contain venison *only.* Wash the venison in vinegar, sprinkle sugar upon it and hang in a cool, airy place for, say, ten days; when used, sponge it over with lukewarm water and dry with a soft cloth; bone, trim away all the skin and cut into pieces 2 in. square. Line a baking dish entirely with good stiff paste (see below); put in the pieces of meat, fat and lean together, or if there is not fat enough add a thin slice of the firm fat of the loin or neck of mutton; season with pepper and salt; put over ½ ℔ butter and pour in ¼ pt. stock or water; cover with thick pastry, ornament, make an opening in the centre, and lay a sheet of letter paper over it; bake. While baking put the bones and trimmings into a stew-pan with powdered mace, salt, pepper and 3 pts. of water; simmer till strong and pleasantly flavored and reduced to less than half the quantity; strain, let cool and remove the fat. When the pie .s done enough heat the gravy with a little lemon-juice and port; pour it into the pie so that the gravy will penetrate all parts. Serve hot or cold. If the undercrust is omitted the pie will not need to bake as long. Unless the pastry is thick it will be burnt up before the meat is none enough. The venison is often partially stewed before being put into the pie.

The pastry for venison pasty should be good and short, but stiff. For a rich pasty it may be made in the proportion of 10 ozs. butter to 1 ℔. flour, and worked to a smooth, stiff paste with 2 eggs and lukewarm water. For an ordinary pasty, rub 3 or 4 ozs. butter into 1 ℔. flour, and work to a smooth, stiff paste with a beaten egg and lukewarm water.

VENISON PIE.

Proceed with venison alone as, for Venison and Hare Pie.

WASHINGTON PIE.

Line a buttered oblong tin mould with short paste; fill the pie with alternate slices of pork, bacon and apples; season between each layer with chopped onion, pepper and salt, and chopped sage-leaves; pour in good gravy; cover the top with paste; egg it over and bake 1½ hours.

WOODCOCK PIE.

Line the edges of a dish with good puff-paste; place at the bottom, a slice of thin veal well seasoned with pepper, salt and pounded mace; place on this a slice of thin lean ham. Pluck four woodcocks carefully, so as not to injure the tender flesh; do not open them, but season with salt, pepper and mace, covering them with layers of bacon; pack them closely into the dish and fill up the empty space with hard-boiled plover's or hen's eggs; pour over them 1 pt. beef gravy, so strong that it will jelly when cold; cover with pastry, ornament and finish as usual.   It should be eaten cold.

WOODCOCK PIE—RAISED (COLD).

Bone four woodcocks; put the bones and trimmings into a saucepan with a shallot, a small onion and a sprig of thyme; cover with stock and let simmer till the gravy is strong and good.   Remove the gizzard from the trail, pound and mix it with forcemeat.   Place the woodcocks, skin downward, open upon a board; spread over them a layer of forcemeat; then 2 or 3 sliced truffles and another layer of forcemeat; fold the skin over and restore the birds to something of their original shape.   Line a pie-mould with pastry; put a layer of forcemeat at the bottom; place two woodcocks over this, covering them with a few slices of truffles and a thin layer of forcemeat; put in the other two woodcocks with a little more truffles and another layer of forcemeat; place over all some thin slices of bacon. Cover and finish.   Half an hour after it has been taken from the oven, pour in a little of the gravy from the bones, which should be strong enough to form a jelly when cold.

WOODCOCK PIE—RAISED (HOT).

Divide four woodcocks into quarters; line a pie-mould with pastry and fill it with alternate layers of forcemeat and pieces of woodcock; cover and bake; take out of oven and pour into it some good brown sauce made of the trimmings of the woodcock stewed in beef gravy. Serve hot upon a dish covered with a napkin.   If liked a hollow place may be left in the centre of the pie, into which a piece of the crumb of bread, covered with fat bacon, may be placed whilst the pie is being baked; when done enough this hollow may be filled with sliced truffles mixed in brown sauce.

YALE PIE.

Put 3 ℔s. or 4 ℔s. steak, seasoned with pepper and salt, into a dish. Cut in pieces two chickens; lay them on the steak and over them put 1 doz. oysters without the liquor; add ½ doz. hard-boiled eggs; pour in ½ pt. strong ale and cover with fresh mushrooms and ½ ℔. calf's-foot jelly; cover with paste and bake in a brisk oven.

YORKSHIRE HARE PIE.

Remove all the flesh from a hare in as large pieces as possible—that is, take out the fillets, remove the shoulders and hind quarters, and bone them; cut all the meat into collops about ¼ in. thick and set them aside on a plate; with the carcass and trimmings and a calf's foot make some well-seasoned aspic jelly; prepare also some thin slices of ham and hard-boiled eggs, and finish as Yorkshire veal pie, using aromatic seasoning. These pies may be varied by using pork, veal, mutton, venison, poultry or any kind of game, instead of veal or hare.

YORKSHIRE PIE.

Bone a goose, or hare, two grouse and four snipes; spread them out on the table; season with aromatic spices, pepper and salt; fill them with pork-sausage meat; sew them up with string; bake them until done; proceed with them in the usual way, using thick slices of cooked ham and sausage meat in place of forcemeat. When the pie is baked, pour in the reduced stock from the bones; and when cold the next day, garnish the top with aspic jelly.

YORKSHIRE VEAL PIE.

¾ lb thin slices ham or streaky bacon (previously par-
boiled),

1½ lbs. veal collops,
4 hard-boiled eggs,
Sufficient aspic jelly.

Pour a thin layer of aspic jelly at the bottom of a pie-dish, and upon this place in neat circles a layer of veal collops; season with pepper and salt, chopped parsley and shallot; then put a layer of ham, and upon this a layer of hard-boiled eggs cut in slices; repeat the seasoning and aspic jelly, and so on, until the whole of the ingredients are used up. Cover the pie-dish with stiff flour and water paste; bake on a baking sheet containing a little water to prevent the possibility of the aspic jelly contained in the pie from being dried up. Bake 1¼ hours in a moderate oven; when done, set in a cold place till the next day; it may then be turned out whole on a dish, garnished with fresh parsley.

CHAPTER V.

FISH PIES.

Salmon, trout, codfish, turbot, haddock, mackerel, etc., —indeed any kind of fish tolerably free from small bones, are adapted to this purpose. Whichever kind is intended for the pie should be freed from skin and bone, etc., and cut into large scollops; a mould should be lined with paste, a thin layer of Bechamel sauce spread over the bottom, and over this place a close layer of scollops of fish; season with chopped mushrooms, parsley and shallot, fillets of anchovies, capers, nutmeg, pepper and salt, and slices of hard-boiled eggs; repeat the sauce, fish, etc., until the pie is filled up; cover in the usual manner; bake 1½ hours and serve.

From 2 lbs. to 3 lbs. of fish is the quantity supposed to be used in reference to above recipe.

In place of the Bechamel sauce, forcemeat may be used or oysters and bread crumbs; and the seasoning may be varied according to taste.

Fish pies may be served with any sauce desired, separately in a boat.

CARP PIE.

Line the edges of a pie-dish with a good light crust; stuff a medium-sized carp with oyster forcemeat; sew it up to prevent this escaping, and lay it in the middle of the dish; put round it pieces of eel about 1½ in. long, which have been already partly cooked. Take ¾ pt. of the liquor in which the eel was stewed; put it with a gill of port, a little salt and cayenne, an onion stuck with cloves, and a blade of mace; let these simmer gently till reduced to ½ pt. gravy, which may be thickened with flour and butter; pour this over the fish; cover with crust and bake.

COD PIE.

Steep over night the middle cut of a small cod, in salt and water; wash well and season with cayenne, pepper and salt. Put a little good stock or broth into a pie-dish, with small pieces of butter; place the fish in the dish; cover with paste and bake. Serve with sauce made as follows: ½ pt. cream, spoonful of broth, a little grated lemon peel, and a small piece of roux. Allow it simply to come to a boil, and when the pie is baked enough, raise the crust and pour the same over the the fish.

COD PIE—FRESH.

Fill a deep pie-dish three parts full, with pieces of fresh cod about 2 inches square; season with salt, cayenne and grated nutmeg; lay 2 dozen oysters on the top, with bits of butter over them; cover with a good crust and bake.

COD PIE—SALT.

After soaking the cod for 12 hours, simmer ¼ hour; cut into pieces about 2 inches square. Place a layer of sliced potatoes, half boiled at the bottom of a pie-dish, then a layer of fish, and one of sliced onions, partly boiled; season each layer with pepper and pounded mace (no salt). Melt some butter and mix with it mustard, catsup, and essence of anchovies; pour this over the pie; cover; bake. If preferred, mashed potatoes may be spread on top of the pie, in place of the pastry.

CRAB PIE.

Boil a moderate-sized crab, and, when it is done, pick out the meat, and mix with it a little butter, pepper and salt, and if too liquid, bread crumbs, sufficient to give it the proper consistency, after adding three spoonsful of vinegar. Clean out the shell, and place the mixture in it, covering it slightly with bread crumbs; heat it before the fire or in the oven; brown it with a salamander, sprinkle a little cayenne over it, and it will be ready for serving.

EEL PIE (1).

Wash and skin 1 ℔. eels; cut them into 2 in length; line the bottom of a pie-dish with a slight layer of force-meat, on the top of which place the eels, with a seasoning of chopped parsley, one shallot, grated nutmeg, the juice of half a lemon, and pepper and salt to taste; pour over it some strong gravy. Bake, and when sufficiently done, heat $\frac{1}{2}$ pt. bechamel sauce, and pour into the pie, before serving. Oysters may be used in place of forcemeat.

EEL PIE (2).

Having skinned and cleaned 2 lbs. large sized eels, divide them into pieces 2 or 3 in. long. Cut off the heads, tails and fins, and boil them with lemon peel, a shallot, a blade of mace, and as much veal or mutton broth as will cover the eels in the pie-dish; thicken with butter and flour, and add the juice of half a lemon; when strained and cool, turn the broth into the pie-dish over the eels, sprinkle with pepper, salt and chopped parsley, and cover with puff-paste. Bake in a moderate oven: or the eels may be stewed first for $\frac{1}{2}$ hour and finished in the pie.

FISH AND OYSTER PIE.

Clear the meat from the bones of any cold fish which has been left over from a previous occasion. Cod, haddock, sole, or plaice are best for the purpose. Place a layer of the fish in the bottom of the pie-dish, and sprinkle it with pepper and salt; over this put a layer of bread crumbs, on which place a few oysters, a little chopped parsley and grated nutmeg, and repeat the layers till the dish is full. Before covering, pour over the pie the liquor of the oysters, and a little melted butter or white sauce; it may be covered with strips of puff pastry, laid trelliswise, or it may be simply covered with bread crumbs. Bake for about twenty minutes.

FLOUNDERS PIE.

Clean and dry well in a cloth some flounders; boil and separate the fish from the bones; boil the bones in a saucepan with 1 pt. of the water in which the fish was boiled, parsley, lemon-peel, pepper and salt; when reduced to the quantity required for gravy, make a crust and line a pie-dish; put bits of butter in the bottom, then a layer of fish; strew with chopped parsley and sprinkle with flour, pepper and salt; proceed thus until the dish is full, pour in the gravy, and bake with a top crust.

HALIBUT PIE.

Take 4 lbs. fresh halibut (the middle of the fish is best); season with salt, pepper, cayenne and powdered mace. Take off the skin, cut the flesh into thick slices, and put them into a pie-dish with $\frac{1}{4}$ lb. of butter, broken into pieces, and a little anchovy sauce. Line the edges of the dish with pastry, cover and bake.

HERRING PIE.

Choose some herrings with soft roes; scale and clean them well; cut off the heads, tails and fins; split them open, take out the bones, and season their inner surface with salt and pepper Line the edges of a buttered pie-dish with a good crust; spread over the bottom a layer ½ in. thick of equal parts of finely minced appl s and onions; place the herring on this, and cover with an-other layer of apples and onions; sprinkle the surface with grated nutmeg and finely shred lemon rind; place pieces of butter on top, pour in a little water, cover and bake.

LING PIE.

Take 3 ℔s. of the thin part of a salt ling, wash in two or three waters, and let soak for 2 hours; put it into a fish-kettle with as much water as will cover it, and let boil slowly until done. Take off the skin, and put layers of the fish into a pie-dish, with four hard-boiled eggs cut into slices, chopped parsley, with salt, cayenne and pounded mace strewn amongst them; add 3 ozs. butter, in small pieces; pour over the fish ¼ pt. gravy. Line the edges of the dish with a good crust, cover, egg and bake. Before serving pour a cupful of warm cream into the pie.

LOBSTER PIE.

Pick the meat from two medium sized, freshly boiled lobsters, and cut into neat small pieces. Bruise the shells and spawn in a mortar; put them into a stewpan with ¼ pt. water, vinegar, pepper and pounded mace; simmer gently until the goodness is extracted; strain the gravy, thicken with 1 oz butter rolled in flour, and let boil again. Line the edges of the pie-dish with good puff paste; put in the pieces of lobster, strain the gravy over them, strew finely grated bread crumbs over them; cover and bake.

LOBSTER AND OYSTER PIE.

Pick the meat from the tails of two freshly-boiled lobsters; cut into neat pieces and season with pepper, salt and pounded mace. Bruise the shell and spawn, and make a little gravy from them. Pound the flesh from the claws and bodies, to a small paste, mix it with a slice of bread finely grated, 6 ozs. butter, vinegar, pepper, salt and nutmeg. Line the edges and sides of a pie-dish with good puff paste; put in the slices of lobster, then 2 doz oysters with their liquor, and afterwards the pounded meat; cover and bake. Before serving, strew a little of the gravy from the shells, into the pie.

MACKEREL PIE. (1)

Clean three middling sized mackerel, taking out the melts and roes which are in the composition of a force-meat, to stuff the fish. Add bread-crumbs, chopped parsley, onion, mace, pepper, salt, butter, and an egg or two, to cement the whole. Sew up the fish neatly and lay them into an ordinary oval flat dish with an edging of good mashed potatoes or a puff paste. Balls of force-meat will enrich the dish, and some rich sauce may be poured over the fish when baked; but both forcemeat and sauce should be delicately prepared. Cover with bread-crumbs, and put bits of butter over the fish; bake.

MACKEREL PIE. (2)

Proceed as for cod pie, but do not salt them till used.

OYSTER PIE. (1)

Butter the inside of a shallow pie-dish rather thickly, and line the edges with a good puff-paste. Open and beard 2 doz fresh oysters, lay them in the dish, season with salt, cayenne and pounded mace; sprinkle over them finely-grated bread-crumbs. Mix the strained oyster-liquor with the same quantity of thick cream and a little lemon-juice; pour over the oysters; cover the pie and bake; $\frac{1}{4}$ lb of the kidney fat of a loin of veal, or a small boiled sweetbread cut into thin slices, may be put into the pie with the oysters.

OYSTER PIE. (2)

Cook 1 qt oysters in about 1 pt milk, for five minutes; add 3 ozs cracker dust, $\frac{1}{4}$ oz pepper, and a little sage; fill the pies; cover and bake.

PATE OF FISH.

Boil and mash smoothly, with 1 oz. butter and a spoonful of milk or cream to each pound, as many potatoes as will make a border about 3 inches high within the rim of the dish; 3 lbs. of potatoes will do for a moderate-sized dish; raise this border, ornament it, brush over with beaten eggs and bake till lightly browned; have ready crab or other fish, stewed in sauce, and when the potatoes are colored, put in the preparation and serve very hot.

To prepare the fish. Take 2 lbs. cold boiled fish, carefully picked from bones and broken into small pieces; warm in 1 pt. good white sauce, richly flavored; stir gently over the fire until the fish is hot; turn the whole into the hollow in the centre of the potatoes.

To prepare the crab. Pick the meat from the shell,

mix with it ⅛ of its bulk in fried grated bread crumbs; season with salt, cayenne and grated nutmeg; pound in a mortar; moisten with gravy thickened with flour and butter; add a spoonful of sherry and stir over the fire till quite hot; squeeze over it the juice of a lemon, and it is ready for use.

PILCHARD AND LEEK PIE.

Trim off the coarser leaves from four or five large leeks; cut the white parts only into equal lengths and scald them in salted water; lay them in a pie-dish, the edges of which are lined with plain pastry; put between the layers four salted pilchards, which have been laid in water the previous day to soak; cover and bake; when done enough lift up the cover, drain off the gravy, and put in a little boiling cream.

PRAWN PIE.

Have as many well-cleaned prawns as will nearly fill a die-dish; season with powdered mace, cloves, cayenne or Chili vinegar; put some butter in the dish, cover with a light puff-paste and bake.

SALT FISH PIE.

Soak and boil the fish; divide the flesh, freed from skin and bones, into neat squares. Take double the quantity in partially-boiled potatoes, thinly sliced, and as many as agreeable of half-cooked sliced onions. Butter a pie-dish thickly, fill it with layers of sliced potatoes, first, hard-boiled eggs and onions; season each layer with pepper and dry mustard; place pieces of butter in the pie; pour over egg sauce, cover and bake. If liked, mashed potatoes may be used to cover the pie instead of pastry; or potato paste may be used.

SALMON PIE.

Remove the skin from about 3 lbs. fresh salmon; raise the flesh from the bones and divide it into pieces convenient for serving; season every piece separately with salt, pepper and pounded mace. Shell 1 pt. shrimps and pound them with 1 oz. butter and a pinch of cayenne. Put the pieces of salmon in a dish, interspersing the pounded shrimp amongst them. Make some fish gravy by boiling the skin and bones in water till the liquor will jelly when cold; fill the dish with this; cover and bake.

SALMON PIE—HOT.

Make a short paste as follows: Take 1 lb. flour and spread it in a circle on a slab; lay in the center the yolk of an egg, 10 ozs. butter, ½ gill water and a pinch of salt; dilute the butter with the liquid and introduce the flour gradually into it; as soon as a firm paste is obtained break it three times with the palms of both hands, gather it up and set it aside for ½ hour.

Take a round pie-mould, butter the inside well and set it on a baking sheet. Make a quenelle forcemeat with 10 or 12 ozs. of the flesh of pike. Remove the skin and bones from about 1½ lbs. fresh salmon and divide the flesh into squares. Chop an onion, fry it in a stewpan with oil and butter, adding a few fresh-chopped mushrooms; whenever their moisture is reduced add two or three raw chopped truffles and pieces of salmon; fry over a sharp fire for a few minutes; season with salt and spices and moisten with half a glassful of Maderia; let the whole boil for a few minutes, keeping the saucepan covered.

Mould two-thirds of the prepared paste into a ball

and roll it out into a thin, circular, flat form; raise the sides of this paste, pressing it between the fingers so as to form the paste into a sort of bag; lift the paste carefully and place it in the mould, covering it well at the bottom and along the sides; cut the paste $\frac{1}{2}$ in. above the rim of the mould and then mask it at the bottom and along the sides with a layer of forcemeat; above the layer place half of the slices of salmon with some of the fine herbs; mask again with forcemeat and pile up the rest of the fish in a dome-like shape, rising above the rim of the mould. Cover the pieces of salmon with another layer of forcemeat, and place over all the rest of the paste rolled out very thin; fasten the two flats of paste on the edges, pressing the paste so as to render it thinner; cut it regularly, in order to be pinched all around with pastry pincers. With the trimmings of the paste prepare a few imitation leaves, which arrange as a rose on the dome, on the top of which form a small cavity; cover it with three small rounds of paste of different sizes, placed one above another like a pyramid; egg and push it into a moderate oven; cover with paper and bake. On taking it out, having put it on a dish, remove the mould and cut the dome all around its center, by which aperture pour into the pie white sauce, reduced with extract prepared with wine and the trimmings and bones of the pike and salmon.

SALMON PIE—COLD.

Cut 2 lbs. raw salmon into squares, larding them with fillets of truffies and anchovies; season with salt and spice; fry them a few minutes with butter in a stewpan; pour over $\frac{1}{2}$ gill of sherry, which must be reduced; re-

move the stewpan back, add to the fish 1 ℔. peeled raw
truffles cut in quarters, seasoned; cover the stewpan and
let all the ingredients coo' together. Chop very fine 10
ozs. lean veal or pork with the same quantity of raw
pike or eel· add to this mince 1 ℔. fresh fat bacon;
pound the whole together and pass through a sieve; season the forcemeat well, with salt and spices and add to
the above the trimmings of truffles, pounded with a little
bacon and passed through a sieve.

Prepare a short paste (see Salmon Pie—Hot). Butter
a cold pie-mould of either round or oval shape, which set
on a baking sheet covered with paper; line it with two-
thirds of the paste and mask the hollow and sides wtih
a thin layer of forcemeat; fill the hollow with the
squares of fish and the truffles and forcemeat
mixed, arrange the preparations in a dome-shape
fashion, rising above the rim of the mould; mask
it with little slices of bacon, and then with a thin round
flat made with the remainder of the paste; cover, decorate and bake. One-half an hour after removed from
the oven, pour into the hollow on the top two glasses full
of aspic jelly, mixed with a little Madeira. Half an hour
after take out of the mould, and let the pie cool 24 hours
previous to being served.

SALMON PIE A LA RUSSE.

Cut 2 ℔s. fresh salmon in slices about ½ in. thick; fillet ½ dozen anchovies; trim 2 dozen olives (removing the
stones by paring off the outer part without altering the
shape); boil ½ dozen eggs; place the whole of these in a
dish. Chop a sufficient quantity of mushrooms, shallots,
parsley, green thyme, sweet-basil, tarragon; put them
into a stew pan with 2 ozs. butter, nutmeg, pepper and

salt; simmer five minutes; add ½ pt. brown sauce and the juice of a lemon; stew the whole five minutes longer.

Have ready 2 ℔s. short paste; roll out ⅔ of it about 1-6th in. thick, and after having thinly spread the inside of an oblong mould with butter, line it with this, and fill with alternate layers of the slices of salmon, hard eggs, olives, and fillets of anchovies, at the same time spreading some of the fine herbs' sauce between each layer; the pie must be covered with the remainder of the paste in the usual manner; bake 1½ hours; dish on a napkin.

These pies may also be made of sturgeon, trout, mackeral, soles, etc.

SALMON AND POTATO PIE.

Free from skin and bones the remains of cold boiled salmon; divide into small pieces, and season 1 ℔. of it with salt, pepper and cayenne. Butter a shallow pie-dish; spread over the bottom a layer of potatoes which have been mashed lightly with butter, milk and the yolk of an egg. Put the pieces of fish on the potato, moisten with any fish sauce, and cover with another layer of potato; roughen the top of the pie with a fork, and put in a brisk oven till the surface is lightly browned and quite hot; serve in the dish it was baked.

SHRIMP PIE (1).

Pick as many shrimps as will almost fill the dish, seasoning with cayenne, pounded mace, salt and vinegar or lemon pickle; a small proportion of essence of anchovies may be added if desired. Butter a pie-dish rather thickly, and line the edges with puff paste; put in the shrimps, pour over them a glass of light wine, and a small cup of rich gravy; cover with puff paste and bake.

6

SHRIMP PIE (2).

Pick 1 qt. shrimps, if they are very salt, season them with only mace and a clove or two. Mince a few anchovies; mix them with the spice and then season the shrimps. Put some butter at the bottom of the dish and over the shrimps, with a glass of sharp white wine. The paste must be light and thin; they do not take long to bake.

A few hard boiled eggs, cut in quarters, may be placed over the shrimps.

SOLE PIE (1).

Split some soles from the bone, and cut the fins close; season with a mixture of salt, pepper, nutmeg and pounded mace; put them in layers with oysters.

SOLE PIE (2).

Clear from bones the remains of any cold boiled sole or cod; put a layer of it in the bottom of a pie-dish; add a little seasoning of pounded mace, pepper and salt, and a few oysters, in the proportion of a dozen to each pound weight of fish. Fill the dish with alternate layers of fish, oysters, and seasoning; add three tablespoonsful of white stock; cover the pie with puff paste, and bake in a moderate oven for half an hour. Boil a teacupful of cream with just sufficient flour to thicken it, and. when the pie has been baked, pour it into it, and serve.

The remains of cold cod may be made into a pie in the same way.

STAR-GAZY PIE.

Take as many fresh herring or mackerel as will fill a moderate-sized dish; scale, empty, open and remove the bones; lay them flat on the table; season the inside of each with salt, cayenne, and chopped parsley; and roll it up neatly. Butter the pie-dish, and sprinkle upon it a thick layer of finely grated bread-crumbs, lay in some of the fish, and fill the dish with alternate layers of fish and bread-crumbs; cover the contents of the pie with a few slices of fat bacon or the fat of a ready-dressed ham; pour over all ½ dozen eggs beaten up with tarragon vinegar, or ¼ pt. cream, if preferred. Cover the dish with a good crust, and bake. Arrange the heads of the fish in the center of the pastry, and when the pie is baked, put a piece of parsley in the mouth of each fish, and serve.

This pie is so named because the heads of the fish are usually placed mouth uppermost in the centre of the lid of the crust, as pigeon legs are in a pigeon pie, and therefore the fish are supposed to be star-gazing.

TENCH PIE.

Butter a pie-dish rather thickly, and line the edges with a good crust; put in the tench; season with pepper, salt and grated nutmeg; place on it lumps of butter, and pour over it claret and water; cover and bake. When the pie is done, pour in some strong gravy through the hole at the top.

TENCH AND EEL PIE.

Bone two tench, and bone and skin two eels; cut the latter in two inch lengths, but leave the sides of the tench whole. Simmer the bones of the fish gently for an hour in a stewpan, with a pint of water, a faggot of savory herbs, two onions, four blades of mace, three anchovies, and pepper and salt to taste. Afterward strain the liquor, and allow it to cool, skimming off the fat. Place the tench and eels in a pie-dish, in layers, having between each a seasoning of one teaspoonful of chopped parsley, the yolks of six hard-boiled eggs, and pepper and salt. Pour part of the strained liquor over all, cover the pie with puff paste, and bake for fully half an hour in a quick oven. When ready, heat well the remaining portion of the strained liquor, and add to the pie.

TURBOT PIE.

Take the remains of cold turbot; free the white flesh from skin and bone; tare it into flakes and season with pepper, salt and powdered mace. Spread it at the bottom of a thickly-buttered baking dish, and pour over it any appropriate sauce, or melted butter; cover with a thick layer of potato paste; bake, and salamander.

WHITING PIE.

Take the fillets of about a dozen small whitings, wash and trim without taking off the skins; season highly with salt, pepper and nutmeg; spread over them forcemeat of crayfish, with truffles or mushrooms; roll up the fillets, quite round, beginning at the small end. When thus prepared, spread some of the forcemeat at the bottom and sides of the pan; place upon it some of the fillets upright, which should thus cover the bottom; pour upon them butter scarcely melted, and place two more layers of the fillets; pour butter over them with two bay-leaves added; finish and bake. When serving pour off all the fat, and mask with a ragout.

CHAPTER VI.
VEGETABLE PIES.

Scald and blanch some beans; cut young carrots, turnips, artichoke-bottoms, mushrooms, peas, onions, lettuce, parsley, celery—any or all of them—making the whole into a nice stew. Bake a crust over a dish, with a little lining around the edge, and a cup turned up to keep it from sinking; when baked, open the lid and pour in the stew.

VEGETABLE PIE (2).

Scald some Windsor beans; cut into neat pieces, young carrots, turnips, artichoke-bottoms, lettuce, mushrooms, celery, and parsley, with green peas; onions and spinach may be added if liked. Stew the vegetables partially in gravy and season with pepper and salt. Trim the edges of a dish with pastry; put in the vegetables, pour the gravy over this, cover and bake. If a *maigre* dish is wanted, use cream or milk, slightly thickened with flour and butter, in place of gravy.

CARROT PIE.

Wash and slice the carrots, and parboil them; put them into a dish edged with a light crust; add pepper and salt, and pour a little water over them; cover with crust, and bake.

HERB PIE.

Wash and boil a little, sufficient parsley, spinach, lettuce, mustard-seed, cresses, and a few leaves of borage, etc.; drain and press out the water; cut them small; mix, and lay them in a dish, sprinkled with salt. Mix a batter of flour, 2 eggs well beaten, 1 pt cream, and ½ pt milk; pour it on the herbs; cover with a good paste, and bake.

LEEK FLAMMISH.

Cut up one doz leeks (previously washed clean and free from grit) into pieces ½ in. long; place these in a basin with ¼ pt good thick cream, seasoning with nutmeg, pepper and salt; mix all well together. Prepare 1 ℔ short paste; divide it into four equal parts; mould these into balls; roll them out to the size and shape of pudding plates, and place them on a baking-dish or tin; with a paste brush dipped in water, wet all around the paste, fill the centre of each with enough of the prepared leeks to fill the flammish, when, by gathering up the sides of the paste, each flat assumes the form of a puckered purse; this must be secured by fastening the plaits together with a wetted small circular piece of paste gently pressed upon their centre. Bake ½ hour.

MACARONI PIE.

Take a piece of gravy beef, cut in small pieces, put it into a saucepan with an onion sliced, and a piece of butter; toss it on the fire till the onion and pieces of meat are browned; then add a glass of white wine, a faggot of sweet herbs, a carrot cut in pieces, spices, pepper and salt to taste, mushrooms, and a fair allowance of tomato-sauce. Let the whole simmer for a couple of hours, then strain, and skim off superfluous fat. Put the boiled macaroni into a saucepan with a piece of butter, plenty of grated Parmesan cheese, and as much of the sauce or gravy as it will absorb; toss it on the fire a little while and put it by till wanted. Make a smooth and stiff paste with 1℔ fine flour, 5 ozs fresh butter, two or three yolks of eggs, two ozs sugar, a pinch of salt, and tepid water, *q. s.* Roll it out to the thickness of the eighth of an inch, and line with it a plain round mould previously buttered, uniting the joints carefully with white of egg. Have ready some very small fillets of breasts of chicken, just cooked with butter in a covered tin in the oven, some cooked ham or ox tongue cut in dice, some truffles, mushrooms, and cockscombs, cut in convenient piec⋅s and cooked in the gravy used to dress the macaroni. Fill the lined mould with all these things in judicious proportion, letting the macaroni, of course, predominate, and adding during the process a little more sauce or gravy and a due allowance of Parmesan cheese; cover up the mould with a disc of paste, unite the edges carefully, and bake in a moderate oven for about an hour. Turn out the mould carefully and serve.

MUSHROOM PIE.

Choose 1 or two 2 doz. fairly large mushrooms; peel and quarter them—cut button mushrooms in half if used instead of the larger kind. Pare and slice ½ doz. potatoes, and put both mushrooms and potatoes into a buttered pie-dish with a little water. Divide 2 ozs. butter into equal pieces, and add, placing on the other ingredients; season with pepper and salt, cover with a good paste, and bake.

Stew down the parings and stalks of the mushrooms in a little water for ½ hour; strain, and when the pie is ready to serve, make an incision in the top and pour in the gravy.

ONION PIE.

Equal quantities of onions, apples, ¼ oz. dried sage, and 2 oz. butter. Cut the onions in two, boil five minutes, and chop them small, adding the sage; season with pepper and salt, and put them in a pie-dish with the butter and a little water. Prepare the apples as for sauce, with a little sugar; lay them over the onions, cover with paste and bake.

PATE OF MACARONI.

Put into a stew-pan 6 ozs. macaroni with a moderate sized onion, and 3 pts. boiling water, seasoned with salt and pepper; let simmer 20 minutes, drain well, and put back into the saucepan with ½ pt. broth; let simmer again until the onion is absorbed and the macaroni tender, but unbroken. Place a layer at the bottom of a deep pie-dish; sprinkle with grated Parmesan and pieces of butter; cover with beef steak, highly seasoned and stewed until tender, in good brown gravy and cut into small thin pieces. If preferred, a fricasseed chicken, minced veal, sweetbread cut into dice, or mushrooms, may be substituted for the beef but they all must be stewed in rich gravy before they are put with the macaroni; fill up the dish with alternate layers of macaroni and meat, the uppermost layer being, macaroni; sprinkle Parmesan over the top, and pour over it ½ oz. clarified butter; put the dish into the oven, and when the cheese is dissolved it is ready to serve.

POTATO GIPSY PIE.

Peel and slice thinly as many potatoes as will fill a moderate sized pie-dish; put them in in layers, and season with salt, pepper and minced onion; pour over a

little water and place pieces of butter on top; cover and
bake; when done enough, pour mushroom catsup
into it, through a hole in the top.

POTATO PASTY.

To make this, a pasty-pan must be procured with a
well-fitting perforated plate and a valve-pipe to screw on.
The meat seasoning and gravy are put into the lower
part, the plate is then laid upon the meat, the valve-pipe
screwed on and mashed potatoes equally spread on the
top; it should be baked in a moderate oven and sent to
the table in the same tin in which baked, with a neatly
folded napkin pinned around it; the cover should not be
removed until the meat is to be served, and an empty
dish should be placed in readiness for it; if properly
baked, the potatoes will be nicely browned, and flavored
like the meat.

The contents of this pie may be varied indefinitely.
Mutton or veal cutlets, pork chops, chickens or rabbits
cut into neat joints and fish of various kinds may all be
used. The meat should be neatly trimmed, nicely
seasoned, and gravy poured over it; the mashed potatoes
should form a crust at least 3 inches thick; 2 ℔s. meat
and 3 ℔s. potatoes will make a moderate sized pasty.

POTATO PIE (1).

Slice three onions and put them in a stewpan with
4 ozs. butter, and 1 doz. potatoes; add 1 qt. water, pepper
and salt; put the lid on, and set the whole to stew on a
rather brisk fire, for ½ hour; by this time the potatoes will
be done, and the water sufficiently reduced to furnish
only enough for the pie; pile the stew up in an earthen

pie-dish, covered with potato paste; bake ½ hour and serve.

Any kind of fish, or shell fish may be added; but when fish is used for potato-pie it should be freed from bone and skin, and simmered with a little butter, pepper and salt, and when done, placed in neat rows on top of the potato stew, previously to the pie being covered in. In this case the pie will require an extra quarter of an hours' baking. Sausage meat is frequently mixed with the potatoes.

POTATO PIE (2).

Skin some potatoes and cut them into slices; season them; also some mutton, beef, pork and veal; proceed as for turnip pie.

POTATO PIE (3).

Peel, slice and wash some potatoes; place them in a deep dish, narrower at the bottom than the top; place the potatoes in layers, then pour over them liquor from mutton bones, that have been carefully stewed for a couple of hours; season with salt; put a thick crust over the top.

A *whistler* is made as above with the addition of 1 lb. onions to every 5 lbs. potatoes. The onions are supposed to be whistling for the meat which is very conspicuous by its absence.

POTATO PIE—TEN TO ONE.

Line the edges of a deep pie-dish with good crust, fill it with either beef steak or slices of mutton, nicely seasoned, and slices of raw potato ⅓ inch thick, allowing 8 or 10 slices of potato to one piece of meat; pour a little gravy or water over the whole; cover and bake; serve very hot.

This is a favorite New England dish.

POTATO PIES.

It is a good plan to have made a tin perforated with holes, and with a handle at each end to fit an ordinary sized pie-dish; this lid should fit down at least an inch below the level of the dish, and before using it the first time it should be washed in boiling soda and water, as new tin is often poisonous.

Cut any cold meat into neat slices, sprinkle over them pepper and salt, minced onions and a little gravy or water, with lumps of butter or beef-drippings; put on the tin lid, and pile upon it as many cold boiled potatoes, mashed with milk, as will fill the space to the top of the dish; bake and send to table in the dish in which baked, with a hot napkin pinned around.

TURNIP PIE.

Season mutton chops with salt and pepper, reserving the ends of the neck-bones to lay over the turnips, which must be cut into small dice, and put on the steaks; put in a little milk and a sliced onion; cover with a crust and bake.

CHAPTER VII.

Patties, Vol-au-Vents.

PATTIES, OR VOL-AU-VENT CRUST.

FOR OYSTERS, CHICKEN, FRUIT JELLY, ETC.

2 lbs. flour,	1 wine-glass rum,
2 lbs. butter,	Ice water.
½ teaspoon salt,	

Puff paste must be made in ice box or very cold room.

Wash butter, squeeze dry, flatten out square; sift flour with salt; put in ice box until next day, to become chilled.

Put ¼ lb. of cold flour on corner of table or dough board and sprinkle rum in the 2 lbs. of flour in large dish or bowl; mix. Break off ¼ of the butter, rub finely into the flour, pour in enough ice water to make a *soft* dough; mix lightly, turn on floured table, roll out to ½ inch thickness. Place butter in center, fold 4 sides over, turn all over. Roll out to ½ inch thickness; be careful butter does not break through; sprinkle with flour; let stand 15 minutes.

Fold once toward you and once from you, making 3 laps; roll out to ½ inch thickness; let stand ½ hour. Fold up again, this time from the sides; roll out to ¼ inch thickness; let stand ½ hour. Repeat this five times in all, from front to side folds, and let last fold stand ¾ of an hour. Cut into shape desired with cutter; place into pan and let stand 20 minutes, and bake in medium oven. If the oven is too hot, they rise too quickly and topple over; if too cold, the butter will run out. Follow all directions closely, not forgetting to use good rum.

PATTIES

May be baked in patty pans or without them, the former being styled French Patties, the latter being preferable. They are usually made with puff-paste and filled with savory ingredients of various kinds; they should be baked in a brisk oven.

If made in pans, lightly grease them; line the moulds with puff-paste ($\frac{1}{4}$ inch thick), fill them with flour, or place a crust of bread in the middle of them, put on the cover, trim the pastry evenly with the moulds, moisten the edges, press them together, and mark them with the prongs of a fork; when baked enough, raise the covers, take out the crusts, and return the patties to the oven for a minute or two to dry; before serving put the proper meat into the place where the bread has been.

When made without moulds, roll out the paste about $\frac{1}{4}$ inch thick, cut into rounds $1\frac{3}{4}$ inches in diameter; place half of them on a buttered baking tin, moisten the edges, place a teaspoon of the proper forcemeat in the centre of each, and cover it with another of the rounds, press the edges securely, egg and bake.

Patties, served hot or cold, should be arranged on a folded napkin.

VOL-AU-VENTS.

A Vol-au-Vent is one of the handsomest forms in which the remains of dishes can be served; it is generally filled with a mince, or ragout, or fricassee of dressed meat; it is made of the lightest puff-paste, which should be prepared an hour or so before wanted, and kept in a cool place. If the paste is not exceedingly light the Vol-au-Vent will not rise properly; in rolling, care must be taken to keep it perfectly square and even at the ends, or the pastry cannot rise evenly; the pastry ought to have six turns, and five minutes should elapse between each turn; brush over with lemon juice, and when doubled for the last time, fold it in such a manner that, when finished, it will be the exact size of the inside of the dish in which it is to be served, and a little more than an inch thick; cut it evenly all round with a knife that has been made hot in water, so as not to drag the pastry; make an incision with a cutter $\frac{1}{4}$ in. deep all round the edge of the lid; press the inner circle away from the outer one with the point of a knife to prevent them closing again; this inner circle when baked will form the cover of the Vol-au-Vent. Put in a well heated oven; in $\frac{1}{2}$ or $\frac{3}{4}$ hour, if it appears baked through, take it out, lift up the cover with the point of a knife where it has been marked, and scoop out the soft crumby centre without injuring the walls of the case; put in the oven a few minutes to dry; fill with the savory mince; put on the cover, and serve on a napkin.

Care must be paid to the condition of the oven; if it is not well heated the pastry cannot properly rise; if the heat is *too fierce*, the surface will be set before the heat has penetrated through the pastry, and this will also keep it from rising. When it has risen a couple of inches, and before it acquires any color, cover the Vol-au-Vent with paper to keep it from browning too quickly. If, accidentally the walls of the Vol-au-Vent should receive any injury, a little piece of pastry should be stuck in the thin place, with white of egg. The appearance of the Vol-au-Vent will be improved if it is brushed over with egg after it has risen in the even.

When preparing the ragouts; etc., for Vol-au-Vents, it is very important that the sauces in which the meat is heated should be very thick; unless this is done, the liquor will be in danger of oozing through the crust, and this will entirely spoil the appearance of the Vol-au-Vent. Also the meat should be simmered only in the sauce; if allowed to boil, it will in all probability be hard and unpalatable.

VOL-AU-VENTS—SMALL.

Prepare the pastry as for large vol-au-vents: roll out ½ inch thick; have two cutters, one double the size of the other, if fluted, so much the better; bake, and when done enough, lift off the covers and scoop out the insides as before; dry the pastry and fill the cavities; put on the covers and serve hot or cold.

A LA FINANCIERE.

When about to send to the table make a vol-au vent case hot; place it on a dish; garnish with a financiere ragout (see below). The top may be finished by placing in it a larded sweetbread surrounded by decorated quenelles, or truffles and crayfish.

Financiere Ragout. Place in a stew pan, ready cooked, a few cockscombs, button mushroom, truffles, quenelles, scollops of sweet breads; add a half pint good brown sauce, flavored, if possible, with game, a glass of sherry or Madeira, and a pinch of cayenne; boil together three minutes and serve as garnish for vol-au-vents, etc.

A LA NORMANDE.

Fillet a large sole, put on a buttered dish, and sprinkle

upon it a finely minced onion, previously parboiled; pour
upon it as much milk or light wine as will barely cover it,
and bake till done enough; divide it into neat slices of uniform size, and put them in a stewpan with an equal quantity of oysters which have been plumped in their liquor,
mussels which have been shaken over the fire in a stew-pan
till their shells open, mushrooms stewed in butter, and
small pieces of the crumb of bread fried in butter till lightly
browned; take as much veloute or other appropriate sauce
as will cover the ingredients; put it into a sauce pan, and
stir in the oyster liquor, the mussel broth and the gravy
from the sole; let simmer till thick; beat the yolks of two
eggs in a basin; mix a spoonful or two of the sauce with
them, and add to the rest; simmer the suace without
allowing to boil, and pour it over the fish; let all heat
very gently for three minutes, and the ragout will be
ready for the vol-au-vent.

BEEF PATTIES—(PODOVIES).

Take ½ doz. slices under-dressed roast beef, with a
small portion of fat; shred finely, season with salt, pepper
and chopped onion or shalot. Roll out ¼ ℔ puff-paste
very thin; lay spoonsful of the mince upon it, one inch
apart, and moisten the pastry round the meat with a
little water; cover with a piece of pastry; press together
the portion round each little ball of mince, and stamp
rounds out with a cutter; pinch the edges and fry the
patties in hot fat until bright colored; drain on blotting
paper; serve piled high on a dish.

BEEF PATTIES. (1.)

Take thick slices of stale bread, cutting them of the
desired form and size, with a tin cutter; scoop out the

middle to receive the mince, as prepared below; dip each piece of bread into cream, and when drained brush with the white of egg, and dredge bread crumbs over them; fry in fresh butter, fill with the mince made hot and send to table on napkin.

To prepare the filling.—Mince $\frac{1}{2}$ lb fresh suet; put it, to 1 lb each of beef and veal, cut into small pieces, but not chopped; season with pepper, salt, pounded allspice, and mace; mix all together; when wanted for patties cut up a little parsley, and shred one blade of shalot, very finely, to mix with it. Bake in patty pans or buttered saucers.

These patties are good cold, and may be warmed up at any time.

BEEF PATTIES. (2).

Shred 1 lb undercooked beef, a little fat and lean together; season with pepper or cayenne, salt and onion or shalot.

CHEESE PATTIES.

Line some tartlet tins with good puff paste, and half fill them with the following mixture: Put $\frac{1}{4}$ lb cheese, cut into small pieces, in a mortar with salt, pepper, raw mustard and a small piece of butter; pound smoothly, and add by degrees the well beaten yolks of three eggs, and a tablespoon of sherry; mix thoroughly, and just before the patties are to be baked, add the white of an egg beaten to a solid froth.

CHICKEN PATTIES. (1).

Take three or four old chickens after having them well cleaned; put them in about 3 or 4 quarts cold water, well seasoned with salt, pepper, thyme, celery,

7

etc., and well garnished with carrots and onions. When it commences to boil take them out and let them get cold; take off all the meat, letting the carcasses reboil in the same stock; cut the meat in small square pieces. Let the stock boil down until reduced to 1½ quarts, and strain through a towel. In a small sauce pan put three spoonsful of flour with two of butter and mix well until almost brown (but not dark); add the stock in which the chickens have boiled, and stir constantly till it comes to a boil; then take the yolks of four eggs, mixed with a little cream and one ounce butter; bind the whole together; strain the same, adding the juice of a lemon and a little butter, as required; mix with this sauce, the chickens already cut up. Warm the patty pans and fill.

CHICKEN PATTIES. (2.)

Proceed as for veal patties, using chicken in place of veal.

CHICKEN VOL-AU-VENTS.

Take the bones from a boiled chicken and cut the meat into small cubes, adding a few mushrooms, cut up in a similar manner, and a bit of lean, boiled ham, finely minced. Make a sauce of well reduced chicken broth, adding a few yolks of eggs, a pat of butter and a glass of cream; season with salt, pepper, nutmeg and the juice of a lemon; into this put the minced chicken, etc., and place in a sauce pan over the fire: Warm up the cases and line them from the mass with a spoon. Serve on a dish with a folded napkin undeaneath.

DRESDEN PATTIES.

Take the outer crust of a stale French roll, divide the crumb into slices, and then into rounds, with a tin cutter;

make the slices sufficiently thick to allow of the middle being scooped out. Dip the croustades into milk, drain well, smear with egg and cover with fine bread raspings, fried in butter to a pale brown. Fill with compote of fruit; or with minced fowl, ham, and tongue; or with oysters, mushrooms, etc.

EEL PATTIES.

Skin and wash some middle-sized eels, and after having cut them into pieces 1 inch long, soak in salt and water one hour; when drained, put them into a stew-pan with just enough hot water to cover them; add salt, pepper, a blade of mace, a little lemon peel, and a sprig of parsley; when the fish will separate from the bone, after ten minutes gentle stewing, divide each piece into two, puting them aside until the broth has stewed a little longer, when remove the lemon-peel, mace, etc.; thicken with butter and a little flour; flavor with lemon-juice or vinegar, and return the pieces of eel to the broth.

EGG VOL-AU-VENTS.

Mince two truffles; put them into a stew-pan with two tablespoons of thick cream; add four eggs that have boiled twenty minutes, chopped fine; season with salt, pepper and nutmeg; when the mixture has simmered five minutes, fill the cases and serve hot.

FISH PATTIES.

Pick from the shell of a crab all that is good; pound it in a morter with a small quantity of bread-crumbs, and a seasoning of white-pepper, cayenne, salt and nutmeg; add a little gravy, which thicken with butter rolled in flour; make it hot and squeeze in a little lemon juice. Have ready a wall of mashed potatoes round the inner rim of a flat dish, 2½ inches high; smooth and ornament it with leaves, flowers, etc.; this can be done with a tin-cutter, and, if egged and browned in the oven, will have a pretty appearance. Fill the centre with the fricassee, and salamander.

Small patties may be made and filled with this fricassee.

FOWL or GAME PATTIES.

Take the breast and flesh of chickens, etc.; pass the meat twice through a mincing machine at fine tension; then through a wire tammy, using a little white stock to help it through; season. Mix ¼ lb. of mince to 1 pt. whipped cream; warm up; fill the cases three-fourths full; whip the whites of eggs to a stiff foam, and season with salt; color green with parsley juice; put a cone of this over each patty and warm in the oven; but be careful not to let the egg mixture brown or change color, or the beauty of the dish will be lost. Place on a hot plate covered with a lace paper; garnish with crimson or red flowers, and serve.

GAME PATTIES (1).

Proceed with any kind of game, as for veal patties.

GAME PATTIES (2).

Make a nicely-flavored mince of the remains of game; moisten with a little gravy; warm the mince in a saucepan, put a little in the centre of each patty, and serve hot, piled on a napkin.

HAM AND CHICKEN PATTIES.

Take two-thirds chicken and one-third ham, freed from sinew and skin; mince finely and season with greated lemon-peel, salt and cayenne; put the meat into a saucepan with good gravy, sufficient to moisten it; sqeeze over it a few drops of lemon juice.

KEDGEREE PATTIES.

Boil a little rice, Indian fashion, showing the separate grains; take the fish from the bones of some yesterday's fish, and mince it. Boil some eggs hard, let cool, shell and mince them also. Fry chopped onion in a stewpan, with some butter; stir curry powder into it to taste, also salt. Have equal quantities of fish, rice and eggs. Put them into the stewpan, and stir them up into the curry; then cover with milk, boil up with a lump of *roux* stirred in, set to the usual consistency, and fill into patty-cases.

LEMON PATTIES.

Rub the rind of a fresh lemon with 3 ozs. loaf sugar; crush it to powder, and mix with finely grated breadcrumbs; pour over the mixture $\frac{1}{4}$ pt. boiling milk, and soak for an hour; then stir in 2 ozs. clarified butter and 2 well beaten eggs. Butter some small cups; fill them rather more than half full with the mixture, and bake; when done, turn out on a hot dish and serve with wine sauce.

LOBSTER PATTIES.

A hen lobster should be had. Put some of the spawn or coral into a mortar, or cut smooth and fine with a knife; add butter, and when well mixed, rub through a sieve and put in the sauce. Chop the meat of the lobster rather fine and add to the sauce, with a little essence of anchovy and a little cayenne. Make all hot, and fill the cases.

MARROW PATTIES (1).

The only marrow fit for this purpose is that taken from the bones in the rump. Empty this and chop up the marrow; add pepper and salt, a little cream and a beaten egg. Line patty pans with puff-paste as follows: Roll it out very thin; cover the pans once all over; cut strips about 1 in. wide; moisten the edges of the paste already on, and lay three rows of strip paste, one over the other, moistening each row slightly. Fill the hollow centre with the marrow mixture. Put on a thin coat of paste and bake in a quick oven.

MARROW PATTIES (2).

Take the marrow from the bone, cut it up and parboil in salt and water for one minute; drain and season with pepper, salt, lemon juice and chopped parsley (a bit of shalot if desired); toss these ingredients lightly together until hot; fill the cases and serve.

MUTTON PATTIES (1).

Line some tartlet pans with a good paste; take an equal weight of lean mutton from the fillet, and fat bacon, which pound together; season with salt, spice and cayenne. Place a round ball of the meat into each patty-pan; cover with paste, and make a small hole in the centre; bake in a quick oven, and pour into each patty, through a funnel, a little well seasoned gravy or glaze, before the patties get cold.

MUTTON PATTIES (2).

Cut the lean part of a loin of mutton into very small squares; season with chopped mushrooms, parsley and shalot, pepper and salt, and a little brown sauce or gravy; mix all together in a basin. Fill the preparred patty pans.

OYSTER PATTIES (1).

Plump and beard 2 or 3 doz. oysters; mix very smoothly a teaspoon of flour with 1 oz. butter, put them in a clean saucepan, shake them round over a gentle fire, letting them simmer two or three minutes; throw in a little salt, pounded mace and cayenne; then add, by slow degrees, two or three spoonfuls of rich cream; give these a boil, and pour in the strained liquor of the oysters; next lay in the oysters, and keep at the boiling point for a couple of minutes. Raise the covers of the patties, take out the bread, fill them with oysters and their sauce, and replace the covers.

It is an improvement to stew the beards of the oysters with a strip or two of lemon peel in a little good veal stock for ¼ hour, then to strain and add it to the sauce. The patties should be made small, with a thin crust, and well filled with the oysters and their sauce. The substitution of fried crumbs for the cover will vary them agreeably.

Oyster patties may be served either hot or cold, and should be sent to table piled high on a napkin. They may be baked in patty pans if liked; when so made, line the pans with a good puff-paste, rolled out thin, put a crust of bread in each, lay on the cover, brush the top with beaten egg, and bake in a quick oven; when done, remove the covers, take out the bread, fill with oyster mixture, lay the covers on again, and serve.

OYSTER PATTIES (2).

Line small patty pans with a fine puff-paste; fill each of them with bread crumbs, and cover with paste. Chop oysters into bits, put them into a saucepan with a little grated nutmeg, pepper and salt, a little cream, a little of the oyster liquor, and a small lump of butter. Take the bread crumbs out of the patties and fill them with the oysters, after simmering them for a few moments, and serve hot.

OYSTER VOL-AU-VENTS.

Beard 3 doz. oysters; put the liquor into a saucepan with the beards, mace, nutmeg and pepper, adding the rind of half a lemon and the strained juice; boil up; knead 3 ozs. of butter with a spoonful of baked flour, and stir in; boil till it is reduced to ¼ pt.; strain; add the oysters, simmer five minutes, and stir in 1 gill very thick cream; fill the cases and serve.

PATTIES DE CREME DE VOLAILLE.

Make a *puree* of fowl, cooked in milk (no salt). Use the milk in passing the *puree* through the tammy; put the whole over the fire in saucepan, with two tablespoonfuls of desiccated white vegetable soup; stir till the *puree* is quite thick, then season with salt. Have puff-paste cases ready; three parts fill with the *puree;* decorate the top with white of egg, whipped to a stiff foam, colored with saffron, spinach, cochineal, etc.; season with salt, and dry in the oven, but do *not color*. Set on stands, with lace-paper under the pastry, and a centre-piece of flowers rising out the middle of the stand.

PETITS PATTIES.

Cut some chicken in dice; put it into a saucepan with some Bechemel sauce, well seasoned with a shalot; reduce it a little and let it get cold. Line some patty pans with rather thin puff-paste; put a little of the meat in each.

Sprinkle them over with bread crumbs and bits of butter. Bake 20 minutes in a quick oven.

PIGEON VOL-AU-VENTS.

Divide two freshly killed pigeons into neat joints.
Put two veal sweetbreads into a saucepan, cover with
luke-warm water, and set over the fire till the water
boils; lift them out and plunge at once into cold water;
cut them into neat pieces of uniform shape and size, and
bind them securely together with twine. Put the sweetbreads with the pigeon, into a stewpan, pour a cupfull of
water over them, adding an onion, a bunch of parsley, a
bay leaf, a slice of fat bacon, $\frac{1}{2}$ oz. butter rolled in flour,
pepper and salt; simmer gently an hour; remove the
twine from the sweetbreads, strain and thicken the gravy,
if necessary; fill the Vol-au-Vents. The sauce must be
very thick or it will soften the light paste.

PIGEON-PATE, CHAUD.

Boil 4 ozs. lard in $\frac{1}{4}$ pt. water; stir while hot with 1 ℔.
flour and a little salt, and work the whole into a stiff,
smooth paste; shape $\frac{2}{3}$ of it as for raised pies, fill with
bran or flour; roll out the remainder, place on top as a
lid, ornament, egg and bake; when done enough cut out
the lid, remove bran, and fill with stewed pigeons; put
with them stewed mushrooms, or any other garnish, and
pour a little poivrade sauce over the whole; serve as hot
as possible.

The shells may be made and baked the day before
wanted, and put into the oven to heat, when the pigeons
are ready for serving.

PODOVIES.

See Beef Patties.

POTATO PATTIES.

Take as many large well-shaped potatoes as it is intended there should be patties; wash well and bake; take them out before quite done enough, so that the skins may not be injured, and carefully cut off the top, and scoop out the inside with a spoon; mix with the floury part a little thick cream, a piece of butter and a pinch of salt, together with sugar, lemon or cinnamon flavoring, and the yolks and whites of 2 or 3 eggs, beaten and added separately. Put this mixture into the hollow potatoes; place them upright, side by side in a buttered dish, and bake in a hot oven.

If liked, savory patties can be made by mixing with the potato flour a little pounded veal and ham, cream, salt, pepper, lemon peel, grated nutmeg, and mushroom catsup.

RABBIT PATTIES.

Free from skin and sinew the white meat from a cold-dressed rabbit; mince finely with portions of suet, Bruise the bones, put them into a stewpan with salt. pepper, grated nutmeg and lemon peel; let simmer until the gravy is pleasantly flavored; thicken with flour and butter, and stew the mince in this till quite hot.

RABBIT PATE.

Bone and cut in pieces two young rabbits. Chop small $\frac{1}{2}$ lb. each fresh pork and veal fat; mix with a laurel leaf, a shalot, thyme and parsley (finely shred), pepper, salt and powdered cloves. Lay the rabbits and minced meat in a pie-dish lined with slices of fat bacon: pour a glass of brandy over the whole, and cover the top with slices bacon; bake, and when done enough, serve the pate in a flat dish, garnished round the edges with slices of pickled beet-root, or pickled capsiums.

SHRIMP PATTIES (1).

Pick the shrimps and cut the tails in two pieces. Put the heads and shells into a saucepan and boil gently with sufficient water to extract the flavor; thicken the liquor with arrowroot, egg yolks or flour, to the consistency of cream; moisten the shrimps' tails with the same; season with salt (if necessary), cayenne, grated nutmeg or scraped horse-radish, or 2 or 3 pounded anchovies; or the seasoning may be omitted if liked. Fill the cases while the preparation is hot.

Sometimes shrimp patties are served with bread-crumbs sprinkled over them, and without the pastry covers.

SHRIMP PATTIES (2).

Proceed with shrimp as for lobster patties; the shrimps of course are not cut up; color with lobster coral or a few drops of prepared carmine.

SHRIMP VOL-AU-VENTS; BOUCHEES.

Use same preparation as for Shrimp Patties.

SWEETBREAD VOL-AU-VENTS.

Soak two large fine sweetbreads in water for a couple of hours; boil them quickly for 10 minutes, and throw them into cold water; when cool, dry them perfectly, cut them into small pieces, and dredge with flour. Melt 2 ozs. butter in a saucepan, put in the pieces of sweetbread, add one-third pint white stock, the strained juice of a lemon, 2 tablespoons of sherry or Madeira, a bunch of sweet herbs, the thin rind of $\frac{1}{2}$ lemon, half a blade of

mace, two cloves, pepper, salt and grated nutmeg; let
the sauce boil up once, skim, and let the sweetbreads
simmer gently until done; take them up, strain the sauce,
and mix with it gradually the yolks of two eggs, beaten
up with sufficient cream; stir the sauce over the fire a
minute or two, but do not let boil.

This dish will be much improved if a few mushrooms
and browned potatoes are added, in the shape of balls,
when the Vol-au-Vent cases must be at least six inches in
diameter.

TURBOT PATTIES or VOL-AU-VENTS.

Take the white meat of the turbot freed from skin and
bone; mince finely and season with pepper and salt. Put
into the stewpan a few spoonsful of thick cream;
thicken by boiling with butter rolled in flour; when
quite hot put the minced fish into it that it may also
heat.

TURKEY PATTIES.

Mince very finely a little of the white meat of a cold
dressed turkey, adding a small proportion of grated ham;
stew this gently for a minute or two in as much melted
butter or good gravy as will barely cover it; add a spoonful of thick cream; season with grated lemon-rind, white
pepper, salt and powdered mace.

VEAL AND HAM PATTIES.

Mince finely 6 ozs. lean veal and 3 ozs. dressed ham.
Put ¼ pt. cream and ¼ pt. white stock into a saucepan;
thicken this sauce with white roux or with a small piece
of butter rolled in flour; simmer till it is smooth and
coats the spoon; add pepper, salt, cayenne, and a flavoring of grated nutmeg and lemon rind with a little lemon

juice. Put in the minced meat and simmer gently, stir all the time till quite hot; it must not boil or it will be hard.

VEAL PATTIES (1).

Boil $\frac{1}{4}$ ℔. veal cutlet till firm; save the liquor; chop the veal fine and add to white sauce. Reduce the reserved liquor one half, then add to the sauce with cayenne and salt. The sauce must not be too thin. A little essence, or a small portion of ham, chopped very fine, is a great improvement; a few drops of lemon juice may also be added.

VEAL PATTIES (2).

Mince first separately, and afterwards together $\frac{1}{2}$ ℔. lean veal and 2 ozs. ham; add a tablespoon flour, a little grated Parmesan, the rind of a grated lemon, grated nutmeg, pepper and salt. Put the mince into a saucepan with strong veal stock that will jelly when cold, to moisten it; stir over a gentle fire $\frac{1}{4}$ hour; add cream and lemon juice.

VEAL PATTIES (3).

Mince $\frac{1}{2}$ ℔. dressed lean veal free from skin and fat, and $\frac{1}{2}$ doz. oysters separately; moisten with veal stock which will jelly when cold; mix with it two tablespoons of thick cream, the oyster liquor, and a little grated lemon rind. Put the sauce with the mince into a saucepan, and let it get quite hot; put in the oysters for $\frac{1}{2}$ minute, and serve.

VEAL PATTIES (4).

Cut into strips 1 ℔. dressed lean veal free from skin and gristle; mince finely with $\frac{1}{4}$ lb. lean ham. Put the bones and trimmings of the veal into a saucepan with 1

pt. water, a bunch of parsley, ½ doz. peppercorns, a blade
of mace, and a little thin lemon rind; simmer for an
hour or more till strong and pleasantly flavored;
strain, let get cold and free from fat. Put the minced
veal into a saucepan with as much gravy as will moisten
it; add a little cream and a piece of butter rolled in
flor; stir the mince over a gentle fire till hot and smooth.

If preferred the mince may be baked in the cases; but
it is best to bake the pastry separately, as the mince
hardens in baking.

VEAL PATTIES—FRIED.

Mince ½ ℔. dressed lean veal and ¼ ℔. ham; season
with salt, cayenne, grated lemon rind and nutmeg; mix
with a hard boiled egg chopped small; moisten with
stock that forms a strong jelly when cold; add a little
cream. Roll out thin some good pastry; place on this
little mounds of mince about 1 inch apart; place over all
a piece of pastry stamp the covered mounds out in
patties with a round cutter; moisten the edges and
press the pastry together round the mince. When
wanted, drop the patties into hot fat and fry a light
brown; drain and serve on a napkin garnished with
parsley.

If preferred, these patties may be baked in a moderate
oven.

VEAL VOL-AU-VENTS.

Cut some lean veal into small thin round slices; beat
with a cutlet bat and fry till lightly browned; cover with
rich brown thick gravy, highly flavored; put with them a
few fried forcemeat balls, and serve the Vol-au-Vents on
a napkin.

Small Vol-au-Vents may be filled with the savory preparations recomended for veal patties.

VEGETABLE PATTIES.

Prepare a macedoine of vegetables; moisten with nicely flavored white sauce.

VENISON PATTIES.

Chop cold bits of venison, and heat with some of the gravy; season with pepper and salt; fill some patty pans and cover the top with crust; bake brown.

CHAPTER VIII.

Savory Boiled Puddings.

(For the method of preparing Suet and Butter Pastes—also preparation of pudding basin etc., see Part II, page 36).

BEEF STEAK PUDDING.

Cut and flatten some rump steak, with a moderate proportion of fat; season with pepper, salt and fine herbs; fill a lined pudding basin with it; add a little good stock, cover with paste; tie over with a cloth and boil 3½ hours.

BEEF STEAK AND OYSTER PUDDING.

Cut some fillets of beef into thin slices; season and put them into the prepared basin, in alternate layers, with 3 doz. oysters; add some stock and finish as above.

CALVES' HEAD PUDDING.

Stamp out with a round cutter some pieces of calves' head, which has been previously dressed; mix with 1 pt. brown sauce, reduced with two glasses of sherry; add to this 1½ doz. balls of veal etc. quenelle, cooked in stock; put into a prepared basin and boil 2½ hours.

CALVES' HEART D'UXELLES PUDDING.

Roast a calf's heart in buttered paper; when done and cold, take the best parts and cut into convenient pieces; then sweat some prepared mushrooms, three shalots, and some parsley, all chopped fine, in ¼ lb butter, over the fire; add 5 yolks of eggs and a couple spoonsful of brown sauce; mix, season etc.; boil 2½ hours.

CALVES' TONGUE AND BRAIN PUDDING.

Wash and remove the outer skins from six calves' brains, and boil them in vinegar and water; egg and bread crumb with fine herbs, and bake on a buttered cutlet-pan in the oven for ¼ hour; cut up two cooked calves' tongues in slices; place them round the lined basin; fill the center with the brains and some reduced white sauce; finish and boil 1½ hours.

CURRY CALVES' FEET PUDDING.

Make a good curry of two calves' feet as follows: bone the feet and boil them in water till nearly done; chop up four onions very fine and fry them in ¼ lb. butter; add 2 tablespoons of curry powder, the calves' feet cut into convenient pieces, and some stock; season to taste; add a little cream, and set at the corner of the stove, stirring occasionally until done; put into a prepared basin, finish and boil 1½ hours.

CHICKEN AND HAM PUDDING.

Cut up two chickens into small pieces, and likewise a proportinate quantity of ham cut rather thin; place this in prepared basin in alternately seasoned layers; add some chicken broth; finish and boil 2 hours.

EEL PUDDING.

Skin and cut two large eels into inch lengths, seasoning with pepper, salt and chopped parsley; fry in a cutlet-pan with butter; put them in some brown sauce, reduced with fine herbs, and a couple glasses of sherry; put the whole into prepared basin, finish and boil 2 hours.

FROG PUDDING.

Put a canister full of prepared frogs into pudding

8

basin with some prepared mushrooms, and ½ doz. truffles cut in slices; mix with ½ pt. reduced white sauce; finish and boil 1½ hours.

GIBLET PUDDING.

Cut and prepare a set of goose giblets; boil them until tender, in broth flavored with a bouquet of vegetables and a little fresh basil; line a prepared basin with pieces of fillet of beef seasoned; season the giblets, mix them with some brown sauce, and put in the center of the pudding; finish and boil 2 hours.

GROUSE PUDDING.

Fillet eight grouse; saute in a cutlet-pan with 3 oz. butter, some prepared mushrooms chopped, pepper and salt; add to this while hot, three yolks of eggs; mix with the raw fillets; put into prepared basin with a little gravy; finish and boil 1¾ hours.

HARE PUDDING.

Fill the prepared basin with the fillets of two fine hares, cut into scallops and seasoned; 1 doz. button onions blanched and slightly fried or passed in butter, some prepared mushrooms, a little red currant jelly, 2 ozs. melted glaze, and some stock; finish and boil 2 hours.

IRISH STEW PUDDING.

Make a good Irish stew; put it when cold into prepared basin; and boil 2 hours.

KIDNEY PUDDING.

Fill a prepared basin with about 1½ doz. sheeps' kidneys, skinned, cut into slices, dipped into clarified butter, and seasoned with fine herbs, pepper, salt and lemon juice; finish and boil 3 hours.

KIDNEY AND BEEF PUDDING.

Fry in butter, enough bullock's kidney, cut into thin slices, to half fill the pudding, and place it in prepared basin, with alternate layers of fillet of beef cut thin, and seasoned with pepper and salt, fine herbs, and a little lemon juice; add some stock, and boil $2\frac{3}{4}$ hours.

LAMB AND GREEN PEAS PUDDING.

Line a prepared basin with nicely seasoned neat pieces cut from a small leg of lamb; fill the centre with boiled green peas, adding some white sauce, and a layer of the lamb on top; finish and boil $1\frac{1}{2}$ hours.

LAMB'S TAIL PUDDING.

Cut and prepare the tails as for ox tail pudding, finishing as follows: Reduce 1 pt. white sauce, flavored slightly with fresh basil and a glass of sherry; season and boil $1\frac{1}{2}$ hours.

LARK PUDDING.

Saute 3 doz. larks in a cutlet pan with butter and fine herbs; cut with a circular cutter $1\frac{1}{2}$ doz. rounds of raw ham; place all in a prepared basin, season, add some stock; finish and boil 2 hours.

Lark Dumplings.—Bone 1 doz. larks; stuff them with quenelle, and a small truffle in the centre of each; enclose each one in suet or butter paste; tie up in cloths; boil and serve with half glaze.

LIVER AND BACON PUDDING.

Cut some calf's liver in thick slices, saute or fry them in a buttered cutlet pan for a few minutes, with some fine herbs; cut them into convenient pieces and place them in alternate layers, with a proportionate quantity

of bacon, in a prepared basin; add ½ pt. brown sauce, reduced; finish and boil 2 hours.

MACKEREL PUDDING.

Take one or two mackerel; thoroughly clean them,
removing the heads, fins and tails; cut into blocks of about
2 inches; take a quarter of the weight of fish in pickled
pork, rather fat, cut it into dice, and season with pepper,
salt and parsley, or a little fennel; put into a prepared
mould, and boil an hour or more.

MUTTON PUDDING.

Cut up some of the lean, and a proportionate quantity
of the fat of a loin of mutton into convenient pieces;
season each piece; fill a prepared basin; sprinkle some
fine herbs on top; add some stock; finish and boil 2
hours.

MUTTON PUDDING—HARICOT.

Fill a prepared basin with 1 doz neat braized mutton
cutlets, and the same of boiled turnips cut into the
same shape; season; add brown sauce; finish and boil 1½
hours.

OX CHEEK PUDDING.

Boil an ox cheek in stock till tender; when cold, trim,
bone and cut into square pieces; boil 1½ doz. button
onions, and the same of carrots and turnips cut out with
the vegetable scoop; fry in butter, and mix these vegetables with the pieces of cheek and about ¼ lb. glaze; put
into a prepared basin, with a little stock; finish and boil
2½ hours; serve with strong gravy.

OX TAIL PUDDING.

Cut two ox tails into pieces, stew them until tender in

weak broth, remove the meat from the bone, and add to 1 pt. brown sauce, reduced to nearly one-half; mix with two glasses sherry, and some prepared mushrooms, sliced; season to taste; place in prepared basin; boil 2½ hours.

PARTRIDGE PUDDING.

Proceed with three partridges, as for Pheasant Pudding.

PHEASANT PUDDING.

Trim and cut two pheasants into members, putting the backs into a stewpan with a little stock; draw a good essence over the fire from this; strain and add two glasses of sherry; season the members, and put all together in prepared basin; finish and boil 2 hours.

PIG'S FEET PUDDING.

Prepare and boil some pig's feet, reserving the large bones; reduce some white sauce, adding chopped parsley and the finished feet; season and fill prepared basin; boil 1½ hours.

PIGEON PUDDING.

Trim eight or ten pigeons; cut them in half, and proceed as for grouse pudding, with the exception of filleting them.

QUAIL PUDDING.

Cut up the remnants of quail which may have been left from dinner; season; put them into a reduced brown sauce; fill a prepared basin; finish and boil 1½ hours.

RABBIT AND PORK PUDDING

Cut up a young rabbit; well season some neatly trimmed pork cutlets; place them in layers with some

streaky bacon, in prepared basin and a little chopped
onion fried in butter; finish and boil 3 hours.

RAGOUT PUDDING.

Fill the prepared basin with the following mixture:
put into ½ pt. brown sauce, two throat sweetbreads,
blanched, skinned, and cut into pieces; ¼ lb. cock's
combs, boiled tender; the yolks of ½ doz. eggs, boiled
hard; some prepared mushrooms; six slices of cooked
ox tongue, and the same of ham, cut with a circular
cutter; and three truffles, sliced; finish and boil 1½
hours.

ROMAN PUDDING.

Butter a basin and line it with boiled macaroni, round
like a beehive; have ready veal, ham, tongue, chicken or
cold game, all cut very finely; 1 oz. Parmesan cheese,
nutmeg, salt, pepper; lemon peel and cayenne, 2 eggs
and a cupful of cream; mix altogether, and fill the
basin; boil ½ hour, glaze and serve with brown sauce. ·

RICHELIEU PUDDING.

Take 1 lb. cold meat, 2 oz. fat or suet, chopped fine;
have ready some bread previously soaked in milk, a
little chopped parsley, thyme, lemon peel, pepper and
salt; mix well together with 2 well-beaten eggs; butter
a mould, fill and boil 3 hours; turn out on a dish and
serve with white or brown sauce. It is equally good
when eaten cold.

SAUSAGE PUDDING.

Take 2 lbs. pork sausage; remove the skins, form
them into balls; beat up on a plate one egg with fine
herbs, pepper and salt; roll the balls into this, and fry

them of a light brown; fill prepared basin with them; add a little brown sauce; finish and boil 1½ hours.

SHEEP'S TONGUE AND BRAIN PUDDING.

Proceed as for Calves' Tongue and Brain pudding, using more of the sheep's in proportion.

SMALL BIRD PUDDING.

Pick and clean 1 lb. small birds, larks, sparrows, etc.; slightly fry or saute them in a cutlet-pan, with herb mixture and a pat of butter; place them in a prepared basin with ½ lb. rump steak, and some fat bacon cut up thin; season, add a little stock, finish and boil 2½ hours.

SNIPE PUDDING.

Cut ten snipes in half, remove the trail, place the snipes on a dish, and season with cayenne, salt and lemon juice; chop and fry two onions in a little butter, when rather brown, mix in a dessert spoon of flour; stir over the fire two minutes, then add some fine herbs, and moisten with ½ pt. port wine; boil this almost five minutes, and then add the trail; put the snipes into prepared basin, add a little stock and the mixture; finish and boil 2 hours.

SQUAB PUDDING (DEVONSHIRE).

Cut the mutton from the loin, with a proportionate quantity of fat; fill prepared basin with this, in alternate layers, with sliced onions and apples; season each layer with pepper, salt and sugar, (sugar to predominate); add a little clear stock; finish and boil 2½ to 3 hours.

SQUAB PUDDING (SOMERSETSHIRE).

Proceed as above, substituting pork for mutton, and adding a little sage to the other seasonings.

SWEETBREAD PUDDING.

Blanch four veal throat sweetbreads; skin, cut them into pieces and put them into a buttered cutlet-pan, with prepared mushrooms chopped fine; fry for a few minutes; fill a prepared basin, add a little stock and two glasses of sherry; finish and boil 2 hours.

TENDRON AND GREEN PEAS PUDDING.

Place a dish of tendrons, after being well seasoned, into a prepared basin, with some fresh boiled green peas, and a little white sauce; finish and boil 2 hours.

THREE DECKER PUDDING.

Line a pudding basin with suet paste; put at the bottom a layer of mutton cut up and seasoned; put a little stock to this, and cover with a thin layer of the paste; on the top of this put a layer of pork cut up and seasoned, with the addition of a little sage and chopped onion; add some stock, and cover with a thin layer of paste as before; lastly, put in a layer of fillet of beef cut up and seasoned; add some stock to this, cover in and boil 3 hours.

TRIPE PUDDING.

Cut into square pieces 2 lbs. of the rich part of tripe, cook it in milk; when done, strain off; reduce 1 pt. white sauce to half; add to this a puree of onion, and then mix in the tripe with a little of the milk; put into prepared basin and boil 2½ hours.

VEAL AND HAM PUDDING.

Take 2 ℔s. fillet of veal, cut into thin scallops, and put into prepared basin, with a proportionate quantity of slices of ham; cut neatly, and fill in alternate layers with the veal, and fine herbs, pepper and salt; add ½ doz. spoonsful white sauce; boil 3½ hours.

VENISON PUDDING.

Boil some of the best parts of a neck of venison; cut it in slices and lard it coarsely with pieces of fat bacon, rolled in chopped parsley; place the pieces, seasoned well, into a prepared basin; add a little stock, some red currant jelly, and a little game glaze melted; finish and boil 2 hours.

YACHT PUDDING.

Cut small rounds of pieces of the salt round of beef, the same of veal and mutton cut from the neck, a duck cut up small, some pickled pork and onions, and potatoes in slices; mix the whole well together; season highly; put into prepared basin; add ¼ lb. glaze melted and diluted with water; finish and boil 3 hours.

CHAPTER IX.

VEGETABLE AND GARNISH, ETC., PUDDINGS.

BEETROOT AND ONION PUDDING.

Fry two rather large finely chopped onions in a stew-pan, with 3 ozs. butter and some grated horse-radish; when of a light brown color, remove it from the fire, and add two boiled beetroots chopped fine; season with salt, pepper and mustard; mix this with Yorkshire pudding batter (see below), and finish as there directed; serve with roast beef.

BRUSSELS SPROUT PUDDING.

Proceed as for cabbage pudding; dish and garnish with a few Brussels sprouts, reserved for the purpose.

CABBAGE PUDDING.

Boil two cabbages; press them on a sieve; take out the stalk and chop fine; put it over the fire with 2 ozs. butter, 2 ozs. glaze, a teaspoon of sugar, pepper and salt to taste; remove from the fire; add 4 yolks of eggs; steam in a prepared mould until perfectly set, and serve with half glaze, as a second course, or garnish vegetable pudding.

CARROT PUDDING.

Boil the red part of ten or twelve carrots; when done, press and chop them very fine; put into a stewpan over the fire, with 3 ozs. butter, a little sugar, pepper and

salt; stir this over the fire for a few minutes, and finish
as for cabbage pudding.

CHEESE PUDDING.

Mix with ½ ℔. Cheshire cheese, grated, 2 eggs, half a
dariole mould of clarified butter, one dariole mould of
cream, and a spoonful of bread crumbs; mustard, salt
and pepper to taste; bake in a small dish, lined with`
puff paste.

CHEESE PUDDING (Welch).

Melt ½ ℔. grated Cheshire cheese and one egg with old
ale; mix in two tablespoons of bread crumbs, and a few
bits of butter; salamander and serve.

CHEESE PUDDING—MACARONI TIMBALE.

Build a timbale of macaroni (Indian), and fill carefully with the following: Thicken ½ pt. milk and ½ pt.
cream over the fire with 3 ozs. butter kneaded with flour;
work this over the fire until it assumes a smooth paste;
add ¼ ℔. grated Parmesan cheese, a spoonful of ready-
made and another of French mustard; cayenne, pepper
and salt, 4 yolks and 2 whites of eggs; steam.

CHESTNUT GARNISH PUDDING.

Peel, skin and boil in weak stock, about 1 doz. chestnuts, pass them through a sieve into a stewpan, with 2
ozs. butter, 1 gill cream and a lump of glaz'; season to
taste, and finish as for cabbage pudding, serving with
turkey as a garnish pudding.

CHICKEN PUDDING.

CREME DE VOLAILLE.

Fillet one large fowl, or two small ones; scoop the
fillets away with a knife until they are reduced to a pulp;

pound the chicken pulp in a mortar with 1 oz. fresh
butter; add to this the yolks of 4 or 5 eggs, one at a time,
pass the whole through a fine wire seive; place it on the
ice in a basin; stir in lightly ½ pt. whipped cream; then
beat up the whites until they are stiff, and stir them
lightly into the mixture; season to taste with salt and
cayenne; fill it into a plain buttered mould; place the
mould in a stewpan with a little boiling water; let it
steam at the corner of the stove, being careful not to let it
boil; when set firm enough, turn it carefully out on its
dish, and serve with a little half glaze poured round it.

FISH PUDDING.

Take 2 ℔s. of any cold fish, chop and pound it, adding
minced onion, parsley, prepared mushrooms, pepper,
salt and 2 eggs; line a plain mould with slices of fat bacon, put in the fish pudding, cover with fat bacon, and
bake 1½ hours; when done, turn it out on its dish,
remove the bacon, and serve with brown sauce; or cold
with marinade.

FRENCH BEAN PUDDING.

Cut two hundred french beans into diamonds; boil
them very green; strain and put them into a cutlet pan,
with a pat of butter, a little chopped parsley, and season
to taste; pass over the fire for three or four minutes; put
into about ½ pt. white sauce; add 6 yolks of eggs, and
finish as for cabbage pudding.

GARNISH PUDDING FOR ROAST GOOSE.

Fry three finely chopped onions and the same of apples,
with a pat of butter, sage, pepper and salt to taste; add
this to Yorkshire pudding batter, and finish as there
directed.

GREEN PEAS PUDDING.

Make a stiff puree of green peas; reduce the puree in a stewpan, with a piece of glaze, 2 ozs. butter, sugar, salt and pepper to taste; add to this, when off the fire, five yolks of eggs; line a prepared mould with green peas boiled carefully; fill in the puree; steam, and serve with white sauce, round the base.

HAM GARNISH PUDDING.

Take enough fried bread crumbs to half fill a prepared pudding mould; mix with this ¼ ℔ grated ham; put the whole in a basin, with 3 ozs. clarified butter, and a cold custard of six yolks and four whites of eggs, and ½ pint cream; season; pour into the mould; steam, and serve with roast chicken, etc.

JULIENNE PUDDING.

Cut a quantity of Julienne roots as for soup; boil them for two minutes; strain, and fry them in a stewpan, with 2 ozs. butter and a teaspoon of sugar; add ¾ pt. white sauce; remove from the fire, add seven yolks of eggs, and finish as for cabbage pudding.

MUSHROOM PUDDING.

Cook sufficient prepared mushrooms; chop them up very fine; mix with ½ pt. white sauce; stir in 8 yolks of eggs; season to taste, and finish as for cabbage pudding, serving with white sauce.

ONION PUDDING.

Boil 1½ doz. onions; drain, pass and rub them through a wire sieve; put the puree into a stewpan, and stir it over the fire to evaporate the water; add ½ pt. double cream, still reducing it over the fire until it nearly detaches from the sides; add 1 gill of white sauce; remove from the fire; add 7 yolks of eggs, and finish as for cabbage pudding.

OYSTER PUDDING.

Take a round French loaf about the size of a pudding mould, cut the top off, scoop out the crumbs quite close to the crust, spread the outside of the case with butter, and a band of foolscap paper round it; place it in a baking sheet, and fill in alternate layers—6 doz. raw oysters, horned and bearded, and bread crumbs fried in butter of a light brown; bake 1½ hours in a moderate oven, putting a few pieces of butter on the top; remove the paper, and serve hot.

PEAS PUDDING.

Boil ½ pt. split peas in a bag or cloth until soft; when done, turn out into a stewpan, and stir over the fire, with 3 ozs. butter, and some mashed potatoes; season to taste; add 3 eggs; tie up in a buttered and floured cloth as an ordinary pudding; boil ½ hour, and serve with boiled pork.

POTATO PUDDING (1).

Mash some boiled potatoes firm; add 2 ozs. butter, 1 gill double cream, salt and pepper to taste, and the yolks of 5 eggs; put into prepared mould; let it set in a moderate oven; turn it out on its dish; glaze it lightly, and pour Steward's sauce round the base.

POTATO PUDDING (2).

Mash some potatoes, adding a little milk; season to taste; put into a Yorkshire pudding tin, and finish as for Yorkshire pudding.

RHUBARB GARNISH PUDDING.

Skin, cut into pieces, and boil a bundle of rhubarb; drain on a sieve, press and put into a stewpan; evaporate the water over the fire; add 2 oz. butter, ½ gill cream, pepper, salt and sugar to taste; remove it; add 6 yolks of eggs, and finish as for cabbage pudding.

SPINACH PUDDING.

Boil, press and pass through a wire sieve some spinach as for a dish; put it into a stewpan over the fire and stir into it one gill double cream and a pat of fresh butter; season to taste with a little nutmeg, etc.; remove from the fire and finish as for cabbage pudding.

TONGUE GARNISH PUDDING.

Proceed as for Ham Garnish Pudding, using grated tongue.

TURNIP PUDDING.

Boil and press as dry as possible eight or ten turnips; pass them through a sieve; stir them over the fire to extract all the water; add ½ pint double cream, pepper, salt and sugar to taste; when sufficiently reduced, remove from the fire; add ½ dozen yolks of eggs, and finish as for cabbage pudding, serving with white sauce.

WINDSOR BEAN PUDDING.

Boil and skin sufficient Windsor beans to make enough puree to fill a prepared mould; put the puree into a stewpan with 2 ozs. butter, a little lemon juice, chopped parsley, a piece of glaze and a half gill cream; season and finish as for cabbage pudding, serving with white sauce.

YORKSHIRE PUDDING.

Put into a basin six ounces flour; mix four eggs in smoothly with a little milk; add 1½ pints milk, and a little salt; butter a Yorkshire tin; make it hot; pour in the batter; place it under the roasting meat; brown on both sides; when done, cut into squares and dish; serve with roast beef.

CHAPTER X.

Meat and Fish Batter Puddings.

BATTER FOR BAKED MEAT PUDDINGS.

Put about ½ ℔ flour into a basin; mix smooth with a little milk; add about 1 pint milk with 3 beat eggs, and pinch of salt; use according to recipes.

CHICKEN BATTER PUDDING.

Place at the bottom of a buttered pie dish, a chicken cut up into small pieces, and each piece dipped into clarified butter, and seasoned with pepper and salt; put a layer of cooked tongue at the top; fill up with batter and bake.

CURRY BATTER PUDDING.

Make a curry (see curry calfs' feet pudding); place it it in the bottom of a buttered pie dish, and fill up with a batter of ground rice boiled in milk, and a couple of beat eggs; put a few pieces of butter on the top and bake.

FISH BATTER PUDDING.

See turbot batter pudding.

IRISH BATTER PUDDING.

Put a layer of fillets of beef, seasoned with fine herbs, at the bottom of a buttered pie dish; fill up with a batter of mashed potatoes. thinned with milk; season, add four eggs and bake.

LAMBS' FRY BATTER BUTTER PUDDING.

Cut up a lambs' fry and place it at the bottom of a buttered pie dish; season and add some fine herbs to this; pour over it batter, and bake.

LAMBS' HEAD AND MINCE BATTER PUDDING.

Boil and bone two lambs' heads; place at the bottom of a buttered pie dish; parboil the liver; mince and add it to batter; season to taste; fill up with the batter and liver; bake.

LIVER AND BACON BATTER PUDDING.

Proceed as for lambs' fry batter pudding, using slices of calves' liver and bacon, in proportion.

PIGS FRY BATTER PUDDING.

Cut some pigs's fry into convenient pieces; lay it at the bottom of a buttered dish; season, pour over it batter, and bake.

RABBIT BATTER PUDDING.

Place at the bottom of a buttered pie dish two rabbits cut into joints, and seasoned with fine herbs, pepper and salt; cover with a layer of streaky bacon; fill up with batter and bake.

TOAD IN THE HOLE.

Butter a pie dish, and place at the bottom 1½ lbs rump steak, beat with the cutlet chopper; spread with fine herbs, and fold into three; season well; pour over this the batter, and bake about an hour.

TURBOT BATTER PUDDING.

Form a thick batter with 1 lb flour and 1 quart milk,

9

two shalots, a bay leaf, chopped parsley, thyme, salt, pepper and grated nutmeg; stir and boil the batter over the fire until thick, then remove, stir in $\frac{1}{2}$ lb butter and the yolks of 3 eggs; pass this through a tammy, and pour some into the bottom of a buttered dish; place over this a layer of cold turbot, boned, then a layer of batter and fish in alternate layers, finishing with the batter; strew the top with grated Parmesan cheese, bake for 20 minutes in a moderate oven; salamander and serve.

All other Fish batter puddings may be made in the same manner.

CHAPTER XI.
Timbales.

Timbales are French dishes, so named from timbale, a metal cup, because they are generally made in plain moulds, either round or oval. They are excellent and pretty, but diffcult to make, as they require both care and practice; they resemble our raised pies. The outer case may be constructed of short paste, macaroni, rice or other substances, and they may be filled with any nicely flavored fricassee of fowl or game; or with fruit and sweetbreads.

PASTE FOR HOT TIMABLES.

This should be a little more delicate than for a cold pie, and therefore requires more butter. Take 1 ℔ flour, a little more than ½ ℔ butter, 2 yolks of eggs and a pinch of salt; work with a half glassful of water, making the paste as smooth as possible; then proceed as follows: butter a plain mould all over; decorate the bottom a little and and the sides by using some of the same paste, and adding some pounded sugar, as the paste will take a trimmer shape; spread the paste over the board, cut a piece the size of the bottom of the mould (using the mould to measure with) and cover the bottom of the mould and all the decorations, without disturbing them; water the ornamented paste as above; stick the other paste lightly over, and cut a bit to put all round over the decorated parts; roll a little paste also to stick the whole together round the bottom; fill the mould with beef suet chopped fiue, aud make a cover of the same length; bake and when done empty it for use.

These timbale cases may be used for macaroui, fricassee, blanquettes of every kind, etc.

SMALL TIMBALES.

Butter a dozen dariole moulds thoroughly; cut with a round cutter trimmings of puff-paste large enough to fill the mould; have a bit of paste the same form as the inside of the mould, but not so large; put the round piece over the latter, let it fall all around and then introduce this into the mould; press equally everywhere with the fingers to keep the paste the same thickness; cut off all the paste above the rim, fill the mould with trimmings of paste, and put on a false cover to prevent the paste from taking a bad color; bake, and when done, empty the inside, and garnish as desired.

For *pates au jus* (with gravy), fill the inside with godiveau (see godiveau pies) and bake with false covers; when done, take off the cover, open with a knife to let in a spoonful of Espagnol sauce, and cover with small covers made of puff paste; serve hot.

Small Timbales can be filled with any savory preparation desired. They are also used for all sorts of entrees; fruit, jelly, cream, truffles, etc.

CAULIFLOWER TIMBALES.

Cut the flowerets of three cauliflowers; boil them carefully but not too much; place them in a cutlet pan with a pat of butter; pepper, salt and Parmesan cheese to taste; pass over the fire for a few minutes, and finish as macaroni timbale (1).

FRENCH TIMBALES.

Line a round well-buttered mould with short paste; put a thin layer of forcemeat to correspond. Lard a piece of the fillet of veal, about 3 lbs, and cut in thick slices, across the grain; fill up the mould with alternate layers of the veal, small thin slices of boiled ham, and forcemeat, seasoning with herbs and spices. Roll out paste for a cover, even round the edges and securely close; pinch, ornament, egg and bake. When done and the heat has passed from it, pour in a thin glaze through the top, made from the bones and trimmings of the veal, and some jelly of calf's foot.

INDIAN TIMBALES.

Boil and dry about ¼ ℔ rice, with the same weight of turbot, and 3 hard boiled egg minced up; moisten with white sauce, a spoonful of curry paste and half a grated cocoanut; finish as macaroni timbale (1); garnish with with rice sprinkled with Parmesan.

ITALIAN TIMBALES.

Boil some Italian paste in consomme until done; finish as for macaroni timbale (1).

LOBSTER TIMBALES.

Proceed as for oyster timbales, with a lobster, cut up into small dice, adding a little essence of anchovy.

MACARONI TIMBALES (1).

Butter a round plain mould; stick all round the sides and bottom with some broken vermicelli; line with puff paste cuttings reduced with a little extra flour; fill the centre with flour and bake; when done take out the flour

and turn the case out the mould.   Have some macaroni
boiled and cut into inch lengths; put into a stewpan
with some supreme sauce; add 2 yolks of eggs, ¼ ℔ Parmesan cheese, a teaspoon mustard, salt and cayenne to
taste; put over the fire for a few minutes; fill the timbale
case and turn it over into its dish and serve.

MACARONI TIMBALES (2).

Cut some firm boiled macaroni into not quite ½ in. in
length; build these round the bottom and sides of a prepared mould, with the open pipe against the mould, to
represent when turned out, a honeycomb; line very carefully with any quenelle, filling the centre with a mixture
as for Richelieu Boudin (which see); cover in with
quenelle; steam and serve with supreme sauce, round the
base.

A great variety may be made from this.

MACARONI TIMBALES (3).

Honeycomb eight buttered dariole moulds as for macaroni timbale (2), cutting the macaroni much shorter;
fill carefully with quenelle; steam and serve with supreme
sauce; a salpicon may be introduced with care.

MACARONI TIMBALES A LA MINUTE.

Proceed as for macaroni timbale (2) only winding the
macaroni round the bottom and sides of the mould, instead of honeycombing it.

MACARONI TIMBALES—INDIAN.

Proceed with some macaroni which has been tinged
with saffron, as for macaroni timbales (2); line carefully
with veal quenelle; fill the centre with a mince of calves'

head curried (see Curry Calves' Feet Pudding); close over
with quenelle; steam and serve with a curry sauce round
the base, and rather a large spoonful of boiled rice at
each end.

MACEDOINE TIMBALES.

Drain the liquor from a canister of macedoine vegetables, and finish as for macaroni timbale (1).

MACKEREL ROES TIMBALES.

Take the soft roes of four large mackerel; (do not wash
the fish, for the roes would turn black and soft); put
them into melted butter, without any salt; cover with
the butter and either bake or let them sweat on the stove,
taking care not to let them break; when done, lay them
on paper to drain; dust with salt and cut into neat
small dice; finish, as usual, using Bechemel sauce.

NOUILLE TIMBALES.

Make and blanch some nouilles, and finish as for Macaroni timbale (1).

ORSINI BOMBS.

Make ten timbales of macaroni, as for macaroni timbales (2), in dariole moulds; steam, dish, and mask with
brown sauce.

OYSTER TIMBALES.

Take about 6 doz oysters; blanch them slightly, remove
the beards; thicken ½ pt. cream with some arrowroot,
and 2 yolks of eggs; season to taste, add the oysters to
this, and fill; serve in timbale case, as for macaroni timbales (1).

PETITS CHOUX TIMBALES.

Bake some petits choux, in the form of small balls; shortly before using throw them into some strong consomme; boil up for a minute over the fire; flavor with Parmesen cheese, cayenne, pepper and salt; stiffen with arrowroot, and serve as for macaroni timbales (1).

PRAWN TIMBALES.

Prepare 50 fine prawn, and proceed as for oyster timbales, adding a little essence of shrimps.

SPANISH TIMBALES.

Peel and blanch 3 doz. button onions; put them into a cutlet pan with a pat of butter, a dust of sugar, and 1 oz. grated Parmesan; fry of a light brown; prepare some mushrooms, drain and mix with the onions; put them into a stewpan with some brown sauce; thicken with three yolks of eggs, and serve as for macaroni timbale (1).

VERMICELLI TIMBALES.

Blanch enough vermicelli in consomme to fill the timbale case; finish as for macaroni timbales (1).

CHAPTER XII.

Savory Fritters (Beignets), Rissoles and Cromesques.

Fritters should be dipped in batter (see part 2, chapter XI) and fried quickly in hot lard; drain and serve with a little cayenne and salt.

Rissoles after being prepared according to recipes, are put in small portions into paste cut and finished as follows: Work some extra flour into trimmings of puff-paste; roll out very thin; stamp out with a 3½ in. cutter; place a portion of the mixture into the middle of each round; egg the edge, and double into the form of a turn-over; egg the rissoles, and roll them in broken vermicelli or bread crumbs; fry in hot lard; drain on paper, and serve on a napkin with fried parsley.

BEEF AND GHERKIN RISSOLES.

Cut some cold roast beef and four gherkins into small dice; put into some brown sauce reduced; spread on a plate to cool, and put small portions of the mixture into the paste; finish as above.

CALF'S HEAD FRITTERS.

Cut some cold calf's head in rounds with a circular cutter; mask them in cold reduced brown sauce, flavored with a little fresh basil and sherry; season to taste, and finish as directed above.

CHEESE FRITTERS.

Make a petit choux, season with 2 ozs. grated Parmesan, a teaspoon of mustard. salt, cayenne, etc. to taste; form them into balls; fry in hot lard until very light and thoroughly done; drain on paper, and serve with a dust of Parmesan.

CHICKEN RISSOLES.

Proceed as for turkey rissoles with cold roast chicken, adding some cold ox tongue, cut into dice.

Rabbit rissoles are prepared in a similar manner.

COD RISSOLES.

Mince up some cold cod; put into white sauce, reduced with a little elder vinegar, and seasored with cayenne and salt; finish as directed.

Salmon rissoles are similarly prepared from cold salmon.

CROMESQUES OF SWEETBREADS.

Blanch two throat sweetbreads; skin and cut them up into dice, with some cooked ox tongue and a few truffles; put this into some reduced white sauce; season to taste; let it cool on the ice; roll them into oblong pieces about the size of a croquette; wrap each one carefully in a piece of pig's caul; dip in batter, fry, drain, and serve on a napkin with fried parsley.

A great variety of these can be made.

EGG RISSOLES.

Poach ten eggs and place them delicately on the back of a fine hair sieve; when cold, stamp off the superfluous white with a round cutter; season and enclose them carefully in the paste, and finish as usual, using bread crumbs instead of vermicelli.

GROUSE RISSOLES.

Cut the breasts of three cold roast grouse into dice using the backs to flavor some brown sauce, by making a strong essence of them; reduce the sauce; add the mince to it; cool and finish.

Pheasant and Partridge rissoles are prepared in a similar manner.

LEVERET RISSOLES.

Cut up into small dice the fillets of a tender roast leveret; put into a good brown sauce, reduced with a little red currant jelly and port wine; finish.

LITTLE DEVILS.

Make a petit choux, adding ¼ lb grated Parmesan cheese seasoned very highly; spread on a buttered sheet; when cold, stamp out with a round cutter, egg and breadcrumb; fry in hot lard, drain and dish on a napkin; sprinkle with Parmesan and serve.

LOBSTER RISSOLES.

Cut a lobster up into small dice, and mix with white sauce, reduced with a little of the spawn and a very little anchovy sauce; when finished and dished, stick a piece of the horn into each, before serving.

MUTTON RISSOLES.

Cut some small dice of cold loin of mutton and a couple of eggs boiled hard; mix this with white sauce, reduced, season and finish.

Pork Rissoles are made as above, omitting the eggs, and adding a little of the stuffing.

OYSTER FRITTERS.

Remove the beards from 4 doz. large oysters; lay them on a sieve; throw them into fritter batter; pick them out one by one; fry in hot lard; drain and serve on a napkin, with a dust of salt and cayenne.

OYSTER RISSOLES.

Blanch and beard 4 doz. oysters; put them into a strongly reduced white sauce; season to taste and finish as usual.

RUSSIAN FRITTERS.

Mix six very thin pancakes (see chapter XII. pt. 2, English pancakes), seasoned with pepper, salt and chopped parsley; make a good salpicon of sweetbreads, mushroom, tongue and truffle, chopped and put into reduced white sauce; put this on the ice to cool, and spread each of the pancakes with it; roll and cut them into 1½ inch lengths; dip into fritter batter and fry in hot lard.

SALPICON RISSOLES.

Cut into dice some prepared mushroons, truffles, sweetbread, and tongue; put them into some reduced white sauce and finish.

TENDRON FRITTERS.

Mask cold tendrons with cold reduced white sauce; dip them in fritter batter; fry, etc.

TURBOT FRITTERS.

Cut some scallops of cold turbot; marinade them in oil, vinegar, salt, pepper and chopped parsley, for four hours; pick them out of this; dip into batter; fry etc.

TURBOT RISSOLES.

Cut some cold turbot and a little lobster into dice; mix with white sauce reduced to taste; finish.

TURKEY RISSOLES.

Cut some of the breast of a cold roast turkey, with a little of the (chestnut) stuffing, into dice; have ready some reduced white sauce; mix carefully together and finish.

VEAL RISSOLES.

Cut small dice from a cold roast fillet of veal; mix this with some white sauce, reduced, adding a little chopped mushrooms; finish as usual.

VENSION RISSOLES.

Cut up into small dice cold roast vension, adding little of the fat; mix with brown sauce, reduced, with little red currant jelly and 1 oz. glaze; season and finish.

WHITING RISSOLES.

Set four fillets of whiting in the oven on a buttered baking sheet; season the fillets with pepper, salt chopped parsley, and the juice of a lemon; mince the whole fine with the essence, and add to it a little white sauce thickened with four yolks of eggs; finish as usual.

Sole rissoles are made in the same way.

CHAPTER XIII.

BOUDINS.

(For Boudin Moulds, see Part 2, Chap. 1).

BEEF PALATES, BOUDINS.

Boil two palates of beef for four or five hours until done; skin, press, and when cold cut them out with ½ in circular cutter; put them into a reduced brown sauce, with a few slices of mushroons; line a boudin mould with quenelle, put the mixture in the middle, cover in with quenelle, and steam; serve with Bohemian sauce.

BEEF PALATES' BOUDINS (Small).

Cut the palates of beef, dressed as above, in small dice; put them into reduced white sauce; let this cool; line eight dariole moulds with quenelle; fill the centre with the mixture; cover in with quenelle; steam and serve with Bohemian sauce.

CALVES' TAIL BOUDINS (White).

Cut two calves tails into joints; stew them until tender; remove the bone from the best pieces; put the meat into reduced Bechamel sauce, flavored with basil; line a boudin mould with quenelle, fill with the mixture; cover in with the quenelle; steam and serve with white sauce.

CALVES TAIL BOUDINS (Brown).

Proceed as for Calves' tail Boudin (white), substituting reduced brown sauce for bechamel; and serve with half-glaze.

CARDINAL LOBSTER BOUDINS.

Shell and chop up a lobster very finely; pound it in a mortar, adding by degrees towards the last its weight of double cream; add enough lobster spawn to color, and one egg; season and pass through a wire sieve; fill the boudin mould; steam and serve with Cardinal sauce.

COD BOUDINS.

Proceed as for Turbot boudins.

CHICAGO BOUDINS.

Make a quenelle as for pheasant boudin, using pheasants, partridges or grouse etc.; roll it with a little flour into balls about the size of croquettes; roll them in egg, and then into chopped truffle; blanch in stock; dish in a circle, and centre with mushroons and white sauce erduced; pour white sauce round.

D'UXELLES BOUDINS.

Make a rabbit quenelle, roll it out with a little flour into the form of a roll-pudding; poach it in consomme; when cold, mask it with D'Auxelles sauce; then egg and bread-crumb it; fry in hot lard and serve with half-glaze.

Veal may be substituted in place of rabbit.

EEL BOUDINS.

Line the boudin mould with with a quenelle of whiting or other fish; fill the center with some pieces of eel, dressed and thrown into some reduced Steward's sauce, and the yolks of 2 eggs; cover with quenelle; steam and serve with tata cold sauce.

FOIES GRAS BOUDINS.

Cut 1½ ℔s. calf's liver, ½ ℔. fat bacon, ¼ ℔. lean ham, into dice; put into a good sized stewpan with two spoonfuls of fine herbs; sweat it at the corner of the stove for 1½ hours, stirring occasionally; season with pepper, salt, and a little herbacious mixture; pound in a mortar with 1 gill double cream and 5 yolks of eggs; pass through a sieve; fill a boudin mould; steam, and serve with half-glaze.

FOIES GRAS BOUDINS (Nouille).

Make and blanch some nouille paste in the form of rings; stick these all round the inside of a boudin mould; carefully line the mould with foies gras, as above, so as not to disturb the rings; fill in with nouilles blanched in strips, and put into reduced brown sauce; fill in with the forcemeat; steam, and serve with half-glaze.

FOWL BOUDINS A LA LUCULLUS.

With all the meaty part of a fowl, prepare some veal forcemeat, and when finished, incorporate therewith two spoonsful of puree of mushrooms, and use this to form some quenelles with tablespoons, filling the centre of each quenelle with small pellets of puree truffles; the quenelles are to poached in the usual way in boiling water, and when done, are to be drained, and dished up in a croustade: some white sauce is to be poured over the quenelles, and a border of truffles placed around the base.

FRENCH BOUDINS (1).

Make some quenelle; divide it into two equal parts; roll them up with a mixture of minced sweetbread, tongue, truffles and mushrooms, thrown into reduced white sauce and cold salpicon, in the centre; poach them in stock; when cold, egg and bread-crumb them; fry in hot lard; drain, and serve with half-glaze.

FRENCH BOUDINS (2).

Make the boudins as above, with the exception of using partridge or chicken quenelle, and forming them in the shape of birds; cut the necks, heads, wings and tails in bread, which fry in butter; and when the puddings are fried and dished, stick the necessary ornaments in their respective places.

GROUSE BOUDINS.

Ornament a boudin mould with truffles; line with a quenelle of fillets of grouse, fill with a financiere mixture of cock's combs cooked, prepared mushrooms, and truffles, thrown into reduced white sauce; fill over with quenelle; steam, and serve with grouse sauce.

GROUSE BOUDINS A LA STANLEY.

Prepare some forcemeat with a couple of grouse, reserving the carcasses to make sauce. Finish the forcemeat by incorporating therewith two spoonsful of stiffly reduced sauce; form the boudins with two tablespoons, introducing small pellets of croquette preparation of truffle, tongue and mushroom, seasoned with chopped chives; when the boudins have been poached, drained, and become cold, they are to be masked over with some game sauce, finished with three yolks of eggs, egged, crumbed and fried in hot lard; they are then to be dished up with a ragout of artichoke bottoms, and the remains of the sauce is to be poured round the base.

LEVERET BOUDINS (1).

Make a quenelle of fillets of three leverets; coat the interior of the mould all over with chopped truffles; steam, and serve with venison sauce.

LEVERET BOUDINS (2).

Decorate the bottoms of some dairole moulds with a large ring of boiled white of egg, the interior of the ring filled in with a round of truffle; fill with leveret quenelle; steam, and serve with venison sauce.

MUSHROOM BOUDINS (1).

Make a boudin of veal quenelle, filling the centre with prepared mushrooms thrown into reduced brown sauce; cover in with quenelle; steam, and serve with truffle sauce, with chopped mushrooms in it.

MUSHROOM BOUDINS (2).

Fill some dariole moulds, buttered as usual, with quenelle, to which 2 doz. prepared mushrooms, first chopped, have been added; steam, and serve with truffle sauce, and a neat button mushroom on top of each.

NORMANDE BOUDINS (1).

Line the boudin mould with whiting quenelle, and fill with the following mixture: 1 doz. mussels scalded, $\frac{1}{2}$ doz. button onions cooked, $\frac{1}{2}$ doz. prepared mushrooms, and 1 doz. oysters bearded and cooked; mixing all together in reduced white sauce; cover in with quenelle; steam, and serve with Dutch sauce.

NORMANDE BOUDINS (2).

Fill eight buttered dariole moulds with whiting quenelle; steam, and dish them in a circle on the dish; centre with the above Normande mixture, and serve with with Dutch sauce.

NORMANDE BOUDINS OF SOLES—SMALL.

Prepare a quenelle of soles; line the boudin mould with this; fill the centre with prepared mushrooms, oysters, truffles, and a few button onions, all well finished, and put into reduced white sauce; cover in with quenelle; steam, and serve with Steward's sauce.

NORMANDE BOUDINS OF SOLES.

Fill eight dariole moulds with quenelle of soles; steam and dish them in a circle; centre with the Normande mixture, and serve with Steward's sauce.

PARTRIDGE BOUDINS.

Make some quenelles of fillets of partridges, adding two tablespoonfuls of brown sauce, fill the boudin mould and serve with brown sauce.

PHEASANT BOUDINS.

Line a boudin mould with a quenelle of fillets of pheasants; centre with a financiere mixture as for grouse boudins; fill in with a quenelle; steam, and serve with half-glaze.

PHEASANT BOUDINS A LA RICHELIEU.

Take a cold pheasant and pick the meat from it; remove the skin and sinews, and pound the flesh in the mortar to a smooth paste. Mix its weight with the same quantity of potatoes or panada and six ounces of fresh butter. Mix these thoroughly, pound them together, and season highly with salt, cayenne, and a trifle of mace. Bind together with the yolks of four eggs, one at a time, two tablespoonfuls of white sauce, and, last of

all, two tablespoonfuls of boiled onions, chopped small.
Spread this mixture out on a dish and make it up into
small cutlets, about 3 in. long, 2 in. wide, and $\frac{1}{4}$ in. thick.
Drop these carefully into very hot water and poach
them gently for a few minutes. The water must not
boil. Take them up, drain, and let them get cold; then
egg and breadcumb them, and fry them in hot butter a
nice pale color. Make a gravy by peeling and frying
four onions in butter till lightly browned, dredge an
ounce of flour over them, and pour upon them half-a
pint of stock, a glassful of claret, the bones of the pheasant, and pepper and salt. Simmer over fire for twenty
minutes, strain through sieve, and it is ready for use.
Serve the boudins in a circle with the gravy round.

PIG'S FEET BOUDINS.

Line a boudin mould with quenelle, and fill up with
two pigs feet, boned, cooked, cut into convenient pieces,
and thrown into a reduced white sauce, and a little parsley chopped fine; cover in with quenelle; steam and
serve with Steward's sauce.

POTATO BOUDINS.

Prepare some potatoes (see mashed potato pudding);
line the boudin mould with it; fill in with macedoine
vegetables mixed with reduced white sauce; cover in
with potato; make it hot in the hot closet; turn out on its
dish, and serve with Steward's sauce.

QUEEN'S BOUDINS (1).

Make a quenelle of about $\frac{1}{2}$ doz. rabbits, using the
fillets only, adding two tablespoonsful of white sauce;
line the mould with the quenelle, and put in the
centre, prepared mushrooms chopped and boiled up in

a reduced white sauce; cover in with a layer of quenelle; steam, and serve with white sauce.

This is also made with a quenelle of fillets of chicken; serve with supreme sauce.

QUEEN'S BOUDINS (2).

Butter eight dariole moulds; fill with chicken quenelle, and steam; when dished mask with supreme sauce, and place a round truffle on the top of each.

RICHELIEU BOUDINS.

Ornament a plain boudin mould, prepared as usual, with truffles cut fancifully; line the mould carefully with veal quenelle; three parts fill with the following mixture: put into reduced white sauce, some prepared mushrooms, truffles, cooked sweetbreads, and tongue, cut into rather large dice; cover in with a layer of the quenelle; paper and steam; serve with supreme sauce.

This may also be made with a quenelle of fillet of rabbit; serve with half-glaze.

SALMON BOUDINS (1).

Fill a boudin mould with salmon quenelle made with raw or cooked salmon; steam and turn out on a bed of tata sauce, in a cold dish; serve immediately.

SALMON BOUDINS (2).

Fill ten dariole moulds with solmon quenelle; steam and turn them out on a plate; mask them with Cardinal sauce, thickened with 2 yolks of eggs; dish them on a bed of tata sauce, in a cold dish.

SALMON BOUDINS—ITALIAN.

Pound some cooked salmon, mixing in by degrees its weight of double cream; season and color as for lobster

boudins; add 3 yolks of eggs; and pass the whole
through a wire sieve; fill a boudin mould; steam and
serve with Cardinal sauce.

SUPREME BOUDINS.

Make a delicate quenelle of fillets of chicken, with
which line the buttered and papered boudin mould; cut
some slices from the middle of a cooked ox tongue, and
build them up against the quenelle, thus leaving an interior coating of tongue:—fill the centre with scallops
of chicken and truffles, tossed up in reduced white
sauce, cover in with a layer of quenelle, and paper and
steam; serve with supreme sauce.

TRUFFLE BOUDINS.

Make a veal or other quenelle, mix with it ¼ ℔ truffles
chopped very fine, line the boudin mould with this; cut
eight truffles into slices, and mix them with a reduced
brown sauce; fill with this; cover in with quenelle, steam
and serve with truffle sauce.

TURBOT BOUDINS.

Fill a boudin mould with a quenelle of cooked turbot,
suitably seasoned, steam and serve with Dutch sauce.

Small Turbot Boudins are made as above, in dariole
moulds.

TURKEY BOUDINS (1).

Line a mould with quenelle made from the fillets of a
a small turkey; fill with a dozen or more chestnuts,
peeled and boiled in stock, and put into reduced brown
sauce; cover in with quenelle; steam and serve with
chestnut sauce.

TURKEY BOUDINS (2).

Fill some dariole moulds with turkey quenelles, as above, introducing in each a fine chestnut, also prepared; steam and serve with chestnut sauce.

VENISON BOUDINS (1).

Chop, pound and pass some lean venison, mixing in by degrees, its weight of double cream, one whole egg and one yolk; season well; steam in the boudin mould, and serve with venison sauce.

VENISON BOUDINS (2).

Steam the above quenelle in dariole moulds, laying a round of the venison fat at the bottom of each; serve with venison sauce.

VERMICELLI BOUDINS.

Put on the fire 1 pt. of milk with a pat of butter and a pinch of salt; when boiling, stir in enough broken vermicelli to form a stiff paste; set it at the corner of the stove for a few minutes, and fill in 8 or 10 buttered dariole moulds with it; when cold, turn them out; scoop out the centre; warm the boudins in the hot closet just before serving, and fill with a hot salpicon of truffles, tongue, sweetbreads, etc., cut into dice and mixed with reduced white sauce; manage to turn them over into their dish, and serve with Bohemian sauce.

WHITING BOUDINS.

Make a quenelle of whiting, with which line the boudin mould; fill the centre with a small lobster chopped up fine, and mixed with a little white sauce, reduced with some live lobster spawn passed through a sieve; mask over with quenelle; steam and turn on to its dish; serve with Cardinal sauce.

CHAPTER XIV.

Savory Souffles—Fondues.

(MAYONAISE SOUFFLES.)

Small Souffles may be made of any the following mixtures exactly as the larger ones, except they are baked in crimped paper cases, (sold for the purpose) in place of the Souffle lining. Where any special directions are needed for these small Souffles, they are noticed under each recipe. For Souffle cases, see Part 2, Chap. 1.

CHEESE SOUFFLE (Fondue) (1).

Moisten ¼ lb. flour with ½ pt. milk, the same of cream, and ¼ lb. butter, stir over the fire until it forms a paste, remove and add 8 yolks of eggs, ¼ lb. Parmesan cheese, and season to taste; beat up the whites stiff, pour into souffle lining, and bake 30 or 40 minutes, serve with Parmesan sprinkled on top.

Place upon the *small* fondues a small square of gruyere cheese, bake as usual.

CHEESE SOUFFLE (Fondue) (2).

Put into a stewpan ¾ pt. milk, ¼ lb. butter, and 5 ozs. flour, work this over the fire to a smooth paste, remove and add 3 ozs. Parmesan cheese, 2 ozs. gruyere, cut into small dice, season to taste, add 8 yolks of eggs, and at . the last the whites beat stiff; bake in a souffle lining about ½ hour.

CHICKEN SOUFFLE.

Take the breast and white parts of a cooked fowl;

chop it very fine, pound it in a mortar with three spoonsful of reduced white sauce, and the same of double
cream, 2 ozs. butter, salt and pepper; mix with the yolks
of ½ doz. eggs; rub the whole through a sieve; beat five
white of eggs stiff, mix gently together; bake in souffle
case 20 minutes.

GARIBALDI SOUFFLE (Fondue).

Mix lightly in at the last some boiled macaroni cut in
strips, vermicelli, or Indian paste, to cheese Fondue
(2) mixture, just before placing it in the lining. For
the small fondues, cut the macaroni into very small
pieces, and bake the mixture in paper cases, colored red
on the outside.

GROUSE SOUFFLE.

Pound and sers in the lean parts of four roast grouse;
add six spoonsful of brown sauce, one of chopped mushrooms, and one of melted game glaze; season to taste;
add six yolks of eggs and pass; beat the whites; mix and
bake.

LAMB SOUFFLE.

Take some lean meat from a cold leg of lamb; mince
and pound it, adding a little chopped mint, a spoonful
of sugar, one of vinegar, six of white sauce, ½ doz yolks
of eggs; season and pass; beat the whites stiff; mix
lightly together, and bake.

LEVERET SOUFFLE.

Pound the fillets and best pieces of meat of a fine
cooked leveret; add 4 spoonsful of brown sauce, one of
red current jelly, and ½ doz. yolks of eggs; season and
pass; add the beat whites of five eggs and bake.

LOBSTER SOUFFLE.

Shell and chop two lobsters up fine, adding six spoons-ful of Cardinal sauce, a little essence of anchovy, and ½ doz. yolks of eggs; season; pass; mix with the whites, beat, and bake.

Small souffles are served with a piece of lobster on the top of each.

MAYONAISE ANCHOVY SOUFFLE.

Boil ½ doz. eggs hard; chop them up and mix with the fillets of 2 doz. anchovies cut into small pieces; proceed with this in alternate layers as for mayonaise chicken souffle, flavoring the mayonaise with a little of the essence of anchovy.

MAYONAISE CAULIFLOWER SOUFFLE.

Boil the flowerets of two good cauliflowers: drain, and when cold, marinade, and proceed as for mayonaise chicken souffle.

MAYONAISE CHICKEN SOUFFLE.

Boil a chicken until tender; remove the bone; let it cool; take the best pieces, mince them up, and put into a dish, and well marinade with oil, vinegar, pepper and salt; whip up some good (but not too stiff) aspic. Put a layer of the whipt aspic at the bottom of a souffle lining; put a thin layer of mayonaise (see tata cold sauce) over the whipt aspic, and over this a layer of the minced chicken, seasoning each layer with white pepper, salt and Tarragon vinegar; proceed thus in alternate layers until about three inches above the edge of the souffle lining, finishing with the whipt aspic; set in the refrigerator until required. When about to serve, remove the paper, place the lining on the silver souffle-case, sprinkle the top with fried bread crumbs (cold), and serve with a plate of chopped aspic, to hand round.

Grouse, Partridge, Pheasant, etc., mayonaise souffles are made in a similar manner, using the fillets of each. So also mayonaise souffles of *salmon* or *lobster.*

MAYONAISE CRAB SOUFFLE.

Proceed and finish as for mayonaise chicken souffle, with the exception of placing the eatable part of the crab altogether in the centre of the souffle in a bed of mayonaise, instead of alternate layers of it.

MAYONAISE CUCUMBER SOUFFLE.

Peel and slice two cucumbers very thin; marinade in oil, vinegar, pepper and salt, and proceed as for mayonaise chicken souffle, in alternate layers, with the exception of mincing up the cucumber.

MAYONAISE EGG SOUFFLE.

Boil ten eggs hard; when cold, cut them across into rather thin slices; marinade and proceed as for mayonaise chicken souffle. If Plovers etc. eggs are used, cut them in two lengthways, but do not marinade.

MAYONAISE GREEN PEAS SOUFFLE.

Boil 1 qt. green peas until tender; when cold proceed as for mayonaise chicken souffle.

MAYONAISE ITALIAN SOUFFLE.

Take the breast of a boiled chicken and cut it into strips; mix with it half the quantity of cooked ox-tongue and a third of olives cut in the same manner; let this lay in a marinade of vinegar, pepper and salt for ten hours; proceed as for mayonaise chicken souffle.

MAYONAISE LETTUCE SOUFFLE.

Prepare and shred up very fine the best parts of eight lettuces; marinade and finish in alternate layers as for mayonaise chicken souffle.

MAYONAISE MACEDOINE SOUFFLE.

Open and drain a canister of macedoine vegetables; steep in a marinade of oil, vinegar, pepper and salt, for two hours, and proceed as for mayonaise chicken souffle, with the exception of placing the vegetables in the centre of the souffle dish in a bed of mayonaise.

MAYONAISE OYSTER SOUFFLE.

Blanch and beard 6 doz. oysters; proceed as for mayonaise chicken souffle, placing the oysters in alternate layers, but do not marinade or cut them up.

MAYONAISE POTATO SOUFFLE.

Chop up five cold potatoes and two cooked beetroots, not too fine, marinade these for two hours in oil, vinegar, pepper, salt and chopped parsley; proceed with alternate layers as for mayonaise chicken souffle.

MAYONAISE RABBIT SOUFFLE.

Fillet four rabbits, flatten and saute the fillets in a cutlet pan with a pat of butter; marinade, and proceed as for mayonaise chicken souffle.

MAYONAISE SMALL SALAD SOUFFLE.

Wash and dry in a cloth a punnet of small salad, with which proceed in alternate layers as for mayonaise chicken souffle.

MAYONAISE SPINICH SOUFFLE.

Cook a large dish of spinach, season and flavor well, flatten it out on a dish to cool, and proceed as for mayonaise chicken souffle, with the exception of mixing the spinach with the mayonaise, instead of alternate layers of it.

MAYONAISE SOLE AND PRAWN SOUFFLE.

Proceed with the fillets of two soles as for mayonaise whiting souffle, adding 3 doz. prepared prawns, whole.

MAYONAISE TURBOT SOUFFLE.

Proceed with $\frac{3}{4}$ ℔ of cooked turbot as for mayonaise chicken souffle, seasoning with elder instead of tarragon vinegar.

MAYONAISE WHITING SOUFFLE.

Fillet four whitings, set them in the oven on a baking sheet, with some butter, white pepper, salt and lemon juice; proceed as for mayonaise chicken souffle, adding some chopped parsley.

MUTTON SOUFFLE.

Proceed with 1 ℔ lean cold mutton, as for vension souffle. For small souffles, introduce a thin piece of fat on the top of each.

NOUKLES OF PARMESAN.

Make a petit chou, seasoned with salt, cayenne, and a little mustard; make into balls and and blanch for about ten minutes or so in boiling water, strain and place them lightly in a souffle lining, with alternate layers of Parmesan cheese grated, half fill the lining with good consomme; bake ¾ hours and serve with sprinkled Parmesan cheese.

PARTRIDGE SOUFFLE.

Proceed as for pheasant souffle, adding a spoonful of chopped truffles.

Small souffles are served by sticking one of the feet, cleaned and blanched, on each souffle.

PHEASANT SOUFFLE.

Pound the lean part of a fine pheasant with two tablespoonsful of chopped dressed ham, three of brown sauce, three of double cream, one of melted game glaze, seven yolks of eggs; pass, beat, and add the whites beat stiff; bake.

PIGEON SOUFFLE.

Pound the fillets of four pigeons that have been previously served; add four spoonsful of brown sauce and four yolks of eggs; season to taste and pass; beat the whites, mix and bake.

PLOVER SOUFFLE.

Proceed as for pigeon souffle, serving with fried bread crumbs on the top.

PRAWN SOUFFLE.

Prepare about 6 or 8 doz. prawns, and proceed as for lobster souffle. The *small souffles* are served with a small prawn on the top of each.

RABBIT SOUFFLE.

Remove the meat from two fine boiled rabbits; mince and pound it, adding about five spoonsful of double cream, a pat of butter, and five yolks of eggs; season to taste; pass; add the whites beat stiff; mix and bake.

SALMON SOUFFLE.

Pound 1 ℔ cooked salmon with three spoonsful of white sauce, three of whipt cream, and a little essence of shrimps; season to taste; add ½ doz. yolks of eggs; pass; mix with the whites beat stiff, and bake. The *small souffles* are served with tata cold sauce in a boat.

SOLE SOUFFLE.

Proceed as for Whiting souffle with the fillet of three soles.

SHAKESPEARE SOUFFLE.

Mix ½ pt. whipt cream with 6 ozs. Parmesan cheese; stir gently into this the yolks of seven eggs; mix lightly in the seven whites beat firm; season well; pour into a souffle lining; bake 10 or 12 minutes, and serve immediately.

TURBOT SOUFFLE.

Take 1 ℔ cold turbot; chop and pound it, adding two spoonsful of elder wine, a little grated horseradish, three spoonsful of white sauce, three of double cream, and the yolks of seven eggs; pass; mix in the whites beat stiff, and bake. The *small souffles* are served with grated horseradish on the top of each.

VEAL SOUFFLE.

Take about 1 ℔ of cold fillet of veal, mince and pound it with a little of the stuffiing, adding six spoonsful of reduced white sauce, and two of double cream; season to taste; add ½ doz. yolks of eggs and a little grated ham;

pass through a sieve; beat up; mix the whites in lightly, and bake in soufile lining 20 or 30 minutes.

Small Souffles of *Veal.*—Put a small quantity of above mixture into each of eight or ten crimped paper cases; put to this two or three pieces of the veal stuffing cut in dice; fill up with the mixture and bake.

VENSION SOUFFLE.

Take 1 ℔. of the lean part of a cold haunch of venison and proceed as for leveret souflle, adding 2 ozs. melted butter, and introducing about 2 ozs. of the fat, cut thin, during the process of filling the souffle lining. Before baking *small souffles* of venison, place on the top of each a thin piece of the fat, cut with a round cutter.

WHITING SOUFFLE.

Fillet and set in the oven three whitings; chop and pound them with six spoonsful of double cream and a pat of butter, season to taste, add ½ doz. yolks of eggs; pass and add the beat whites; bake.

WOODCOCK SOUFFLE.

Pound the best part of some cold woodcocks, add six spoonsful of double cream, season to taste, add eight yolks of eggs, pass through a sieve, beat the whites; mix and bake.